THE

STONE
COLD
TRUTH

World
Wrestling
Entertainment®

POCKET BOOKS
New York London Toronto Sydney

THE
STONE
COLD
TRUTH

Stone Cold Steve Austin

with **Jim "J.R." Ross** as told to
Dennis A. Brent

Foreword by
Vince McMahon

POCKET BOOKS, a division of Simon & Schuster, Inc.
1230 Avenue of the Americas, New York, NY 10020

Photos and letters on pages 10, 14, 19, 26, 27, 29, 34, 39, 42, 45, 49, 59, 67, 71, 94,
96, 106, 117, 161, 184, 201, 236 Courtesy the Williams family.

Photos on page 77, 80, 81 Courtesy of Buddy Meyers.

ISBN: 978-1-4767-5168-9

First Pocket Books hardcover edition October 2003

10 9 8 7 6

POCKET and colophon are registered trademarks of Simon & Schuster, Inc.

Designed by Richard Oriolo
Visit us on the World Wide Web
http://www.simonsays.com
http://www.wwe.com

Manufactured in the United States of America
For information regarding special discounts for bulk purchases, please contact Simon &
Schuster Special Sales at 1-800-456-6798 or business@simonandschuster.com

I'd like to dedicate this book to my
two daughters, Stephanie and Cassidy,
and, of course, to my family for the
way I turned out.

—STEVE "AUSTIN" WILLIAMS

ACKNOWLEDGMENTS

Steve Austin would like to thank Nicole Dorazio at WWE
for making his life so much easier.

Dennis Brent would like to thank the following people:
From World Wrestling Entertainment, thanks to:
Jim "J.R." Ross, Stacey Pascarella, Barry Werner, Keith
Greenberg, Dr. Tom Prichard, Michael P.S. Hayes, and
Bob Clarke. Also much thanks to Mike Fazioli, Aaron
Williams, and Brian Solomon from WWE Publications
for their tremendous help in transcribing many hours of
interviews.

In the photo area, thanks to: Anthony Cali and
Frank Vitucci from WWE Photo and Buddy Myers, the
ringside photographer from World Class Championship
Wrestling in Texas.

Also many thanks to: Raven, Percy Pringle III,
Skandor Akbar, Mick Foley, and Dutch Mantel.

Steve Austin's family and friends were invaluable
with background information on the Texas Rattlesnake.
Thanks to Steve's family, Beverly and Ken Williams,
Jennifer (Williams) Weigand, Scott Williams, Kevin
Williams, Jeff Williams, and Steve's longtime friends,
Rob Webb and Dr. Jimmy Baros. Beverly Williams,
Steve's terrific mom, provided all the great material
from Steve's career and life.

I would also like to thank my editor at Pocket
Books, Margaret Clark, as well as Lynn, my wife, who
was my constant editor/proofreader.

Stone Cold's success story is about being at the right place at the right time and having paid the right amount of dues to get there. It's about having the right amount of audacity, work ethic and intellect to achieve levels of popularity that had never been achieved by any WWE Superstar before.

However, Austin didn't reach this zenith of popularity by himself. He was very quick to understand the team concept, very adept at establishing relationships—not just with other Superstars but with television production, merchandise and licensing and all-around management of the company. But Stone Cold's most effective relationship has always been with the WWE fans.

In short, Stone Cold has "it." He has the ability to relate to an audience and interpret its reactions, coupled with an insatiable desire to perform. These are but a few of the characteristics of the man known as Stone Cold.

This book is about a man who is like no other . . . as you will find in *The Stone Cold Truth*.

—VINCE MCMAHON

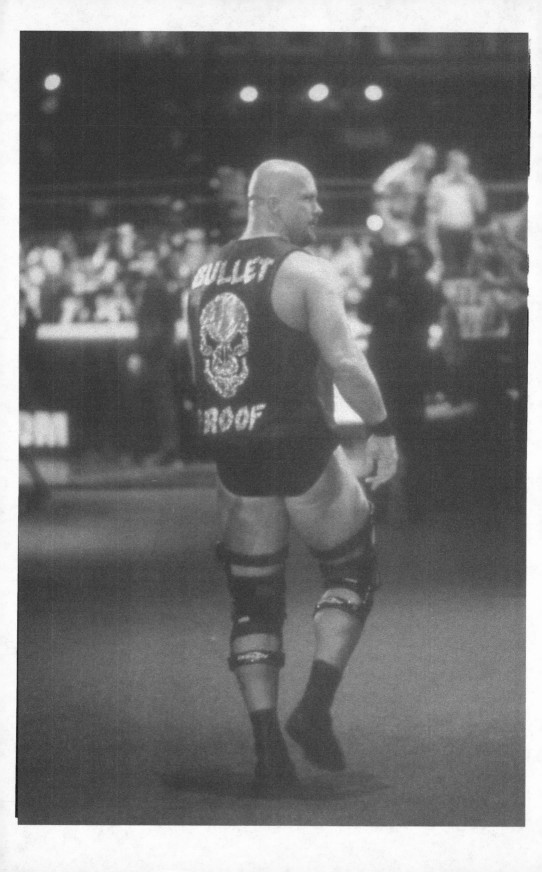

March 29, 2003—
Saturday Night, Pre-
WrestleMania XIX

> When I'm sitting there backstage and
> I'm getting ready to go through that
> curtain, I'm just waiting for that glass
> to break and when it hits, when that
> crowd explodes, I might as well be a
> junkie and I'm hooked on a drug.
>
> —STONE COLD STEVE AUSTIN

Damn, I think I'm dying, dying for sure. I'm getting off the elevator on the twenty-seventh floor of the Grand Hyatt Hotel in Seattle, the night before *WrestleMania XIX*, and my heart's beating so hard it feels like it's going to crack a rib jumping out of my chest.

I'm saying to myself, I'm thirty-eight years old and I'm fixing to freaking die, right here, right now. I'm having a damned heart attack!

And I'm wondering how the hell it could have happened.

I'm Stone Cold Steve Austin—the toughest SOB in World Wrestling Entertainment, better known as WWE. This is Saturday night and tomorrow is *WrestleMania XIX*, the biggest Pay-Per-View event of the year. I'm in one of the biggest matches of my career, wrestling The Rock in my first real match after being out of the business for over eight months.

I've been working out twice a day at the gym and doing nothing but focusing on this match. Mentally, I'm ready, despite all the challenges I've been through in the last couple of years—injuries, surgery and rehab, divorces and—most unexpected of all, maybe—my leaving WWE.

Physically, I look like somebody who deserves the name Stone Cold. But truthfully, I'm a walking disaster area. My back, neck and knees are a mess. I've got two fused discs in my back and others just barely holding together.

But tomorrow is *WrestleMania,* and I need to perform the best I can and put on a hell of a match. Hell, it could very well be the last one of my career. I want to go out in a blaze of glory, like anybody would.

Standing here on the twenty-seventh floor of the Grand Hyatt, my heart pounding against my ribs like a gorilla trying to bust its way out of a cage . . . that wasn't in the plans at all.

I had woken up that morning feeling all right. But the more I thought about it, the problem went back before that morning . . .

The day before, which was Friday, I had bought a couple of those high-energy drinks from the gym. I was in the habit of drinking from three to five of those things a day, plus anywhere from one to two pots of coffee, while I was off and working out. Those drinks are loaded with Ephedra and that Ma Huang crap and lots of caffeine. I should have known with all the warnings about Ephedra, but it never bothered me until now. Famous last words.

I worked out at the gym on Friday and went back to the hotel. I was a little emotional, because I figured this was the last match of my career, so I didn't sleep so well. When I woke up, it was one of those

mornings where you need a crane to pull yourself out of bed, so I opened up one of those energy drinks and drank that thing down.

This was before I had coffee, breakfast, whatever. Then I ordered some room service and drank the other energy drink. And then breakfast came, my normal breakfast, egg white omelet and a large pot of coffee. I drank the whole pot.

Then I called Kevin Nash and went to see him before going to the gym and had a couple more cups of coffee with him. When we went to the gym, I noticed that over the last couple of days the reflexes in my leg were really jumpy. I have what is called a sustained clonuses reflex in both legs, which is an involuntary shaking of nerves, knees, whatever. I was nervous about this whole weekend, this probably being my last match. I was nervous about hurting my neck or back, plus there was all that crap I was putting in my body, and I had been doing this stuff for months on end. Looking back, I think I was wearing myself down.

I went to the gym, but I didn't really work out. I didn't feel like doing a whole lot, so I had kind of a BS workout, a light back workout. I did the recumbent bicycle for my knees, just peddling on it, not really trying to raise my cardio or anything. Kevin had come over after he finished his cardio exercises and we were sitting together talking.

I said to him, "Look," pointing down to my foot.

My foot was resting on the bike pedal, and the reflexes were just firing like crazy in my foot and leg. I said, "Look at that crap."

He looked at my foot as it jumped uncontrollably on the bike pedal, and said, "Jesus Christ."

It was just a lot more jumpy than usual. You could see the muscles twitching away like they had a mind of their own.

When we got through with cardio exercises, we just shot the breeze for a while. Then we crossed the street over to the Grand Hyatt, where we were all staying. There were a lot of fans out there and we signed autographs for a while, and everything was fine. I felt like my normal self. This was about three in the afternoon.

After that, I went through the lobby, got in an elevator and rode it up to my floor. As soon as I got out of that damn elevator, that's when everything started happening.

My heartbeat might be doing 160 or 180 beats per minute. It just feels like my heart's going to jump out of my chest. I've been fatigued in matches before, totally out of gas and winded, but this is scaring the hell out of me. I'm sure I'm having a heart attack.

I start walking to my room, but my feet are going crazy and my legs are shaking uncontrollably every time I lift my weight off them. I finally get to my room, which is right by the elevator, and get the door open.

I say, "Okay, you're having an anxiety attack or something," so I take a couple of deep breaths to settle myself down. Maybe it'll pass, I think. But it doesn't pass. It's still as bad as before.

Hold it together, I tell myself. Getting over to the phone, I call the front desk to see if they have a doctor. I say, "I need someone up here. I need help."

They put me on hold, probably transferring me to someone else. The hell with that. I hang up on them and call back down and say, "I got an emergency. This is Steve Austin and there's something wrong with me. I need some help. I think I'm having a heart attack."

That's when they call Bob Clarke of the WWE Talent Relations Department in the WWE greenroom. In the meantime, Liz DiFabio, one of the WWE executives, just happens to be walking down the hall. I have my door wide open, waiting for some help, so I see her and yell, "Liz! I need help!"

I guess I'm as white as a sheet and I've got some weird kind of look on my face because I'm freaking out. My legs are shaking and I can't make them stop. Liz rushes in to help and then Bob Clarke and Chris Brannan, the WWE *Raw* trainer, come into the room. Then Dr. Robert Quarrells, the WWE team doctor, comes in.

This is all in a matter of a few minutes, I guess. I don't really know. They call the paramedics, but in the meantime they're all trying to settle me down. Dr. Quarrells has got my heartbeat down to 124. Then the EMTs get there and they take my blood pressure. It's 198 or 188 over 105, or something crazy like that. It's normally about 135 over 80.

That "bad feeling" I got when I stepped out of the elevator feels like it's going to come back at any moment. I just want to keep walking

around the room, walking around the room. They all want me to sit down, but I don't want to. I really feel like this is my day to die. It's that kind of feeling.

The EMTs hook a bunch of medical stuff up to me. Then they want to get me to a hospital. Easier said than done.

There are so many fans downstairs, it's a madhouse. We do our best to be inconspicuous, so none of them will know what's going on. A group of us just walk out of the hotel in a pack, with me in the middle. But a bunch of fans see me being taken to a waiting ambulance. There's a funny moment when I look in their eyes and they look in mine, and it's crazy because no one knows what's going on.

Not even me.

We go down to the parking garage, where hotel security has put up a barricade so the fans can't see me being loaded up in the ambulance. I get inside and sit down. But as soon as they close the door, I lie down and they pull the blankets all the way up so no one can look into the ambulance and see who I am.

Finally, we arrive at the hospital, and they keep the blankets pulled all the way up over me so no one can see who they're carting into the place.

I'm thinking, Jesus, Stone Cold against The Rock at *WrestleMania* in Seattle. That's tomorrow, for crying out loud. But I don't think I'm going to be wrestling The Rock at *WrestleMania*. Right now, I'm a helluva lot more concerned about just stayin' alive.

I curse myself for my bad habits of drinking all those high-energy drinks and so much coffee every day. I rarely drank any water. I was just such a big bundle of nerves, with my health and everything else on my mind going into this match, plus my not wanting to stink the joint out. And now it's all just caught up to me—*BANG!*

They take me into the hospital and hook me up to a machine that monitors my heart rate and my blood pressure. They also get an IV going and start giving me some fluids. They end up putting five bags of fluid in me, I'm so dehydrated. An average person might get two bags, but I get *five*.

So here I am, lying in the hospital in Seattle with tubes and wires

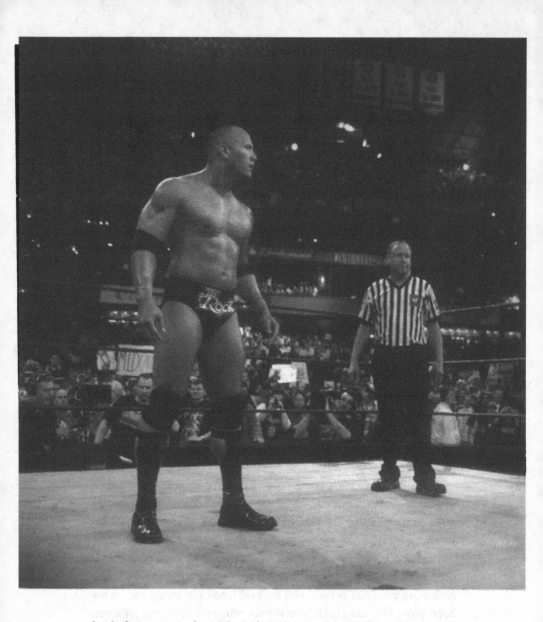

hooked up to me, the night before I'm supposed to face The Rock at *WrestleMania XIX*. It doesn't even seem real. It's like a dream—a bad one. J.R. (Jim Ross) and Vince McMahon arrive while I'm still in the emergency room. After it seems like I'm okay, they leave, thinking I'm coming back to the hotel that night.

Then the doctors decide they want to keep me overnight for evaluation. So J.R. and Chris Brannan come back to the hospital. When J.R.

gets there, he asks me what I ate today, which was practically nothing. He sends Bob Clarke back to the hotel to get me some good food from hotel room service.

When he gets to the hospital with the food, I eat pretty good. That's a good sign. After I finish eating, we talk for a while. Then everybody eventually goes back to the hotel.

I just hang around the room, check out what's on TV and listen to some CDs. The nurse says she's going to give me some sleep medication. Of course, I'm still wound up and wide awake. I've been drinking those energy drinks for eight months, and I had two that day plus all the coffee, so I'm still pretty charged up. I lie in bed for a while just thinking, not falling asleep. It's only now that I start to think I can still work my match with The Rock the next day. I know there are going to be a lot of damn people there, and I've been away from the company for a long time, and there's been a lot of anticipation—on the fans' part as well as my own.

After everything that I've done with this company, and everything this company has done for me, I want to do business with The Rock. I want to do it right. The Rock is going to beat me, and I want him to do it right in the middle of the ring. He's done a lot of stuff for me in my career, and vice-versa, so that *has* to happen. I wouldn't have it any other way.

I lie there in my hospital bed for quite a while, thinking about my

life, my career . . . where it began, where it had taken me, my family, my daughters, my future. And what would happen tomorrow.

Finally, somewhere around three or four in the morning, I calm down enough to fall asleep.

JIM "J.R." ROSS: I had just walked into the greenroom to see how things were going for our staff and talent on what, to that point, had been a pretty uneventful Saturday afternoon. The greenroom is the command center for our staff and talent for *WrestleMania.* It's kind of like going to the only coffee shop in a small town. At some point during the day, everyone drops by the greenroom to see what's going on and to use it as a point of departure for the appearances the talent make at 'Mania. Shane McMahon informed me that Steve had just been taken to the hospital. Steve had gone through hell the previous eight months or so. Some of it he had brought on himself, and some he had little or no control over. Stone Cold deserved a break and something kept telling me that this story was going to have a positive ending. When we walked into the emergency room, Steve was hooked up to a slew of monitors that were supposed to keep an eye on his heart rate and blood pressure. I could tell he was glad to see us because he tried to crack a few jokes. But the Texas Rattlesnake was scared, and he had every right to be.

Eventually Steve's vital signs started to improve, but the doctors wanted him to stay overnight so they could continue to evaluate his heart function. I suggested to Bob Clarke, who along with trainer Chris Brannan did a helluva job that day and night on Steve, that on the company's behalf, they hop back in the van and go to our hotel and get Steve some food. Steve's appetite returned, to say the least. He ordered two steak dinners and two grilled chicken breast dinners, so I felt confident, as I left his hospital room well after midnight, that Stone Cold would be able to lace his boots up—perhaps for the last time—in just a few hours at Safeco Field in Seattle. Stone Cold had a close call, but he was going to survive, just as he has done his entire life. And what a life it has been. . . .

The Glass, No . . . The Water Breaks!

> If you want some mercy, son,
>
> then take your ass to church.
>
> —STEVE AT HIS BEST

When I was born, there was no sound of "breaking glass" with the Stone Cold entrance music pumping through the hospital on loudspeakers and doctors tossing beers. That would have been pretty cool, but it didn't happen.

My story starts in Austin, Texas. That's where I was

My dad, Ken Williams singing lead

brought into the world on December 18, 1964, as Steve Anderson, the second brother in an eventual line of four brothers and one little sister. My mom, Beverly, is a great lady and a wonderful mother who did her best to raise her boys the right way.

Shortly after I was born, she got pregnant again with my brother Kevin. I guess my biological father, James, couldn't deal with that fact. He took off and left me and my brothers Scott and Kevin with my mom.

My parents got divorced before I ever had a chance to get to know James. I have no memories of the man. Neither does Kevin, who's ten months younger than I am. James showed up once or twice at live events when I was in World Championship Wrestling, and told me his name and told me who he was. He looked like me and talked like me, but I didn't know him. I tried to talk to him, but it was like talking to a stranger. The only things I knew about him were what I had heard from my mom. He had abandoned us and I had no feelings for him. By the same token, I had no animosity toward him.

After Mom and my biological father divorced, she moved us from Austin to Victoria, Texas. Mom raised us right, hard as it was on her. She was a single mother with three kids—my older brother, Scott, me and my younger brother Kevin.

Then she met a wonderful man named Ken Williams, and every-

thing kind of took off from there. It was "a marriage made in heaven," as they say, as Ken fell in love with my mom and all of us kids too.

Ken Williams was a real Texan, a man who traveled on the road on weekends playing guitar and singing in a country-western band, was a part-time rancher with his family and sold insurance as his regular job. He had played running back at Rice University on a football scholarship. He worked hard all his life, was in his thirties, but was not married.

Ken always said he was at the point in his life where he was ready for a family, so he married my mom, adopted my brothers and me as his own and moved us to Edna, Texas, a much smaller town than Victoria. We were somewhat middle class, but we had to work for whatever money we wanted for spending. A few years later, my brother Jeff and my little sister Jennifer were born and added to the family.

Edna was just a regular little Texas town. I remember the city limit signs and how they would change the population numbers on them. For a long time the number was 5,332, and then it went to 5,650. After I left, I think it went all the way up to 6,000. Now I think its back in the five thousand range.

At the time I was growing up, I think Edna had three or four red lights and a Dairy Queen. About three years ago, they got a few other fast-food places, a Whataburger, a McDonald's and a Sonic. But I was already long gone by then.

The high school graduating class was a little over a hundred kids. We went from Double-A to Triple-A football, depending on our enrollment that year. I think they had two or three motels in town, and only one theater. It eventually went out of business. Edna had a couple of feed stores a few tire stores, a couple of drive-in grocery stores and a Ford and a Chevy-GMC dealership.

The town finally got a Wal-Mart a couple of years ago, but there wasn't any such thing there when I was growing up. It was just a little-ass town a hundred miles south of Houston on Highway 59, too small to attract the notice of a big retail chain.

Victoria was another town twenty-five miles farther down south. If you went shopping, you sure didn't go to Edna! You'd go to the mall in Victoria, which had a population of about fifty thousand. Or if you real-

ly wanted to go big time, you went to Houston, which was a hundred miles away.

Anyway, Edna was where Ken decided to raise us.

I want to say something about Ken Williams. What a hell of a man he is. Ken is the only father I've ever known, and I love and respect him as my own. In our family, the word "step," as in stepdad or stepson, was never used. When someone asks me who Ken is, I always say he's my dad. He is my real father in every sense of the word.

For anybody to take on the kind of responsibility he did is really something. I don't know if it's something I'd be willing to do. I've always respected the hell out of my dad for that. He's a great man that I really respect. He taught me my sense of humor and my values, so he is my dad one hundred percent, in my opinion.

My dad raised us right—firm, but fair. He kicked my butt many times when it was called for. And my brothers and I did a lot of crap to deserve getting our butts whipped too. We were always doing some kind of stupid stuff.

And then there's my mom. I absolutely love her to death. She has been my inspiration, along with my dad, for everything I have done in my life. I have relied on her for support, love, advice, taking advantage of her wisdom and experience.

I have screwed up plenty of things in my life. That's all a part of living. Through all of my screwups, my mom has understood and helped me in any way she possibly could. It has been one of my missions in life to make her proud of me and to never embarrass her. I love and respect her more than any other person in this world. I'll help you read between the lines. *Don't mess with Stone Cold's mom!*

I have to say I have the best parents in the world.

BEVERLY WILLIAMS (MOM): Family has always been very important to me. I had a situation that was not very good with my own parents, so I went overboard wanting to create a happy situation for my own kids. Ken's parents were wonderful grandparents. My children have so many memories of those grandparents. And Steve still goes to the nursing home and visits his grandma and sends mail, magazines and

posters to the nursing home. A few weeks ago we were up there visiting her and she had this big magazine with Steve on the cover in her hand. She told Ken, "Tear that cover off that magazine Steve sent me, and put it on my wall." So everyone in the nursing home has to go to Edith's room to look at that. Those things are so important to us.

KEN WILLIAMS (DAD): I'm learning now that he listened to us when he was growing up! That makes you proud, that you contributed some good things. He did a heck of a lot on his own too. He's self-motivated.

MOM: I believe in fate. But a lot of times an opportunity may be there and is not recognized. Steve's always had very high goals. He sets his own goals. Steve is going to do it his way. But even back in school, in athletics and everything, Steve was always tougher on himself than the coaches were. If he didn't perform to his expectations, he'd be terribly disappointed. After the football games at Wharton, a lot of times he'd be upset because he didn't think he played worth a darn. He'd be out there apologizing to a whole car full of people who had come from Edna to see his game.

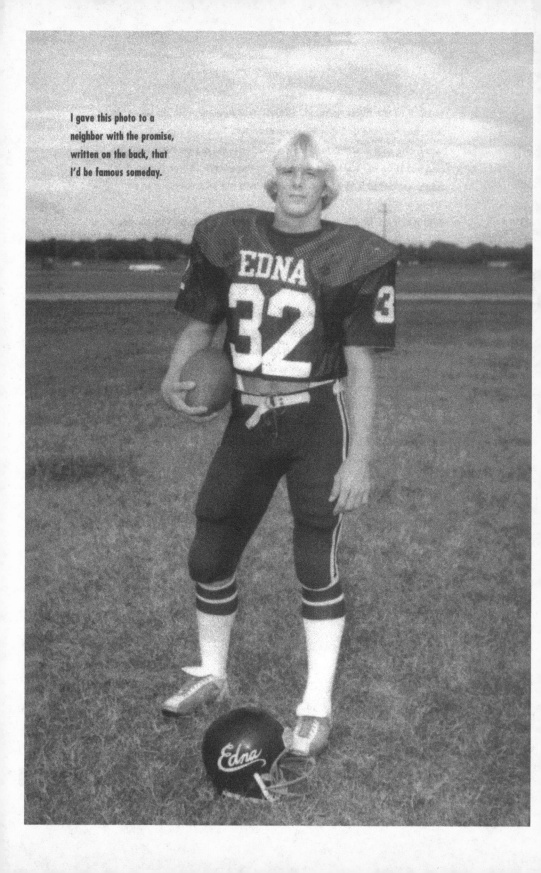

I gave this photo to a neighbor with the promise, written on the back, that I'd be famous someday.

Growing Up in a Small Texas Town

Take the cupcake out of your mouth,
fat-ass, and give me an answer!

—STEVE AUSTIN TO PAUL BEARER

My dad's family had a cattle ranch outside Edna, Texas, and we'd go out there and help with throwing the hay and herding and taking care of the cattle. It was cool, but we managed to always get in some kind of trouble. If I didn't think of something to do to cause some trouble, my brothers did.

Kevin is just like me, only crazier, or maybe I should say "more imaginative." (We were almost like twin brothers, being only ten months apart in age.) Were we bad? Well, yeah, sometimes. We weren't criminal, just ornery. We never got taken to jail, but we did pull some crazy stuff that the whole family laughs about when we all get together on special occasions.

Kevin is serving in the United States Coast Guard and I'm real proud of him. He always said he'd either be a policeman or a soldier. I guess he's sort of both now. And that's a good thing too, 'cause that sumbitch is the real "Stone Cold" and will definitely open up a can of whoop-ass on anyone stupid enough to try on the United States Coast Guard for size!

I was always into athletics. I always played football and baseball, and participated in track. I also really liked the discus throw. A friend and I even tried out tennis one year and somehow went to the state finals. Of course, the only reason I took up tennis was to meet a girl, but we'll get more into that later on.

In high school, I started working out with weights, and my body responded to it. I got thicker and more muscular, "jacked-up," some would say. This paid off, as I got a football scholarship at Wharton Junior College in Texas, and from there I got a full scholarship to North Texas State University in Denton, Texas.

That was a very lucky thing for me in many ways. For one, if I had gone to school out of state, I would not have seen the ads for Chris Adams's wrestling school that aired on *World Class Championship Wrestling,* the Von Erichs' TV wrestling show out of Dallas.

Family has always been real important to me. I'd do anything for my parents, Beverly and Ken, or my brothers Scott, Kevin and Jeff, and my little sister, Jenny—or their families. I'd do pretty much anything for my family, bottom line.

I've screwed up here and there, but I learned some great respect for people from my parents. I do tend to use a lot of four-letter words, but if we're in a restaurant or at a Make-A-Wish appearance, something like that, I'm going to conduct myself accordingly. I pretty much know how to handle myself. But to my friends, the people who know me, yeah, I'm pretty foul-mouthed. Still, I've always respected people. Hell, I treat peo-

ple how I expect to be treated myself. I learned to always say thank you, please, all the right stuff. That's the way my mom and dad brought me up. They taught me respect and the difference between right and wrong.

I wouldn't say I came from a superstrict background, but there were certain things that were going to happen. You were going to do your chores. You were going to take out the trash. We always rotated when it came to doing the dishes, mowing the yard or washing the sides of the house and the windows.

You'd do whatever you had to do. If you didn't, you'd get your ass whupped. At the same time, you weren't going to smart off to your mom or dad, and you weren't gonna cuss. No cussin' and no sassin' mom or dad!

When I was five years old we went to Port O'Connor, Texas, a fishing place we had been going to forever. We rented this bay house and were fishing off the pier when we noticed that all the shrimp boats and fishing boats were coming in. We figured we'd go down there and talk to the fishermen and see what all they caught.

We were walking across this grassy field and stepped into some real-life quicksand. I don't know how prevalent quicksand is in Texas or any other place, to be honest, but this was just like in the movies!

Me and Scott walked right in the middle of this damn quicksand and we were sinking and, damn, I was up to my chest in the stuff. I don't remember freaking out, but Scott had evidently called for Kevin to come bring his fishing pole. So little four-year-old Kevin saved Scott's life and mine by pulling us out.

I guarantee that if he hadn't pulled us out, we would both have been dead. We could not have gotten out of that quicksand without that fishing pole.

I remember when we got back to the house we were renting, Mom and Dad whipped our asses because we were so dirty and muddy! When we finally told them we were stuck in quicksand and almost died, they thought we were BSing them. But it was the real deal—we would have died. Me at five, Scott at seven.

We had another real-life adventure when we were swimming at my Uncle Donnie's house. I looked around and noticed that Kevin had been

down at the bottom of the pool for what seemed like a pretty good while.

My Aunt Pam swam down there, and I jumped in and helped pull him up. An adult there thumped on him and slapped him on the back and revived him, with Kev choking and spitting out all the damn water he had swallowed. He couldn't talk for a day because his vocal cords were all screwed up from swallowing all that water. I don't know how the little SOB made it. I asked him if he had learned how to breathe water. 'Course it was nice to not have him talk for a day.

My folks decided that Kevin needed to see a doctor to make sure he was okay. So we all piled in my mom's Suburban and went with Kevin and everyone to the doctor's office. After looking down his throat and whatever other tests he did, the doctor pronounced Kevin just fine and gave him a sucker. I was POed that I didn't get one! Equal rights! I was part of the damn rescue team and should have got a sucker too!

And it never ended. My brothers and I used to play "prisoner" on these two columns that were out front of our house. One day I was playing around with one of those bicycle security chains with a combination lock on it. I wrapped the chain around myself and one of the columns, and then locked the chain around my stomach. The chain and lock were new, and it sounded like fun at the time.

All of a sudden this big damn bumblebee starts flying around my face and I'm trying to freeze, be still and avoid it. I finally flinched too much and the damn thing stung me right on my eyeball!

Man, I'm squalling as loud as I can squall and I can't get the damn combination lock off because I can't remember the stupid combination. Finally Scott comes out and takes the chain off me, and of course my eye swells completely shut and gets to be the size of a golf ball.

I remember my mom had a big cookie jar on top of the refrigerator, an owl with one eye closed. One of my aunts commented after I got stung, "Look, Steve. You look just like that owl." I don't remember laughing.

Eventually, Jeff joined our brotherly crew. My mother said we were the "neighborhood marauders."

When we moved to Edna my mom had the idea that we should go

around the neighborhood, knock on everybody's doors and see if they had any kids to play with. It worked out pretty good, as we made some good friends from that. But that really was my mom's gimmick for getting our asses out of the house for a few hours—and maybe warning the neighborhood that the "Williams Gang" had moved to town.

Well, we hadn't been in Edna long before we got in trouble. We were going out and ringing doorbells to see where all the kids lived and we came to this one house where nobody was home. But they had a bunch of real nice clay pots with plants in them all across the front of the house. Well, we broke every one of them, every pot they had, and it was a bunch of them—forty or fifty. Damn, we were stupid!

The "Williams Gang" Easter '74, (top row, left-right) Kevin, Scott, me, (bottom row, left-right) Jeff, Jenny.

Then I said, "Kevin, look at this." I pointed to a built-in intercom system by the front door. That was a new deal to me, but I knew what it was. Kevin suggested we come back the next day with a hammer and break it. That must have been when Scott figured we went too far and he snitched on us to the folks.

It was Jeff's birthday, but Kevin, Scott and I had to stay in our room and we got no cake. That was the lightest part of the sentence, as we got our butts whipped as well! Plus, with us being new in town, my poor dad had to go over when the neighbors came back, introduce himself and cut them a check to pay for all the damages. That just goes to show that my dad is a hell of a man. He made no excuses.

He was firm, but fair. One time we were out on the cattle ranch shredding the hay and I uncovered a huge hornets' nest and thousands

of hornets were chasing me and stung me all over. I went home and said, "I quit." Yeah, right. I didn't have no "ball to take home." My resignation lasted only a few hours.

When I was ten or so, it had been raining a whole bunch and we noticed that our neighbors were out of town. We went over to their house and their yard had turned into a field of mud clots. We started picking them up and ended up covering the whole house with mud!

Again, it seemed like a good idea at the time. When it came to getting into trouble, if I didn't think of it first, one of my brothers would. It was kind of neat the way the mud kept sticking, piling up and piling up. Really, we completely trashed the house. The people got home and they put two and two together with some investigation, and they called my father. We got torched on that deal pretty swift. We had to clean their whole house off, apologize and then get punished too. I mean we got our asses whipped! And we deserved it.

Growing up in Victoria, Scott and I were always up to something. One day we got the bright idea of going door to door to see if anybody wanted to buy some cold water. We'd fill up Ziploc bags and put them in the refrigerator and then take them around trying to sell them.

We also set up a stand in the driveway. I remember Scott putting a sandwich board on his back telling people to follow him for a nice cold drink of water—"10 cents." I remember some little girl followed him all over town until she got to our yard and we went ahead and gave her some water for free. We didn't make too much on that venture, but hell, it was my first marketing deal. Seemed like a good idea at the time.

We'd ride our bikes around town and see all these new housing developments they were building, then go back at night and throw rocks through the windows or knock holes in the Sheetrock and, I guess, just mess around and act stupid. That's being malicious though, and I don't endorse it. We never got caught on that one. We would have got our butts blistered.

When you were about to be punished, either you'd have to go out and pick your own switch or my dad would break out his belt. He'd grab your left arm and then he'd proceed to whip the hell out of you. I'd be running circles around him, trying to stay away from the blows, but he

wasn't letting go. He could swing that belt and he'd bust your ass, but it was never child abuse.

I endorse the practice of cutting a switch. We always deserved it, it seemed. We love our dad very much, and know it was all to teach us something. It wasn't anything wrong and I believe in how he raised me. Spare the rod, spoil the child—and we sure as hell weren't spoiled.

My mother is a saint for all the troubles and worries we put her through. Don't get me wrong—she would whip our butts, but we sure made things interesting.

She's a strong, strong lady. I love my mom to death. She can do no wrong in my eyes. Oh, and later in life I learned that my mom went to high school with Virgil Runnels, who would become a professional wrestler—Dusty Rhodes, "The American Dream." He was a few grades ahead of her, but she says he was a good football player and didn't weigh as much as he would later on, "if you will."

My brothers and I would cuss to one another and our friends, but never in front of our parents. In fact, I can remember the exact moment that I first cussed in front of my father.

When I was twelve or so, we were pulling stored hay bales down from the second floor of the barn to where we'd have access to them. Earlier in the day my father had spotted a rattlesnake sneaking in, so he had been on the lookout for it all day. I was up on the second level throwing bales over the side into a truck.

I was moving pretty fast and as I stuck my damn arm in there to grab the next bale I saw that my arm was just inches away from one of the biggest rattlesnakes I'd ever seen. I could see my life flashing before my eyes and had to decide what to do fast!

I yelled, "Oh, shit!" and threw myself out the open second-story bay door to the ground below. My father went inside and got his gun and went looking for the snake.

I was upset about being so damn close to a rattlesnake and almost getting bit. They always scared me and that's one of the reasons I decided to utilize that fear of rattlesnakes and add them to the Stone Cold wrestling character.

Anyway, that was the first time that I had ever cussed in front

of my father. I was really worried about it too—but he never mentioned it.

Recently, I reminded my father of that day. He said that although he remembers the rattlesnake incident like it happened yesterday, he does not recall that I cussed. I guess the situation justified it. Either that or he was so shocked by me jumping out the second story of the barn yelling "snake!" that he was thinking the same thing himself!

My dad always expected us to learn as we go, because sometimes he'd just tell us to do things he thought we should already know *how* to do. One time when I was ten or eleven, my brothers and I were working out at my Uncle Norman's cattle ranch. Our job was to round up the cattle and get them in the pen. When we got them to the gate, they spread out and went everywhere but in the pen. My dad said, "Boys, I said to round 'em up, not to scare 'em the hell off!"

Dad expected us to be these accomplished cowhands. We were on horses, but we didn't know what the hell we were doing. To expect us to be able to round up cattle on horseback at ten or eleven years old or whatever we were . . . man, we were pretty green.

There were only a few things my dad didn't have patience for, and messing up was one of them. But he was usually right when it came down to it.

In this case, he figured we would learn. The cattle were spread all over and wandering off. Dad got on a horse, ran it back and forth in front of the cattle and got 'em to turn around. Then he showed us how to wrangle them to where we wanted 'em to go.

That was so cool. He had to go get a few strays, but we were okay. And we learned.

One thing I could do real well was what they call "throwing the calves." Basically, that meant getting them in a pen and flipping them over so we could give them their shots, mark their ears and so on.

When it was castration time, Kevin would do the smaller ones and I'd handle the bigger calves. We did all that real well, overpowering the cattle, and I think that's where I got a lot of my upper-body strength.

Nowadays, they've got elevated chutes that make it easy. We did it

in a small pen and had to wrestle these strong calves over and hold them down. When we were done with our chores, sometimes Dad would let us ride the calves. It was fun trying to stay on and that's where I probably took my first bumps!

The fact that all the Williams boys are still here is pretty amazing. As a matter of fact, it's a damn miracle!

One time I thought I heard a burglar in our house. I got Scott and we grabbed our shotguns and crept our way into the hall. My dad had given us twenty-gauge pumps for Christmas, so we were ready.

My brother was about ten or fifteen feet in front of me and we heard a noise, so we figured we'd better load up our shotguns and get ready for the showdown with "the burglar." I'd always been extremely safe with a gun, but I was an idiot that night and tested to see if the safety was on—by pulling the stupid damned trigger! *BLAM!!* I had just fired my twenty-gauge shotgun in the house!

Fortunately I had the gun raised to the ceiling, because otherwise I would have shot my brother right in the back. That isn't funny and it's always scared the hell out of me. I was a dumb-ass, but at least I pointed the gun up when I tested to see if the safety was on.

I blew a hole through the ceiling and the roof, and of course everyone jumped like crazy. Kevin woke up and Scott yelled, "What the hell are you doing?" I damn near crapped in my pants, and of course I took a pretty good ass-beating on that one too.

And there never was any burglar. I still don't know what that noise was.

After that, all the guns were locked up in my dad's gun cabinet. We didn't have one at the time, but Dad went right out and bought one—with a lock.

All boys should have a dog, right? When I was twelve or thirteen years old, my dad brought home a dog he found walking down the road. "Look, kids," he said, "here's an early Christmas present!"

We were thrilled with our new dog and named him Socks. Socks was cool and pretty smart. Kevin had a friend from a few blocks away named Anthony. My parents did not really like Anthony. He just always came over at the wrong times and was a pest, and Socks picked up on

that and always growled and gave Anthony a hard time, sometimes chasing him all the way home.

One day we had all just come home from church and Anthony showed up. Again, bad timing on his part. Socks started right in barking at Anthony and was going to chase him home, but I grabbed Socks and assured Anthony that it was okay. I said, "C'mon in, he's okay," while holding Socks back.

As Anthony got about four or five feet from me, I let the dog loose yelling, "GET HIM, SOCKS!" and that dog chased Anthony all the way home five blocks away. We got a big kick out of that. I was always messing with people even back then. Anthony would fall for it every damn time.

MOM: We also had a cute little dog named Leroy, who was kind of dumb. He chased garbage trucks and cars and he got run over one day. The boys were all just boo-hooing away, and they had me crying too over this poor little dead dog. Ken was playing with the band somewhere out on the road, so I called him and told him the news. We were both crying on the phone. The kids were just a mess, and we had to deal with this dead little dog. We went in the backyard and did the whole funeral bit. The boys made a little cross for Leroy's grave. We did that so many times over the years. We probably went through six or eight doggies.

I was a pretty good student in school, and got mostly As and some Bs, and really wanted a football scholarship. I was serious about my grades and all the teachers seemed to like me, even though sometimes I was a class clown. Not really that bad, but I liked to make people laugh if the moment presented itself. Fortunately, I knew when to pick my spots and when to shut up.

I was an easy-to-get-along-with kind of kid and I was friendly to everyone in school. But I only had a few really close friends, as it is with me now. Nothing's changed there.

Because of my good grades, they saw fit to put me in the National Honor Society. There were other kids that got better grades than I did,

but I met all the qualifications and was proud of it. My popularity in school might have helped me a bit. Those silly high school yearbooks voted me Most Popular my first three years and Mr. Cowboy my senior year, which is like Homecoming King, only more manly. In Edna, Texas, being elected Mr. Cowboy was a big deal.

I studied hard, but I was always into the physical fitness thing. Even before I knew what I was doing, I knew it was real important to be in shape to play sports.

In baseball, I played catcher. I was an all-star at that position five years in a row. But I wasn't an all-star because I was the most gifted catcher in the league. I was good, but there were others who had better skills.

The reason I was an all-star was because no one hustled more than I did. If a ball got by me, I'd sprint to the backstop. I was a hustler. Hustle, hustle, always hustle. I never quit. That got me through sports. I was never the best athlete on a team, but I just wouldn't quit.

But baseball wasn't my main focus when it came to athletics. The main deal for me was football. I was attracted to football for lots of reasons. First, every kid in Texas wants to play football. If you were a big, athletic kid like me, that was where you wanted to put your energies. My dad was also an influence, having gone to Rice University on a football scholarship. He was a running back for Rice University in 1958 when they went to the Cotton Bowl against Navy. They lost, 20–7, but my dad scored Rice's only touchdown.

I had no dreams of playing pro football. Later, I wanted to go to college and being good at football was my meal ticket. But I wasn't thinking about college back then. I just wanted to be on the football team.

It was my dad who taught me to bust my ass at everything I did. And if I did something, I needed to do it right the first time so I wouldn't have to come back and do it again. If I got knocked down, I needed to get right back up. And I wasn't ever to let somebody tell me I couldn't do something.

It was good advice. It would help me later on, after I became a professional wrestler.

Back when I was in high school, I was so heavily involved in athletics, so focused on throwing the discus, playing baseball and of course

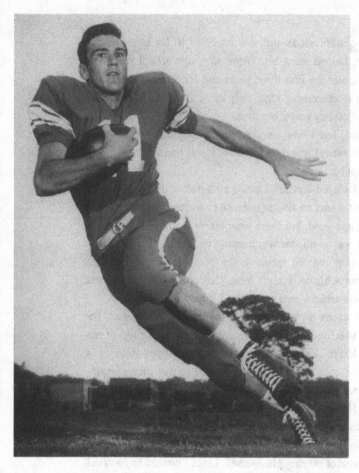
My dad during his
days at Rice.

football, that I got pretty muscular. I had a set of weights out on the back
porch that my mom and dad had bought me and I worked out on those
things all the time.

Of course, I didn't really know how to do it right, but I worked real
hard. I remember on Friday and Saturday nights, I'd be out there lifting
weights all evening. Then I would finally go to bed, and Kevin and all
his hell-raising friends would come over late and be making noise out
on the porch. I'd be trying to sleep and I remember opening the window
and yelling, "Shut the hell up! I'm trying to sleep!" I still can't sleep well
with any noise whatsoever.

In high school I didn't drink beer (believe it or not, although I was

Doing the Sears catalog pose with my brothers Kevin and Scott.

soon to take a crash course). When I was a senior I might have had one or two, but it was not my thing. I was an athlete, pretty much focused on playing sports and making good grades, and I wanted that college scholarship. I wanted to be the best.

When I was in high school, we only lived a block or two from the football field and my dad would go over there and watch us practice and play and he'd always say, "Good game, Steve."

He'd never come in there and gripe at me or tell me what to do, or tell me something I screwed up on. He was always one of my biggest supporters. He always encouraged me, even if I messed up. My folks went to every game they could go to. They are the best.

Neither my dad or my mom was ever overbearing. Sometimes I see situations where I think parents are overbearing to their kids, but my folks were not like that at all. All parents should encourage their kids to succeed. It really means a lot.

Because I didn't drink and insisted on driving, I was always the designated driver for my crazy brothers and their friends. I'd take my mom's Suburban, they'd load it up and they'd all drink beer—they were eighteen or older then—and I'd take 'em to the go-kart track or we'd drive into Victoria and they'd go nuts. Then I'd drive 'em all back home.

One time, we kind of tore up a go-kart track and the old guy who ran the place called the cops on us as we were leaving. The officer pulled us over, but I was driving and I had not drunk anything. After I spoke with the officer, explaining that I was driving everyone home, he let us go. I was my brothers' friends' ticket to a good time. Basically, I was just a big-ass baby-sitter. But we sure tore the hell out of that go-kart track!

As I said, I used to cut up a little in school and get people laughing in class. Sometimes I had something to say that I thought the rest of the class might find entertaining. Once in a while, I went a bit too far.

Then, in the eighth grade, I learned a life lesson that changed everything for me. That year, I had a math teacher named Mrs. Adams. She was a real nice lady, a real pretty lady too, and I was cutting up in her class. And while she was talking, I was running my mouth.

That was the wrong thing to do, because I knew better. But she got on me one too many times. I was really cutting up. I wasn't sassing her, but I guess I was disrespecting her by talking while she was trying to do her job and teach us something.

Well, her husband was Coach Adams of the high school football team. After Mrs. Adams had taken enough crap from me, she apparently told her husband that one of the football players in her class was giving her a hard time.

Well, with me being a big football star in the seventh and eighth grade fixing to go into high school, I was ready for big things. I was ready to be a high school football star on Coach Adams's team.

A few days later after class, here's this big, intimidating coach waiting there. It's Mrs. Adams's husband. He says to me with a lot of bass in his voice, "Are you Steve Williams?"

I said to myself, Well, I guess this guy is noting my football skills. I was a cocky kid, for fourteen years old.

I confidently answered, "Yes, sir," with a big smile on my face.

My first car, a '71 Firebird

He said, "I hear you've been acting up in my wife's class."

To myself, I said, Oh crap, as I looked down at my shoes.

He didn't jump down my throat or yell at me. He looked at me kind of real quietlike and said, "I can make things real hard for you in high school."

I said. "Yes, sir," because I understood exactly what he was talking about. It was that short and that simple. He was intimidating enough that all Coach Adams had to do was look at you. He didn't have to raise his voice. And so from that point on I straightened up—not only in Mrs. Adams's class, but every other class I was in.

Don't get me wrong. When I went on to high school, I still was kind of a class clown, but I sure knew when to shut my mouth! You have to pick your spots.

Then there was the day I bought my first car. It had belonged to this dude we'd see around town and it was sharp! Every time we went to baseball practice or to the baseball park this guy had this car there. It

was a metallic brown '71 Pontiac Formula Firebird, hood scoop, spoiler, white racing stripes down the hood, Crager chrome Supersport mag wheels all the way around, white letter tires. It was a helluva good-looking car.

It originally came with a 455, but when I got it, it had a Chevy 396 in it. It looked great, but turned out to be a real piece of crap. The crossmember motor mount that was under the transmission was lodged in there crooked. There were all kinds of problems with that car. My mom had wanted me to buy my grandmother's two-door Subaru because that would have been a good, economical car to have—fifty miles per gallon and all that.

But no, I had to have this jury-rigged Formula Firebird, because I was cool, right? I paid $1,500 of my own money for it, money I'd earned mowing grass and doing odd jobs. And every weekend my brother Scott, who is mechanically inclined (I'm not), would work on it, fixing it. It was a pile of junk, but it was probably the best-looking car in Edna, Texas.

Then I got a '73 Camaro from my uncle. It had a Corvette 350 motor in it, with a four-speed. That was a nice car. I ended up selling it to my younger brother, Jeff. That was the deal, we had to pay for our own cars.

Nothing in this world is really free. Parents who buy their kids whatever they want aren't doing those children any favors. I know this . . . when you work your butt off for something, you sure as hell appreciate it a lot more when you finally get it.

MOM: Being the mother of four boys was challenging. I did my fair share of spanking, because my husband was in a band, he was gone a lot. Every morning, you might as well have lined them all up for a spanking, because they were gonna need one before the day was up anyway! They knew when I'd absolutely had it with them, and then they'd run to their room and dive under the beds. I'd yank on their legs and pull them out. They still give me hell about that. Sometimes they were awful. It was just boys' stuff, but there was always something going on.

When we lived in Victoria, the nicest, sweetest people lived next door to us and they had one daughter. They really weren't attuned to us, with this wild bunch of boys we had. They were so bad sometimes.

One day, Jim, from across the street, called us and said, "Beverly, I want you to look out the window at what the boys are doing. We're not upset about it, so don't get worried." They had a dirt pile, because they were going to do some landscaping, and it had rained. The boys were just having a ball running and playing with the mud. They were filthy. We had to take them out and hose them off. They were all blond with big blue eyes, and all you could see were those big blue eyes. Steve was especially white-headed. They all were really blond when they were little.

DAD: What one of them couldn't think of doing, the other would. They were always into something. But they never did anything we couldn't forgive them for.

MOM: Steve was such a star in football. We lived one block from the stadium. They were doing well, so we always went to the games. Jenny was real little, and after the game, she'd run to the rail and Steve would come get her and give her and me a big hug. God, he stunk, and he was filthy and sweaty, but she loved it! After every game, he would do that.

Stone Cold Learns About Girls

When I was in seventh and eighth grade in Edna, Texas, I had little girlfriends. I mean, not real girlfriends—crushes, I guess. I remember I was in eighth grade and I was in the band, playing the tuba and the bass horn. One day I was sitting in the back where the tubas and basses go and

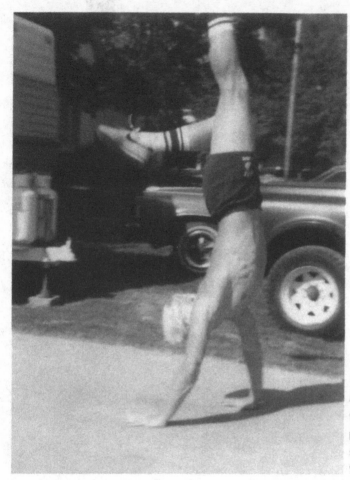

Mom wrote on the back of this photo, "Just showing off." She was right.

some members of the high school band came in to play their instruments for us.

There was this one girl named Kathy. She had on tan pants and she had a star on one of her back pockets. She played the clarinet really well. I later found out that she was three years older than I was, salutatorian of her class, first-chair clarinet and a tennis player. She was just a supersmart person. I immediately fell in love with her. She was pretty

and she had a great body, not like some WWE Diva, but great, with dark brown hair. And I was thinking, God, how am I going to meet this girl?

I was a few grades younger than she was, so I knew I didn't have a chance. Then, out of nowhere, an opportunity came up. This girl played tennis, and the tennis coach, who I knew from playing sports and just goofing around and being friendly, asked me and my friend, Michael Rab, to come out and play tennis.

My wheels started turning. Okay, that would give me a chance to get to know Kathy! I lived about a mile from the tennis courts and Kathy lived on the way to the courts. Michael and I used to walk to the tennis court, but I wasn't going to let anybody see Steve Williams, the big football stud, walking carrying a tennis racket! I couldn't let that happen no matter how much I wanted to get to know this "older woman."

So I'd always lean over and tell my buddy, "Hey, hold my racket while I tie my shoe."

I'd tie my shoe, stand up and start walking, and I'd conveniently forget to take the racket back. My friend would end up carrying it the whole way to the tennis court. I didn't want anybody to think I was some kind of sissy, you see.

Just by playing tennis and being around the tennis courts, I got a chance to meet Kathy. I was shy, but somehow I got to know her. We'd go out to the athletic track and just sit around and talk, and the damn mosquitoes would just be eating us up. One time I worked up the courage to kiss her. I was real nervous, but finally I did it. She was an absolute sweetheart. I'll never forget that first kiss.

We actually ended up being an item, Kathy and I, it started my freshman year in high school—when she was a junior—and lasted a long time. I went to Wharton Junior College in Texas while she was still at Southwest Texas State and got her degree. When I went to North Texas and she had graduated, we moved in together.

We were good for ten years. Then I got this wrestling bug, and Kathy was not a wrestling fan. That was the beginning of the end for us. But I'll tell you that story later on.

Overall, it seems, the wrestling business has allowed me more success in the ring than in romance.

My First Memories of Pro Wrestling

> I don't care if Vince owns this ring, but
> if he gets in this ring, I'm gonna kick his
> ass out of it, and that's the bottom line!
> Why?? 'Cause I said so!
>
> —AUSTIN ON *RAW*

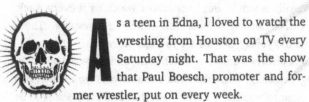

As a teen in Edna, I loved to watch the wrestling from Houston on TV every Saturday night. That was the show that Paul Boesch, promoter and former wrestler, put on every week.

Houston wrestling was the only wrestling show we got in Edna back then. It was a once-a-week deal, one

hour long. I didn't give a damn about the story lines. Back then there weren't hardly any story lines. There were feuds, and there were guys going for the championship belts. That was the draw for me.

Bottom line, I just liked seeing those guys getting in the ring and wrestling each other, punching and kicking each other. I just liked watching it. I remember the commercials from that time too, with I. W. Marks Jewelers putting diamond earrings in Mr. Boesch's huge cauliflower ears, and ol' Mattress Mac. I was always a big Jim McIngvale fan because he was always " . . . *wantin' to s-a-a-a-ave me money!*"

I still have Mac's phone number and we still do things together on occasion. He's a super guy and a workaholic who owns Gallery Furniture in Houston. He's very successful at what he does and extremely honest.

But I remember the guy from way back. I remember meeting with him before *WrestleMania X-Seven* a few years ago in Houston. Jim Mac and I bought the prize-winning steer at the Houston Stock Show right before *WrestleMania X-Seven,* then put it up for charity. That steer, Shorty, went for a million dollars, a world record at the time. And Jim wasn't going to be outbid either. He was serious about it. Those are some high-dollar burgers!

I'm not sure I can explain what drew me to wrestling. You had Jake "The Snake" Roberts, Ted DiBiase, Dusty Rhodes, Ric Flair . . . all those guys would come through Houston and appear on TV. Jose Lothario would come through, "Mad Dog" Buzz Sawyer, a lot of other great wrestling names. I just had to watch wrestling—that smoky arena with one light over the ring, the way I wish it still was today. It was irresistible to me. It drew me to it like a moth to a lightbulb.

My dad didn't watch wrestling. My mom didn't watch and my brothers didn't really watch it. But I remember watching it every week. My sister says she can't remember me watching wrestling. That's because she was too young. She's a lot younger than I am.

My brothers always wanted to watch something else. I'd say, "No, we're watching wrestling, and when the show is over you can watch whatever you want to watch." If I told them that there was going to be something special going on in the ring and sell 'em on the thing, they'd

Here I am at thirteen with my dad's guitar, still dreaming of rock stardom.

watch. I was doing wrestling promos, selling the product back then, and I didn't even know it.

When I was a teenager, I started thinking that being a wrestler would be a good profession for me. I told my brothers that when I was a wrestler, my name would be "The Western Fandango." I don't know why I came up with that crazy name or what it even meant. Shows you how my gears were working. "The Western Fandango, Steve Williams"— I didn't even know what a fandango was, but it sure sounded flashy.

I also wanted to be a rock star. For real. I'm a big music fan and I listen to absolutely everything. Back then, my dad was a huge country-western fan. He plays lead guitar and he sings a lot, so I figured I'd get my dad to teach me how to play guitar.

There we were, doing guitar lessons. Of course, I sucked. I learned a few chords, but I didn't practice enough. You have to practice, practice,

practice, so I quit. I'm not blessed with any musical talent . . . or patience.

Later, I changed my mind and decided that I wanted to learn to play guitar again, so my dad—who has more patience than I do—started teaching me from scratch. Of course, I quit again. But I still wanted to be a damn rock star.

At that point, I went out and bought a bass guitar. My dad knows how to play the bass too, so I figured he'd take yet another shot at teaching me. Besides, I thought, two less strings, it's gotta be easier.

Well, I sucked at the bass guitar too, so I quit that and sold it. Then I said to myself, Okay, I can't play one single instrument.

A rock star who couldn't play anything isn't worth a damn. It didn't leave me a whole lot of options.

But, despite everything, I still had the urge to become a rock star. When I told my parents that I wanted to join a band, they said that was fine. Then I told them that I wanted to play the drums, and they wouldn't let me do that, period.

I had only one choice—to sing. I would be the front man for the band. Anyway, that was the plan.

Kiss was my favorite band growing up. Man, I was the biggest Kiss fan ever. I'd get the headphones on and I'd sing along with all the songs. One day I was singing, "Shock Me," a Kiss song that Ace Frehley sang. I was singing away, doing what I thought was a pretty damn good job, when my brother Kevin came in and slapped the headphones right off my head.

I said, "What the hell are you doing?"

He said, "You suck!"

I said, "What are you talking about?"

And he said, "You've got those stupid headphones on, so you think you sound good. You suck! You're horrible! Take those headphones off and sing without them."

I took the headphones off and I was brutal. Real brutal.

All along, I had thought I was doing good! I thought I was going to be a rock 'n' roll singer and Kevin squashed those dreams right there. Thanks, Kevin. That was it, my singing career officially ended.

Now I buy CDs and listen to the radio. Kevin Williams ruined my dream to be a rock 'n' roll star . . . though I think my lack of musical abilities may have played a small part in it. From then on, I strictly stuck to sports.

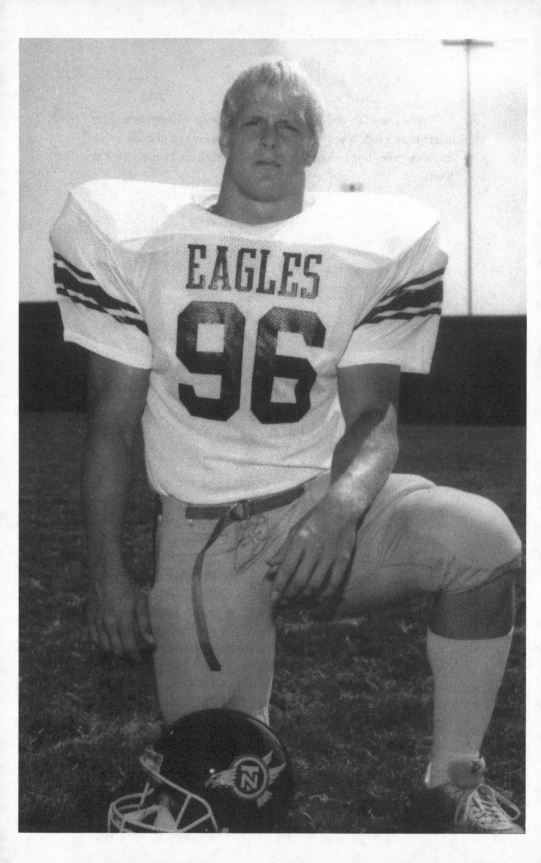

Playing College Sports

s I said before, I loved to play football in high school—that's tackle football, Texas-style—and I was the running back. I was strictly a "north and south" kind of runner who never avoided contact. I'd just run over guys. For three years in a row, starting when I was a sophomore, I was a varsity starter and an All-District running back for the Edna Cowboys.

I started out at 185 pounds and got up to 205 by the time I grad-
uated, so I wasn't a powerhouse by any means. And my offensive line
averaged only about 160 pounds, so I didn't get a lot of blocking. Still,
I managed to flat-out run over some people before they pulled me down.

I was also the discus guy on the track and field team. I even quit
playing baseball because I wanted to concentrate on the discus.

But football was my deal. That was the sport I really loved.

When I came to the end of my high school career, I started looking
around for colleges where I could continue to play football. My dad had
played for Rice University, and of course he was trying to get me in at
Rice. He took me to Houston and we visited the business school and met
the coaches, but they had nothing for me.

Other than that, I got piles and piles of letters from colleges all
over the place, but when it came down to it, I could have gone to Texas
Lutheran College in Seguin, Texas, on a half scholarship, or I could have
gone to Wharton County Junior College on a full scholarship, forty-five
miles from my house.

Well, that was a no-brainer. Of course, I was going to go for the full
scholarship. Hey, it was a chance to be close to home. That was great
because I wasn't one of those kids who wanted to go halfway across the
country to go to school. I loved my family so much that forty-five miles
away was even stretching it for me. So I went to Wharton County Junior
College and played for two years.

At Wharton, they must have decided that I was too slow to play
running back, so they moved me to linebacker. I played linebacker for
two years at Wharton and started all our games both seasons, but I
wasn't very disciplined. I ran all over the field. I liked to hit people.

After a semi-illustrious career as a linebacker at Wharton, I had
three scholarship offers. I could have gone to the University of New
Mexico in Albuquerque on a full scholarship, I could have gone to Texas
Lutheran College on a half scholarship or I could have gone to North
Texas State in Denton, Texas, about thirty-five miles north of Dallas, on
a full scholarship.

The University of New Mexico took me snow skiing and everything
up there in Albuquerque, but North Texas State was in Texas and I didn't

Dear Mom and Company,

Spring training is going pretty good. Everything is okay but the weight program sucks. I'm getting a little tired of it.

I'm ready for summer to get here. Maybe I can find a job in Edna. I forgot to fill an application at the Highway Dept. Oh, well. I need to make some money this summer. I've decided I'm going to buy a street bike if I can afford it. It will sure save a lot of money with these high gas prices.

Well, Scott seemed to be doing pretty good in Huntsville. I think he really likes it up there. Kevin wrote me a letter the other day. Seems like he's doing pretty good, too.

I think someone needs to talk Coach Sappington so Jenny can run the hurdles. That could be her event. She needs to start running them now for the experience. It will help her when she's in high school. She could be a bad ass white girl.

It sure seems like Jeff is having a good time in high school. I think he'll be all right. Seems like he really enjoys the Red Rocker (Camaro).

Well, tell everybody hi for me and tell Dad to take it easy.

Be careful with my stereo.

Love,

Steve

have to leave the state. It was 350 miles away from home, but at least it was in Texas.

That was another no-brainer for me. I wasn't going to do the half-scholarship deal if I could get the full ride. So I packed up and went to attend North Texas State in Denton, Texas, on a football scholarship.

I remember at North Texas I was running the forty-yard dash, and I was clocking in at 4.9. I ran again and it was another 4.9.

The coach who recruited me came over and said, "What are you doing?"

And I said, "What do you mean?"

He goes, "What's with the four-point-nine?"

I said, "That's what I've always run."

He said, "The coach at your junior college said you run a four-point-seven."

I said, "I've never run a four-point-seven in my life!"

These guys at Wharton had padded my stats a bit and said I was faster than I was. If they'd known I ran a 4.9, North Texas State might not have given me the scholarship.

But all the coaches liked me because I ran my ass off on the football field. A 4.9 may have been my fastest time, but I never ran around anybody anyway. I'd always try to run them over.

Being thirty-five miles north of Dallas, I was also about thirty-five miles north of the world-famous Dallas Sportatorium. My North Texas buddies and I would load up on Friday night, drive to Dallas and watch the wrestling matches at the Sportatorium.

Saturday morning, the next day, they'd be doing the TV tapings and I'd be right back there, about ten rows back, watching the guys wrestle again. I've always had a knack for putting myself in the right place at the right time somehow. This was one of those times, because I was getting deeper and deeper into wrestling.

As I said, I had been watching wrestling my whole life. But In Denton, I was exposed to the larger world of Dallas wrestling. I watched *World Class Championship Wrestling* with the Von Erich brothers, and then we started getting Bill Watts's *Power Pro Wrestling* and *Mid-South Wrestling*, hosted by Jim Ross.

So I was playing football, studying and watching my wrestling. And for a while, that was pretty much all I did.

Midway through my junior year at North Texas State, when I was splitting time with one of the starters, I blew out the ACL in my left knee. That was the first of many knee problems in my life. I rehabbed the whole year and came back for my senior year, and started all eleven games at defensive end. Defensive end was a better read for me in college because I was jacking up with the tackle or the tight end rather than sitting back and watching all this movement. I didn't have the discipline to sit back and watch. I liked to attack. Imagine that!

Actually, I didn't like North Texas football a whole lot. It wasn't what I was used to. I was ready to quit at the end of my junior year. And the only reason I *didn't* quit was my dad.

I didn't actually ask him if I could quit, but I was pretty sure I knew what he would say. North Texas had gambled on me and gave me a scholarship. I had given them my obligation to play and if I quit that was going to screw them up.

I knew my dad would be disappointed in me for not fulfilling my obligation to North Texas State, and for taking a scholarship they could have given to someone else. So I forgot about quitting and stuck with it.

After my college football eligibility was up, I still didn't have enough credits to graduate North Texas State. But the team's defensive line coach was good enough to find me a job at Watkins Motor Line, loading and unloading trucks and working on the freight dock. So I worked at the freight dock and made enough money to pay for another semester on my own.

Of course, I got burned out on research papers and all that stuff, but I made it through. But when that semester was over, I was still seventeen class hours short of graduating. Seventeen hours stood between me and a college diploma.

But I was burned out, and I didn't want to do it anymore. So I said, "Screw this," and started working full-time at Watkins driving a forklift. I was still lifting weights and staying in good shape, but I wasn't going anywhere. I didn't have any direction. That's when I started seeing the commercials for Chris Adams's wrestling school on TV, and for the first time I started thinking seriously about getting into wrestling for a living.

In my case, I've never regretted not finishing college. I was talking to a young woman on the airplane just the other day, coming home from Cleveland. We had just gotten to San Antonio and while we were waiting for them to open the doors she introduced herself. She was a sophomore in college, she told me. We started talking about it, how she was doing well in school and all.

I told her I was seventeen hours shy of getting my degree. My par-

ents were disappointed, because I would have been the first kid in my immediate family to get a college degree.

She said to me, "Do you ever regret not going back, or are you going to go back?"

I said, "No on both counts, because I have nothing to prove to myself. With all I've done, I don't need a degree. It's not going to open up any more doors for me. A piece of paper means nothing to me. But as far as you or anyone else is concerned, I'd recommend it absolutely, because it's going to open up a lot of doors for you."

Education is extremely important. I highly recommend it. But for me, at this stage in my life, a piece of paper saying I graduated from college at this point isn't particularly useful. I've been successful without it.

I know my parents were disappointed, and that's a shame. But not having a diploma hasn't been a hindrance to me on the path my life has taken.

If I'd gone to Albuquerque to attend New Mexico University, who knows if I'd ever have gotten into wrestling. But the fact that I was near Dallas, and the Sportatorium was sitting there calling to me, made it all happen for me.

My college education ended, but my wrestling education was just getting ready to begin. And what an education it was! It changed my life forever.

J.R.: Bobby Jack Wright is the current football recruiting coordinator for the Oklahoma Sooners and has long been considered one of the top recruiters in college football. Coach Wright has made a few stops along the way in his long coaching career, including serving on the staff of the University of Texas and on the staff at North Texas State, where he recruited Steve Williams to play defensive end for the Mean Green. Because of my relationship with the coaching staff at OU, I have gotten to know Coach Wright. He once told me that he always thought Steve would not last at North Texas, that he would quit. I listened to the coach's story in amazement. Stone Cold quit? Are we talking about the same guy here? I asked Coach Wright if he thought Steve lacked the heart or the guts to play for North Texas, and the

coach emphatically said, "No!" Steve, like many athletes, had one hel-luva time getting over being homesick! Steve Williams would never quit on the field, but he sure missed his family. He missed his family so much that Coach Wright wouldn't have been surprised if someone had come to him on virtually any morning and said, "Williams is gone. He went back to Edna."

Steve and I had the opportunity to visit with Coach Wright (who, ironically, married a woman from Edna, Texas) at the OU team hotel after the 2003 Rose Bowl victory over Washington State, and we all had a laugh about the homesick country boy from Edna with the motor that never stopped on the football field—a boy who would become one of the most famous wrestlers in the world.

DAD: Steve was always very athletic. He was blessed with a lot of abil-ity. And he always had great size, strength, agility and speed. That combination is pretty rare.

I was always amazed at how supportive Steve was of his little sis-ter. He was off at college doing his own thing, playing ball, lifting weights, working, always busy. Jenny, meanwhile, was a pretty big

Dear Worm, (I mean Jenny)

Hey girl, what have you been up to? You aren't chasing all the guys, are you? What have you been doing this summer? I'm not doing anything but eating, sleeping, and lifting weights.

I sure did like the letter you wrote me the other day. You better write me some more.

You are kind of a brat every once in a while, but I miss you. Have you been acting like you're sick lately? Just kidding. Are you getting a pretty good tan? I'm not. I'm getting ass white as a fish. I mean sheep! No, I just don't have time to get in the sun right now. But I do have a pretty good moon tan. Just kidding, I fooled you didn't I? Well girl, I guess I better go.

Steve

track star in her freshman year of high school. She was on the varsity, and Steve always came to her track meets in these podunk little towns down here. He came to her district track meet in Yokum, and you would've thought she was running in the Olympics. He'd bring down his college friends, and they'd all be up in the stands hootin' and hollerin'. That was always so special to Jenny.

And Now It's Time to Go to School— Wrestling School

7

The whole time I was driving a forklift for Watkins Motor Line, I would come home and watch the *World Class Championship Wrestling* shows from Dallas on TV. I remember they had a graphic of a satellite dish at the beginning of the show, and the satellite dish was beaming *World Class Championship*

Wrestling all over the world. I thought that was the hottest deal I had ever seen.

My buddies and I were going down to the Sportatorium on Friday nights to watch the big main event matches that weren't televised, and then we'd go down on Saturday mornings to watch the TV tapings that went out on the satellite. I'd been thinking about getting into wrestling, but I didn't know what to do or how to get started.

Then they started running TV ads saying that the English-born wrestler, "Gentleman" Chris Adams, was starting a wrestling school, and gave out his contact information. It got my attention. I asked my folks if they would mind if I gave this wrestling a try.

They encouraged me to go try it. They said, "Yeah, give it a shot, as long as it's not illegal or immoral." My mom said I had to change my name though. I told her I was going to change it to "Steve, Son of Beverly Williams from Edna, Texas."

Anyway, I had a fallback position. If wrestling didn't work out, I was still young enough to go back to school or work in the insurance business, and eventually join my father's business after I got enough experience.

For a long time, I had been on a path to be an insurance salesman. So naturally, when I first started college, I was a business major. But accounting kicked my ass and college algebra did too. I was a good student, but math was my weak point. I dropped algebra so many times it was unreal.

But I was going to be an insurance man and eventually take over my dad's business. That's just what I was going to do. I didn't have any other goals once I was out of football.

I remember I once took a career aptitude test in high school, where you fill out all these forms and they give you an indication of what you should pursue in life. When I got mine back, it said I should be a park ranger. I had said I like the outdoors and stuff like that. I don't think I would have looked too good in a Smokey the Bear hat.

I called Chris Adams one day and he said, "Hey, we're going to do seminars for the school, and it will cost you forty-five bucks to go to the seminar. And if you sign up for the however-many-month

course, it'll cost an additional sum, like fifteen hundred dollars."

So I figured, Okay, I'll go check it out. I had nothing to lose but a little time and forty-five dollars.

The seminar was set for an early Saturday afternoon, after the TV tapings and interviews were over and the fans were leaving the Sportatorium. I had long, blond hair at the time and I was pretty jacked-up. I'd been training hard and working on the freight dock. I showed up, and I've never dressed nice my whole life, but I showed up wearing those black Girbaud pants that were in style then with the snap buttons. I had a purple shirt on and a pair of black loafers. So I looked pretty good for me. I wanted to make a good first impression, another of life's important lessons.

I figured there would be a bunch of big, jacked-up guys there, but I was wrong. In fact, I was the biggest guy who showed up. I looked around and some of these guys and girls I saw around me were definitely not in shape. There were thirty-five or forty of us in line for the seminar. It was just a bunch of local people—normal, regular people like you'd see anywhere. And here I was, about 250 pounds, muscular, a decent-looking kid twenty-three or twenty-four years old with long, blond hair. I was standing in line for the school, and people were coming out because the TV tapings were over, and here come the SWAT Team, Samu and Fatu, and those two guys from South Africa, the Simpson brothers.

I'm thinking, Man, here are all these wrestlers from TV, walking right by me.

And then fans started coming up to me and asking me for my autograph. I was saying, "Hey, I'm not a wrestler. I'm here to go to wrestling school, but I'm not a wrestler."

They said, "Well, sign this."

And I said, "But I'm not a wrestler."

And they said, "Yeah, but we know you're going to make it. Go ahead and sign."

What could I have done? I didn't want to be a jackass, so I was standing there writing "Steve Williams" on these pieces of paper.

Pretty soon, we went into the room where they were holding the

seminar and there was Chris Adams. He looked over at me a couple of times and saw something, because of my size, I guess.

He said, "Hey, how you doing? What's your name?"

I said, "Steve Williams."

And he said, "I'm Chris, it's nice to meet you. What's your background?" He gave everybody the same basic greeting, but he came over to me and shook my hand in person.

I told him I had just finished up playing football at North Texas State. Then the meeting started and he began describing the wrestling school. Three or four times he said, and I thought he was referencing me in particular, "Just because you're some big football player doesn't mean you're going to make it in this business. There's a lot more to it than just being a big football player."

I listened to all this, but after the meeting I went up to him and said in a polite way, "You know, you keep talking about football players. I don't know what being a football player's got to do with it, but if you show me how to do this, how to wrestle, I can do it."

I wasn't trying to be cocky or anything, I just wanted to let him know I was paying attention to what he was saying. It kind of pissed me off.

He said, "Okay, Steve, I hope to see you again."

And I said, "Oh, you will," and I signed up.

DAD: At that time, I remember telling him, "You're taking a shot at something that's a high-risk thing. It's hard to be successful in the entertainment business. But I would encourage you to do it now, while you're young. Take a shot at it, if that's what you feel like you want to do." We were all for it. We try to encourage all of our kids to decide what they want to do, as soon as they can. I didn't try to steer them any particular way to do any particular thing. I wanted them to try and figure out what they liked to do—and then get an education and learn how to do it better than the average person, because a person spends so much of his life in his workplace. Even if it's a little less money, if you enjoy what you're doing, it makes all the difference in the world. All the kids have managed to be pretty successful.

The school cost $1,500, just like Chris Adams said. You had to pay weekly, unless you had the money to pay it up front, which, hell, nobody did. Certainly not me. But I had officially started going to wrestling school.

The classes were every Saturday after TV tapings at the Sportatorium. At first, I was very slow to catch on. There was one kid—he weighed about a hundred and fifty pounds—who was a natural. His name was Todd something. He had all these reversals and stuff like that. He made it look easy. He learned to chain wrestle pretty quickly.

Chris was showing us all these holds, and—unlike Todd—I was fumbling through them. I needed repetition. I had never wrestled before in my life. It was awkward. But Chris was cool with me. He kept his eye on me, because he knew I was going to be *his* guy. I was the only guy in the class who had a marketable physique and a "look." He realized that to push his school, he needed a guy who would eventually be ready to do it and succeed, and that was me. Anyway, that was how I learned to wrestle—at Chris Adams's school.

Finally, things started coming along for me. I began to look like I knew what I was doing and Chris said, "Steve, we're going to have your first match pretty soon." I said, "Let's do it."

So after five months of training, I was going to have my first match on *World Class Championship Wrestling* television against a journeyman Cajun wrestler, Frogman LeBlanc. The date of the match was May 11, 1989. It's not a date I'm likely to forget anytime soon.

Was I ready? Not really. I had just been going to this wrestling school, learning a couple of reversals and a couple of moves. You need to know a lot more than that to be a professional wrestler.

Chris Adams had been real nice to me up until that point. Later, I would learn that he hadn't prepared me the way I should have been prepared. At the time, Adams seemed charming and very intelligent to me. I look back at him now and I realize that he was a con man deluxe.

When I broke in, hell, I didn't know what kayfabe was. Now I know it's a signal for wrestlers to close ranks when a fan is approaching, but back then it was just gibberish to me.

Chris Adams didn't try to smarten me up or teach me the "real deal" when it came to pro wrestling. He was just teaching me some moves to use in the ring. I didn't know I wasn't really supposed to go out there and beat the hell out of somebody, or have somebody beat the hell out of me.

Chris didn't tell us, "This is a work, a performance, and you have to protect your partner." No, we were just learning to wrestle. He wasn't exposing the business, he was just teaching us the basics of how to apply one hold or another.

I knew something was up, but no one would come up to me and say, "Hey, here's how we do it." I didn't know how it was going to work. I knew there was something to it, I just didn't know what.

But back then, Chris Adams was my teacher and I was his student, and I trusted him to take care of me. I thought he was a really good guy who had my best interests at heart. I even did a little promo standing beside Chris to advertise his wrestling school, the first of many wrestling promos I would do over the next fourteen years.

Anyway, I had my first television match against Frogman LeBlanc on a Friday night at the Dallas Sportatorium, the place where I had been watching matches as a fan for years. I wrestled under my real name, Steve Williams.

But I had to dress in the janitor's closet. I couldn't dress with the other wrestlers, because I wasn't smartened up yet. I wasn't one of "the boys." I was nervous as hell. The whole experience wasn't shaping up to be what I thought it would be.

As it turned out, I gave Frogman LeBlanc a beating. I must have arm-dragged the poor guy six or eight times in that short match. I put a bunch of armbars on him, and believe me, it was brutal. It was horrible. I had these pretty neat-looking long tights on. I didn't wear short trunks back then. I had good legs, but I always wanted to wear the long tights for some reason.

I was just out of wrestling school, so I was an unknown, but I thought the crowd could have gotten behind me a little more. I was a little disappointed with that aspect of the match. I can't remember what

the finish was, but I beat Frogman LeBlanc, one-two-three. It was a green match, but I got through it.

I remember the referee of the match was Tony Falk, and a couple of times I was a little lost out there. Tony was actually a real good worker in his day. He didn't have a great body, but he was a good worker. He helped me out a whole lot during that match. He called a few things for me and helped me get through it.

After I got out of the ring, Chris Adams came up to me and asked me why I did some of the things I did.

I said, "Well, Tony told me to."

So I think he ended up bitching Tony out a bit, but Tony was just trying to help me. Tony's always been a great help to me. Frogman didn't call anything. He might have said this or that, but he had that really heavy Cajun accent and I've always been half-deaf anyway, so I was probably like, "What?"

But we got through the match. It wasn't anything to be proud of, but it wasn't a disaster either. I got paid forty bucks for it. I had no inkling of what you were supposed to make for a wrestling match, as that had never been discussed with me, but I thought forty bucks was a little light. It turned out that was pretty much the standard pay for Dallas. After I beat Frogman LeBlanc, I went on the road and made even less—twenty-five bucks a match, more often than not.

So it was not bad, as I was still a student. But that first time, my perception was, "I'm on TV. I'm supposed to be making some money for this."

I was a mark, a straight-up mark. I didn't know any better.

"Gentleman" Chris Adams trained me and got my foot in the door in this business at a time when you *had to know somebody* to get in. He was a pile of crap though. That's why I didn't comment when Chris died and the *Dallas Morning News* called me. I wasn't going to run him down in the paper because the guy was dead, but I didn't think a whole lot of him.

I liked him well enough when I first started, but once I got going, he screwed me over too many times. He was just such a picture of insin-

cerity to anyone he ever met. Nobody liked the guy. He was a con man, period.

Anyway, after that match with Frogman LeBlanc, I figured I had started paying my dues in the wrestling business. I wasn't off to a real "stunning" beginning, but I was on my way. I just wanted to learn the business and become the best talent I could.

Then I started getting booked on a regular basis, and they beat the hell out of me every Friday night and Saturday morning for two months. P.Y. Chu-Hi and those guys in Dallas were beating me up with the kendo stick and weightlifting belts, and I still wasn't smartened up all the way. In other words, nobody told me this business was as much showbiz as it is.

When I was breaking in, I used to ride from town to town with Skandor Akbar and Bronco Lubich. Akbar was the evil Middle Eastern wrestler-turned-manager who was born Jim Whebbe, from Vernon, Texas, and Bronco was the longtime *World Class* referee and former tag partner of Angelo Poffo, Randy Savage's father.

Both of these men were former veteran wrestlers who knew a lot about the business and had been all over the world. I was so lucky to be talking with them, learning the psychology of pro wrestling. Their talking to me, telling me how to do things, as we were going up and down the road, was a terrific education in the wrestling business.

We'd be together in one of their cars, and they'd be up front smoking big, smelly cigars and I'd be in the backseat asking them questions and soaking up everything they were telling me. That was a college degree in the old-school ways of doing things. I loved those guys.

Sometimes they'd tell me old wrestling stories. I'd always enjoy hearing those. I didn't have any money then, and they wouldn't charge me for transportation. I'd just sit in the back and ask them questions. Those guys were cool. They knew I was genuinely interested in learning, and they both took me under their wings.

Both Akbar and Bronc were excellent storytellers. When one of them told a story, the way they laughed made me want to laugh too. It was a real good time in my life. Those guys and their wealth of knowledge about ring psychology were tremendous influences on me through-

out my whole career. They also furthered my respect for the wrestling business.

But the guy I came to respect less and less as I pursued a career in wrestling was Chris Adams. Here's a story that young wrestlers can learn from . . .

There was an old, silver-haired guy who booked wrestling shows out of Dallas named Ed Watt—no relation to Bill Watts, the owner and promoter of *Mid-South Wrestling*. Ed was a nice guy. He booked the United States Wrestling Association talent shows and Chris Adams ran his own independent shows. Ed was going to pay me a hundred and fifty dollars a night. This was my second go-around in Dallas after coming back from Tennessee, so I was "known" and could command a bigger paycheck. He booked me for three or four shows.

All of a sudden, I got a call from Chris Adams. He said, "Steve, I need you for some shows on these dates."

I said, "Hold on, Chris, I'm already booked with Ed."

He said, "What do you mean?"

I said, "Chris, I'm already booked with Ed."

He said, "You're not going to work my shows?"

I said, *"I'm already booked with Ed!"*

He goes, "Well, you know I did get you into WCW."

That was crap. I hadn't gone to WCW yet and they hadn't even called me. He was just saying, "Hey, I think they're going to call you," implying that he did something for me. They called me way later, and when they did it had nothing to do with Adams.

But he repeated, "Hey, I did get you into WCW." And I was like, "I can't believe you're holding this crap over my head!" He did train me, for what it was worth, and now he was putting a guilt trip on me.

Then he said, "Look, Steve, if you work my shows, I'll pay you double what Ed Watt was going to pay you."

Money wasn't the thing. It was that he made me feel guilty. So I called Ed up and said, "Ed, this is Steve. Man, Chris Adams is really giving me a hard time about working these shows for you. Do you mind if I work his shows?"

It was clearly something I wasn't comfortable doing, but I was being blackmailed into doing it. So the time came and I worked Chris Adams's shows. But when I got his check in the mail, it only had a hundred and twenty-five dollars written on it.

I called him and said, "Chris, what's the deal?"

He said, "What do you mean?"

I said, "You told me you were going to pay me double what Ed was paying me. Ed was going to pay me a hundred and fifty."

All of a sudden, I heard a click. Chris Adams had hung up on me, like a little chicken.

I couldn't freakin' believe it. I broke my word with Ed Watt, who was always real nice to me, and it wasn't about the double money. It was Adams putting the guilt trip on me. That pissed me off.

I'm sorry he got killed, but the guy did not have good karma. He got shot by a guy, who was supposedly his friend, while having a heated argument that Adams would not back down from. When the case went to court, Adams's friend was found innocent by reason of self-defense.

J.R.: Chris Adams, may he rest in peace, was a con man, pure and simple. He abused women, had a bad temper and generally was not a very good person. However, he was a solid in-ring performer, had a unique British accent that set him apart and was a handsome fellow when he first hit it big with the Von Erichs's World Class Championship Wrestling. Chris was very shrewd. He was a "manipulator," in nonflattering wrestle-speak, but Chris Adams had an eye for talent. He married and dated beautiful women and he could see when a young guy had something special in the ring. Steve Williams had something special that Chris Adams discovered and became determined to capitalize on. There's nothing wrong with capitalizing on business opportunities, but Chris had a problem telling the truth at times, which Steve and anyone else who knew Chris would soon realize. Chris Adams did an excellent job of training Steve Williams in the ring, but luckily, Steve did not acquire any of Adams's negative traits. Steve Williams was Chris Adams's star pupil, without a doubt, and within a couple of years Steve had surpassed his teacher in the ring. I have always felt that if Steve had stayed around Chris on a regular basis after Chris had showed his true colors, that there would have been a terrible altercation between the two. I always felt there was an aura of volatility around Chris, which I guess in a way there was, as he died a violent death.

A "Stunning" Revelation

> Does anyone have a cold
> beer for Steve Austin?
>
> —Austin on *Raw*

Pretty soon, I was wrestling lots of weekend shows in Dallas–Fort Worth and the surrounding area, and doing the televised wrestling shows from Dallas. And I was still using my real name, Steve Williams.

By then, I was working for Jerry Jarrett, who ran

the Memphis wrestling territory and who had had a live television show on WMC-TV Channel 5, on Saturday mornings, for more than twenty-five years. Jarrett had bought the *World Class* promotion in Dallas and renamed it USWA, United States Wrestling Association.

By working for Jerry Jarrett, wrestlers got to work in both territories, Dallas and Memphis, and be seen in two different television markets. Jarrett didn't pay much, but you got a lot of experience and worked with guys who were dedicated to learning the business.

So I was getting my paychecks from Jerry Jarrett, but I wasn't getting them as often as I would have liked. I just wasn't wrestling that much—just Fridays and Saturdays, and working at the trucking company during the week. But I thought I was doing a good job in the ring and finally asked Jerry when he was going to book me full time.

He said, "Hell, Steve, I think you're ready now."

That's when they sent me over to Mid-South Wrestling in Memphis, a pretty famous territory where Jerry "the King" Lawler was usually the champion. They had a lot of television exposure over there, which could only do me good.

So I drove my 1988 Hyundai to the Mid-South Coliseum in Memphis, Tennessee, and was pretty excited the whole way. I remember walking around the dressing room when I arrived. I was the first guy there—a habit I've tried to continue my whole career. I was looking around and in came Ricky Morton, half of the Rock 'n' Roll Express tag team and an awesome worker in his day, smoking a cigarette. Ricky was a big star at the time.

He said, "Hey, how you doing?"

I said, "Hey, I'm Steve Williams."

He said, "Ricky Morton. Can you work?"

Well, Ricky Morton was a workin' son of a gun, one of the best. I said, "Well, I guess that's what I'm here to learn."

He took a drag off his cigarette and said, "Nice to meet you," and walked off. That was my first meeting with Ricky Morton. Little by little, everybody else showed up at the building. Dutch Mantel, the booker, looked at me and said, "Who are you and what are you doing here?"

I said, "I'm Steve Williams, Jerry Jarrett told me to come find you. I'm starting tonight."

He said, "Well, I don't know nothin' about that."

That didn't sound good to me. "Dirty" Dutch Mantel, a Vietnam veteran who looked like Yosemite Sam, is a big, burly guy who's built like a bear and as furry as one too. He has a long beard with a long handlebar mustache and long black hair. At the time, Mantel was a seasoned ring veteran who had been around the world and was booking the Memphis territory. He later came to World Wrestling Entertainment for a while as a character called Uncle Zeb.

I had obviously caught Mantel off-guard. He was the booker in the place, but he didn't know I was supposed to start that night. He didn't even know who I was. And my future had been placed squarely in his hands.

"All right," he said. "Okay, let me think of something. Hang tight and I'll get back to you." Finally he came back and said, "What's your name?"

I said, "Well, it's Steve Williams."

He said, "You can't be Steve Williams here. There's already a wrestler named Dr. Death Steve Williams."

He looked at me a moment longer and said, "All right, you've got fifteen minutes to come up with another name."

I got really nervous. I was in a new territory, it was my first gig there and I didn't want any problems. I was still trying to come up with something that didn't sound stupid when Dutch came back.

"Well," he said, "what'd you come up with, kid?"

I said, "I didn't come up with anything."

He went, "Okay, you're Steve Austin."

I said, "What if I don't want to be Steve Austin? A lot of people watch *The Six Million Dollar Man* TV show, and I don't want to copy anybody."

He said, "You ain't copying anything. It's got nothing to do with that. Your name is Steve and you were born in Austin, right? But if you don't like that name, you've got five minutes to come up with a better one."

The show was about to start and the fans were hollering for us to hurry up. It wasn't exactly the best environment for thinking clearly or creatively.

Dutch came back and said, "What'd you come up with?"

I said, "I still haven't come up with anything."

So he said, "All right, you're Steve Austin."

What was I going to say? I couldn't come up with anything else, so I was Steve Austin. I ended up going out there and telling the fans, "I'm Steve Austin," for however many weeks or months that job lasted. I didn't love the name, but it wasn't a deal breaker for me.

So I made my debut in the Mid-South Coliseum in Memphis and the booker, Dutch Mantel, gave me my name, "Steve Austin." I think it was a week later, over the weekend, that I had my first match.

It was in Lebanon, or some town like that in southern Tennessee, and I was working with a guy under a hood—a mask. I forget his name. Of course, I was green as hell, and Dutch only wanted me to go out there and work seven or eight minutes. When I came back to the locker area, I thought I did pretty well. I walked back through the door and Dutch went, "What the hell was *that* shit?"

I thought it was a pretty good match. I said, "What are you talking about?" He said, "Damn, brother. Chris, come here." He was talking to Chris Champion, a guy who was working his way up the ladder, trying to catch a break. Chris had entered the wrestling business five or six years before me. He had long hair extensions and wore high leather boots up to his knees, and had a rock 'n' roll-type gimmick. He was a good guy to hang out with. I would wind up traveling with him and Dutch quite a bit

Anyway, Dutch Mantel told me, "Put a headlock on Chris."

I got Chris in the hold with his head low on my side. Dutch said, "No, don't do that. Pull him up here under your arm so you can listen to him talk to you."

All of a sudden, I got it. My opponent was attempting to communicate with me, trying to call the match to me, but I didn't hardly hear a word he said. Dutch balled me out for about two minutes, just ripping into me.

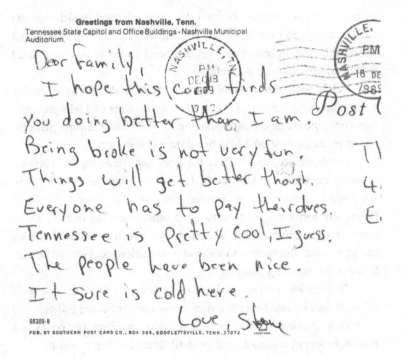

Greetings from Nashville, Tenn.
Tennessee State Capitol and Office Buildings - Nashville Municipal Auditorium.

Dear family,
I hope this card finds
you doing better than I am. Post
Being broke is not very fun.
Things will get better though.
Everyone has to pay theirdves.
Tennessee is pretty cool, I guess.
The people have been nice.
It sure is cold here.
Love, S

68309-B
PUB. BY SOUTHERN POST CARD CO., BOX 308, GOODLETTSVILLE, TENN. 37072

Then he said, "You see that chair out there?" There was a steel chair standing up against the wall. "You get that chair and you sit in the doorway, and you watch every one of those matches out there in the ring. That's the only way you're going to learn."

So from that day on, for virtually my whole career, I've watched every single match on the card. Not so much in the last year or two, but damn near every single match on every card before that. And I did it because Dutch Mantel told me to. He was a big influence on me. "Dirty" Dutch was a damn good teacher and a much better booker than he's been given credit for.

Dutch knew I didn't have any money, but I did have a car, so Dutch and Chris Champion started riding with me. Since we rode in my car and I did the driving, I didn't have to pay for the gas. Sometimes "Dr." Tom Prichard, one of the top heels in the Tennessee territory, came with

us as we traveled around in my 1988 Hyundai Excel, which cost me $154 a month to own. It almost got repossessed several times, but I never let it happen because my brother Scott had cosigned for it and I didn't want to screw up his credit.

Riding down the road and listening to Dutch Mantel run his mouth was a wonderful experience. The guy's a great talker and tells great stories. Great promo guy, great worker and a great mind. Sitting there listening to Dutch, you can't help but learn a few things.

Dutch would always sit in the front seat, chewing *my* chewing tobacco, and Chris would be in the back doing whatever he did—nothing I would recommend to anyone, I'm sure. The more I rode with Dutch, the better we got to know each other—and the better I got to know Dutch's cutting sense of humor. He was just a trained, highly skilled wiseass. But he was a wealth of information too, because he really knew the wrestling business.

One day we were just sitting there, talking. I was asking questions as usual, and he was being real nice to me and explaining things.

Then Dutch said, "You know, if you ever turn heel, you could be a real cocky son of a gun and call yourself 'Stunning' Steve Austin."

So that's how I got the name "Stunning" Steve Austin. Dutch Mantel gave me that one too. Of course, I wasn't trying to be "stunning" with my look. It was more of a mind-set for me. But that was my first bit of education in what a character meant and how I was supposed to "be" it or portray it. For a while, I was riding to the wrestling arenas with Tom Prichard and another wrestler, Brian Lee. We were shooting the bull one time and Tom started talking about gimmicks and personas in detail.

He'd say, "'Prime Time' Brian Lee . . . what's so prime time about you? 'Stunning' Steve Austin . . . what's so stunning about you? You've got these tights and that long hair, but that's about it. Why should the fans think you're such hot stuff?"

He had a valid point and I understood what he was talking about. But I didn't have any money to do anything about it.

When I first went to USWA in Tennessee, Prichard was working against Eric Embry or Jeff Jarrett and he had a damn open cut on his

head for about three weeks where he was gigging every night. It's funny what a person remembers looking back on a wrestling career. To this day, Tom has a forehead full of scars from his matches in the Tennessee territory.

When I first got to Tennessee, I was living in the Congress Inn in Nashville, where a lot of the other wrestlers lived. It was owned by real nice people.

At first, Tom Prichard and I were living on different ends of the Congress Inn, fifty yards apart. But when we started traveling to the shows together and going to the gym together, we ended up living together at the Congress Inn.

That gave me lots of time to pick Tom Prichard's brain. The guy was a big influence on me, because I was watching him every night in the main event. Afterward he'd explain everything to me, why and when he did certain things. Tom was a great worker with a great mind for the business. That's why he's such a great coach for the kids in the WWE developmental program today.

Tom and I lived cheaply by living together, and bought our food once a week. Each time we went shopping, I used my last fifteen or twenty dollars to buy a big-ass bag of potatoes, eight or ten cans of tuna fish and some disposable razors. I was clean-shaven back then.

After about two or three days, I'd be out of tuna fish because that's all I was eating—tuna fish and potatoes. And I couldn't cook the potatoes because I didn't have a stove. My dad had given me and each of my brothers a hunting knife, and I'd use that knife to peel my potatoes and cut 'em up. So for about three or four days all I was eating was raw potatoes that I'd cut with my knife. Literally, that was my whole diet.

Man, I lost a ton of weight. We starved, to tell you the truth. We called Tennessee the "NutriSystem territory," because everybody who went there lost weight. After all, most of us weren't making a dime. There were no guaranteed contracts the way there are today.

Sometimes Dutch and Chris would offer to buy me a hamburger or something else to eat, but I was too proud to take a handout so I never let them buy me food. I'd peel my potatoes, and I'd do my push-ups and put on some baby oil so I'd look good going out for my match. I learned

very early on that a wrestler's look is extremely important. A successful wrestler doesn't have to be a musclehead, but he's damn sure got to be in shape and look like an athlete.

However, after a few days of just eating potatoes, I didn't give a damn anymore and I'd just go out there for my match. I got all flat. I could pull off my jeans without even unbuttoning them, I'd lost so much weight. But that was just the way it was. Again, I knew I was paying my dues and, hopefully, things would get better.

Another guy who helped me out a hell of a lot when I was in the USWA in Memphis was Danny Davis, then known as "Nightmare" Danny Davis. I remember one time I was going down the road, some little spot show, and I was told I was going to work with Danny Davis. That was a big thing for me as he was a very good wrestler and a star.

Before the match, I got together with Danny and he said, "Okay, kid, you ready? I'll just listen to you."

I said, "What are you talking about?"

He says, "Yeah, you call the match."

I said, "Hell, Danny, this is my chance to learn something from you."

He went, "No, no, I've seen you work. You're great. If you need something out there, I'll give it to you. You call the match."

Hell, I went out there with Danny Davis and I called eighty-five percent of the match. That's what kind of nice guy he was. He'd been working how long then? Ten or fifteen years? Of course, he was a great tag-team wrestler. He had a hell of a run in Memphis. I loved working with Danny Davis. He was a very unselfish guy. He helped me understand how to execute a solid wrestling match.

Danny was the first guy to trust my skills to call a match. But over my career I'd say I've called called ninety-nine percent of my matches. Even when I was just starting out, guys would be calling stuff to me in the ring and I couldn't hear 'em. They'd be calling some spots to me, "Uh, kid, one tackle, hip toss, drop down, hip toss, arm drag," and I'd say, "What?"

He'd have to call it to me two or three times so I could understand it.

1) HELL - Sloppy
2) SHINE .
3) Wrestle - You come out on top
4) Heel stop you - take over
5) Heel take hold -
You nearly come out - He cheats
to get on top.
6) Slow come back
LEADING INTO
7) Maniac Come back
8) Slip on banana peel - Lose.
9v) Heel stop you
Then you SURPRISINGLY WIN.

Chris Adams wrote out for me these "rules" for working a heel match.

I've had a hearing problem in one ear since I was a kid. It's not sports or wrestling related, but something I've had since birth.

I had my tonsils and adenoids taken out and was always going to hearing doctors as a kid because I had a lot of fluid in my ears. I never considered it a disability; I just dealt with it. It was something that was

ongoing, and then when I listened to lots of loud rock 'n' roll music and made my loud wrestling entrances, it got worse.

I'm exaggerating when I say I'm half-deaf. But if there's a lot of background noise, I don't hear very well. Outside of wrestling, I lean into people and kind of watch their lips and face. In the arena, in the ring, I just can't hear the other guy.

One time back in Memphis I was working with Undertaker, who was going under the name The Punisher at the time. He was an intimidating guy, pretty jacked up, and had been in the business a good year longer than I was. He was green, but not as green as I was.

He told me before our match, "Well, we'll put over your strength in the beginning, so you'll grab a headlock," and we talked about it for maybe one minute. So we go out in the ring and he was trying to call me a spot. He was making the "sha-sha-sha" noises so the fans didn't know what he was saying. He was telling me, "Okay, kid, one tackle, sha-sha-sha, drop down, sha-sha-sha, hip toss, sha-sha-sha."

I said, "What?"

So he said it all over again.

I said "What?" about three times, and after that third time, here it came. *Bing, bam, boom,* he just hammered me. He couldn't get any high spots out of me so he just beat me up.

So I guess I did have a disability coming in, and that's why I learned how to call a match early on. That way I was the guy talking in the ring, and I didn't have to listen to anybody. I talked and they listened.

It wasn't anything that was a hindrance to me growing up. I just had to try and listen better.

Then there were Gary Young and Billy Joe Travis, who were part of my education too. They were journeymen wrestlers who would go out there and have a killer match, but they didn't get any great breaks. They never had great physiques or were at the right place at the right time. But when it came to working a weekly territory, going around and around and around the horn, these guys were doing something different every night.

I'd ride sometimes with Gary Young. If I did something in a match, he'd say, "Hey, kid," and give me a bit of advice. He showed me how to do different things I hadn't known how to do. He was a big influence on me.

A ton of fine wrestlers, some stars and others not, helped me throughout my time in Memphis. That's one of the great things about this crazy business—people helping each other, the boys helping the boys.

J.R.: The Memphis territory was a unique place by all accounts. Some guys passed through Tennessee and made a few bucks. Some guys literally stayed there their whole careers, like Jerry "the King" Lawler, and endured the cyclical ups and downs of a wrestling territory. Some guys went to Memphis and starved, but got a great education in the process. Steve made virtually no money wrestling in the Tennessee territory, but he was provided with an opportunity to learn his craft and to pay the dues necessary to make it in this business. One thing I can tell you from personal experience is that when you make long car trips with veteran wrestlers, and you are the new guy or the rookie, you had better be a good listener. The old timers do not enjoy hearing newcomers speak, and resent you if you do.

May I suggest that Steve's "tuna and raw potatoes only" diet, which he utilized out of necessity in those days, be one of the last ones you consider if you are looking to lose a few pounds. It would certainly not be AMA approved.

Dallas: Endings and Beginnings

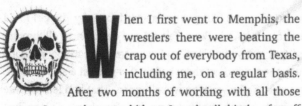

hen I first went to Memphis, the wrestlers there were beating the crap out of everybody from Texas, including me, on a regular basis. After two months of working with all those guys, I was the new kid so I took all kinds of stuff

like getting beaten with leather straps, I decided that it wasn't getting me what I wanted.

Finally, after a few months of starving in Tennessee, the bookers in charge suggested a story line that would send me back to Dallas. I was going to turn heel—become a wresting villain—and go up against my mentor and teacher, "Gentleman" Chris Adams.

I came back to the Dallas USWA group and Chris Adams, and I had a great story line put together. I had been a babyface, a fan favorite, all this time in Texas, but I was going to turn heel against Adams. It was the old "teacher versus pupil" story that has been utilized in our business so often over the years.

The way it started out, I was Chris Adams's friend, former student and tag-team partner, and I was returning to Dallas to help him. We got over with the fans and got cheered. Then, out of the blue, I turned heel on him. That came as a real shock to the Dallas fans.

After a lot of buildup, I beat Adams a few times on TV. I was the cocky ex-student gone bad and then there was Chris, who was over with the fans to a pretty good degree.

Chris Adams technically wasn't the greatest worker in the world, but he did have a lot of great ideas for the business. When it came time for heat, he'd let me get all the heat in the world, and when it came time to win the right matches, he'd have me win the right matches. He was unselfish when it came to business and drawing money.

Also, it was a natural deal to promote his school. And we didn't have all the top talent, so our little bogus program was one of the big drawing cards at the time in Dallas. It sold tickets. Man, we did some great business. It was a believable story—real life, real issues.

In the meantime, I was fixing to get married to Kathy, the girl I had met on the tennis courts back in Edna, Texas. I had dated Kathy all through high school and four years of college, and we were going to the marriage altar even though the road to get there hadn't always been a smooth one.

As I mentioned, Kathy wasn't a wrestling fan. That had led to some growing pains, and I can't really blame her for them. Things just happened.

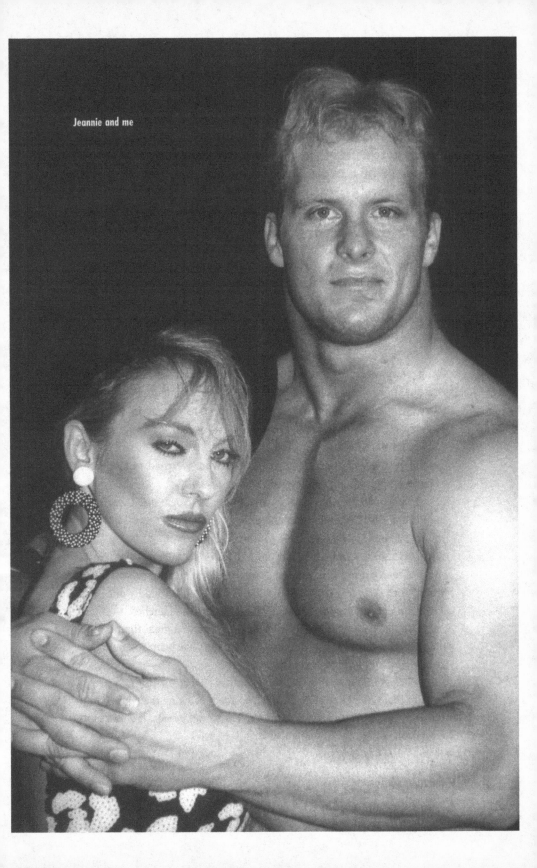

Jeannie and me

At one point, she had had a one-night stand, but at least she told me about it afterward. She was scared to death because it was the first time she had cheated on me, and I had never cheated on her during the ten years we had been together.

That would eventually change.

When we started talking about marriage, it was really just to save the relationship. It wouldn't have survived otherwise. Kathy and I were planning on a Catholic ceremony. At long last, we would be man and wife.

Then Chris Adams suggested adding a couple of women to our ongoing story line. He wanted his real-life wife, Toni, to be on his side and his ex-wife, Jeannie, to be on mine. How could you go wrong with two good-looking blonde women getting involved in catfights all the time?

So, boy, we brought those two women out there and boobs were flying everywhere. They were pulling hair and rolling around and that was hot. It was like going back to Bill Watts's wrestling shows when Missy Hyatt and Dark Journey or Sunshine used to get into it, and we'd go crazy. Missy Hyatt would be swinging that loaded Gucci bag, and ol' J.R. would start yelling about it.

Man, that was some hot stuff. That's what we tried to re-create, because it doesn't get any better than that!

I remember the first time I was introduced to Jeannie. I was talking to Toni, Chris' current wife, and as we were talking, she said, "Have you met Jeannie? There she is, right there."

I had seen Jeannie before, but I had never actually met her. While she was married to Chris Adams, Jeannie had a daughter named Jade. The divorce between Adams and Jeannie had been a friendly one, and Jeannie and Jade used to come down and watch the matches.

Jeannie had beautiful hair, beautiful eyes and a great figure, but I didn't think much of her at the time. I often don't like people when I first meet them, and I didn't like Jeannie at all.

DTA, you know? Don't trust anybody.

At that time, I had some misgivings about bringing the women into the story line. It wasn't that I didn't think it would be hot. It was a matter of how Kathy would feel about it.

I remember thinking, *Hey, I don't know how well this is going to sit with my girlfriend, who's fixing to be my wife.*

But Chris said, "Bring her over and I'll introduce her to Jeannie and make sure everything's cool."

We never did that introduction, but we did the story line with the women, and, of course, everything snowballed from there. I married Kathy—a mistake, as it turned out. Before long, Jeannie and I weren't just an item in the ring. We became an item outside the ring too.

Of course, this took place behind Kathy's back. But eventually, Kathy found out that I had been sharing my hotel room in Tennessee with Jeannie, and she got the marriage annulled. I sure screwed that one up.

I haven't spoken to Kathy since then, but she and my mom still keep in touch. Long ago I had given Kathy a folded-up one-dollar bill for good luck. Just a few months ago my mom told me that she had something for me. I asked, "What is it?" and she said, "You'll know when you see it." It was that same dollar bill. Kathy had put it in a little frame and she had wanted me to have it back for good luck.

That was a classy thing for her to do. I would like to be able to sit down and have a conversation with Kathy someday and just say that I am sorry for being such a jerk back in the day, and that I never meant to be a pile of crap. She is a class act.

Kathy is married now with a nice family. I'm really happy for her. I should have learned more from the mistakes I made in our relationship. It could have helped me in my later relationships with the fairer sex. But I could never do anything the easy way. That's just the way I am.

After I turned heel on Chris Adams in the ring, I seemed cocky and arrogant to the fans who remembered me as a nice kid—so much so that they really began to hate me. My feud with Adams was one of the things that helped draw the houses at the Sportatorium at that time.

You know, it really was a great atmosphere when that place was full. Hell, Elvis played there when he was just getting started in his career. They used to have concerts in that place in the old days.

Then, to add more heat and keep the story going, the bookers in Dallas added Percival Pringle III to the mix—as me and Jeannie's manager. I remember when I first hooked up with Percy. With the brightly colored costumes he wore, he was a real flamboyant guy. Just the way he looked and talked . . . he could talk a hundred miles an hour. He was a great interview and a real smart man, and he was a real big wrestling fan from way back.

At the Sportatorium, on one of the inner office walls, there was a framed photo collection showing all the big stars that had been through there. And sure enough, there was Percy Pringle with Rick Rude.

I had followed Percy's career closely as a fan, and I had always liked the guy a whole lot. And now Percy was *my* manager! I was honored. I was trying to get somewhere in the business and they had hooked me up with a guy who'd had a real good run with so many stars.

I was thinking, God dang, here I am. I got Rick Rude's manager. This is more like it.

Percy eventually made it to WWE as Paul Bearer, Undertaker's manager, and remained in that role for many years.

I really enjoyed working with him in Dallas—he knew how to work that old-school manager distraction gimmick. We had some cool matches together. One time we got to tie up Chris Von Erich, the youngest of the Von Erich family, and we busted him wide open. Another time we tied him and Chris Adams up in a cage with some bailing wire or coat hangers and beat the hell out of both of them. Those were some good times. I was still a newcomer to the business, but I was making progress.

The Dallas and Memphis USWA organizations were a great experience for me, but eventually it became time to move on. I needed to make more money and to continue my wrestling education. After my marriage with Kathy was annulled, Jeannie and I started seeing each other more seriously and became a couple pretty quick. That's when I got a call from World Championship Wrestling.

Jeannie, me, and Percy Pringle III.

WCW—World Championship Wrestling

10

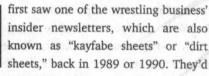

I'll beat your ass in my backyard, I'll
beat your ass in your backyard. Hell,
son, I'll beat your ass up in anyone
out there's backyard.

—STONE COLD TO THE ROCK BEFORE
WRESTLEMANIA X-SEVEN

first saw one of the wrestling business'
insider newsletters, which are also
known as "kayfabe sheets" or "dirt
sheets," back in 1989 or 1990. They'd
been around for a pretty good while, but I just
didn't know about them. You normally see one in a lock-
er room and it gets passed around.

After I'd been wrestling in USWA for a while, and I was done with the story line that had me feuding with Chris Adams, I started working some singles matches with Jeff Jarrett. That worked for me, as he was the number one babyface there. I was also doing some independent wrestling shows booked by Ed Watt, but I was only earning a few hundred dollars a month.

About that time, somebody wrote something good about me in one of those insider newsletters. Grizzly Smith, an agent for WCW who was the father of Jake "The Snake" Roberts, sat down one day and read about this rookie from down in World Class who was doing pretty well and then went to USWA.

It was me, of course, that he was reading about. Word got to Dusty Rhodes, who had been a popular wrestler in his day and was booking talent for WCW, and Dusty Rhodes called Tom Prichard about me.

One day when we were riding down the road, Tom said, "Hey, Steve, I think WCW is interested in you. Let me give Dusty Rhodes a call for you."

This was in 1991. I had been in the business for two years—and I was thinking, Wow!

I knew that WCW would give me the chance to earn more than a few hundred dollars a month. A *lot* more.

WCW was owned by Ted Turner, who was a big wrestling fan, and the shows were televised all over the world on SuperStation TBS. (That was before WCW was sold to WWE in 2001.)

At that point, I was fixing to leave USWA anyway. Portland Wrestling had given me a call. Sandy Barr, the promoter in Portland, had asked me to join his promotion as a heel. "Scotty the Body" Levy, who later became Raven, was about to move on and he had been one of their top heels. They needed someone to replace him.

They said, "We've seen you and you're a good-bumpin' heel," which meant that I could fly around the ring for the hero.

If you're going to be a heel, it helps to be a good bump taker. You'll be taking a lot of them. As a matter of fact, I don't think a wrestler can be a great money-drawing heel if he can't take plenty of bumps.

So I was pretty much on my way to Portland when I got a call from

Magnum T.A., Dusty Rhodes's assistant and a former wrestler. Magnum called me at home and spoke with Jeannie, saying he was calling for Dusty Rhodes and WCW. When Jeannie answered, he liked her voice a lot, so at his request, she sent in some pictures too.

As soon as I got home, I called back, saying, "Hey Magnum, this is Steve Austin. I was told to call you."

He talked to me for a little bit and he said, "Well, are you a heel or a face?"

I said, "I've been a heel for a bit."

He said, "All right, why don't you come down?"

I didn't know this at the time, but Jim Ross had mentioned my name to Dusty several times also, having seen my work in Dallas. I was flown to CNN Center in Atlanta, and they stuck a contract under my face. I signed it. All that mattered to me was I was making $75,000 a year, $1,442 a week!

Wow, that was great! That was way up from what I had been making. And I ended up more than doubling my contract the next year, from $75,000 to $156,000.

But even at seventy-five, I thought, *Okay, I'm making some money now.* My parents were happy for me, even though I was still doing that crazy "wrestling thing." I was on my way up.

Right on the heels of me going to Atlanta, Jeannie ended up there too. So I moved to Atlanta and she followed me there a little while later.

J.R.: When I moved to Atlanta from Dallas to work for the Turner-owned WCW, I continued to watch as much wrestling on TV as I could, because I was, and still am, a huge wrestling fan. It was on Atlanta Channel 69 that I began to see Steve wrestle on a regular basis. Obviously, he had a good, athletic look, but what impressed me the most was his engine. He was in perpetual motion, it seemed. A buzz saw without breaks. I always thought if this guy can learn to do a promo, can learn to talk, he could be special. I spread his name around the WCW offices and spoke to the higher-ups about this kid. It's funny, but when older wrestlers are asked to consider new talent, they usually resist. The old timers never go away gracefully, it seems,

when they ascend to the coveted office job many have sought for years. Magnum T.A., who had been severely injured in a car accident that cut short a very promising wrestling career, did listen—and made the call to Steve about joining us in Atlanta. Ol' Magnum, ever the ladies man, liked British-speaking Jeannie's voice and her 8-by-10's weren't bad either, so we ended up with two new talents instead of one. WCW hired Steve, though I don't think they ever really knew what to do with him. But the same can be said, I suppose, about many wrestlers during the Turner era.

In WCW, they started me with a valet, Vivacious Veronica, who was wrestler Rex King's old girlfriend. Then they put me with Jeannie, who was working as Lady Blossom, just a few weeks later—without any story line reason. They just swapped them out. Dusty Rhodes selected that professional name for Jeannie because her chest was "blossoming out of her top," or so the story goes.

I remember the first night I was there, they told me they were going to put the TV title on me. The reigning TV champion was

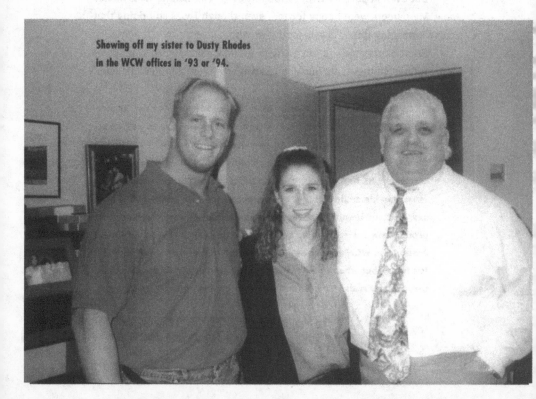

Showing off my sister to Dusty Rhodes in the WCW offices in '93 or '94.

"Beautiful" Bobby Eaton, another one of my favorite hands—just an awesome damn wrestler, especially when it came to tag-team matches.

I had a ton of respect for Bobby. He had always been a supernice guy to me; one of the nicest guys in the business. And here I was taking the damn belt off of him the first time we met. He could have treated me like garbage, but he didn't. I've always respected him for that.

Bobby would become one of my favorites to work with. I'd ask him all kinds of stuff. He couldn't really tell you why he did anything, plus you couldn't understand hardly a word he said with his Alabama drawl and his "mouth full of marbles." But he had incredible timing. He couldn't explain it, but it was a pleasure and an education going out there and working with him.

Bobby Eaton was the consummate professional. Top-notch.

I wish his career had ended on a better note, but unfortunately, a lot of guys don't save their money and seemingly fade away. I hear that he's still working some indy shows here and there in the area where he lives, and he's probably still a great worker.

Anyway, that first night with WCW, I was going to do an in-ring interview with Missy Hyatt. They said, "Go!" and they were playing this music—mine, I guessed. I walked into the ring and all of a sudden I heard, *"From Hollywood, California,"* and I was thinking, Who the hell are they talking about? And they go, *"'Stunning' Steve Austin!"*

I thought to myself, I'm not from Hollywood, California! But that's how the Hollywood thing came about. They just said it on WCW TV. That's where that part came from, as best I can remember.

As I got into the mix at WCW, I got to work with a number of legendary wrestling names who had come from the NWA [National Wrestling Alliance]. When Ted Turner bought Jim Crockett Promotions and turned it into WCW, he also acquired all the NWA big stars' contracts. There was Ric Flair, Dusty Rhodes, the Four Horsemen—all the big, nationally known names who would come through Houston every now and then—all of whom I had loved to watch. Suddenly I was getting to work with these guys!

"Nature Boy" Ric Flair was a big influence on me. I didn't really ask him any questions, but he always put on a wrestling clinic anytime he

was in the ring. I watched what he did in the ring and I learned from it. I have all the respect in the world for Ric Flair.

"Ravishing" Rick Rude was a guy that—well, we just hit it off. I don't know why we did, but it was after we got put together in the Dangerous Alliance in WCW. He was into fishing, being he was from Minnesota, but Paul Orndorff and I got him into shooting and hunting. I liked being with him because he always told you straight up what he was thinking, 24/7.

I watched Rick closely because he really understood his character and was great at it. His heel psychology was so sound, so strong, and he was considered one of the smarter guys around. We just got along. We traveled together, stayed at hotels together, stuff like that.

Once, I tried staying in the same room with Rick. He beat me to sleep and what snoring that man generated! You would have thought a Mack truck was backing into the room. I was yelling, "Shut up!" over and over again. He'd roll over and stop for a while, but then he would start up again. This went on all night. After that experience, Rick and I still traveled together and stayed at the same hotels, but we never stayed in the same room again.

Arn Anderson was always one of my favorite wrestlers when I was a kid. I'd watch tapes of him and Ole Anderson fighting the Rock 'n' Roll Express or the Midnight Express in the NWA in a steel fence cage, and that was the greatest tag-team wrestling I'd ever seen. Then I got to work with him and against him, and that was a wonderful experience. Arn was another guy who helped me out a whole lot.

He also performed one of the most intelligent, well-thought-out promos in the business. When that guy talked, he didn't yell or scream. He just calmly explained things to you. Ole's was another promo I liked. He'd scare you right through the TV screen.

Another guy like that was The Assassin, Jody Hamilton. I never got to see too many Assassin promos, but I heard he was phenomenal.

I wasn't really in any programmed feuds, but I really enjoyed a lot of my matches and working with certain people. One of the highlights, to me, was a time when I was working a tag match on TV—me and Big Van Vader against Arn Anderson and Ric Flair. It went about forty min-

utes on TV and the whole match was called in the ring, not all discussed beforehand. I loved it.

I worked with a lot of great hands back then. Brad Armstrong could work with anybody. That guy was as smooth as silk. He was like Ricky Steamboat, in a way—another guy you went out there with and never had to say a word to. He knew the finish and how to get there. I knew how good he could be. I'd call all the spots in the ring and we'd just wrestle.

I got in with a pretty good group of guys in WCW—the Dangerous Alliance, managed by Paul E. Dangerously, now known as Paul Heyman. It was me, Rick Rude, Arn Anderson, Larry Zbyszko and Barry Windham. I learned a lot from being around these guys. Of course, Rick Rude was the crown jewel of that whole group. I'd just sit back, watch and learn. It was good company to keep.

Larry Zbyszko was real old-school, but a good worker. Barry Windham was always cool. The thing I liked about working with Barry so much was this was a big guy. He was six-foot-six, six-foot-seven, close to three hundred pounds at one time, and he'd just step up on the apron and glide through the ropes like a cat. Definitely one of the most graceful big guys I've ever seen.

A lot of big guys won't take bumps or sell for smaller guys. But not Barry. Big as he was, he took bumps for anybody he was working with. He'd work with Tully Blanchard, who was much smaller than he was, and he'd sell for Tully like anybody else. And Barry is a second-generation worker in the business, with his dad being Black Jack Mulligan.

I'd travel with Barry and referee Pee Wee Anderson, and Barry was cool as hell. I remember one time we rented a Cadillac and Barry was riding shotgun and Pee Wee was in the back, and Barry said to me, "Wanna drive, kid?"

Of course, I'd never driven a Cadillac before, so I was looking at all the controls on the dashboard while I was driving. I almost ran that car right off the road. I had to quickly jerk it back on.

Barry looked over at me—he was always reading a hot-rod magazine or something like that—and said, in a real dry voice, "You okay?" That was it. Barry never got upset. He'll probably live to be a hundred.

Barry was also one of the best all-time drinkers in the business. Barry could drink with anybody in the business, and the next day never show it a damn lick. He could drink all night long, and come back the next day and do it again. That guy could put down some alcohol. But I always enjoyed working with him. We had good chemistry—he'd let me call a match, or he'd call parts of it. A great talent.

Probably the most memorable WCW event I was involved in was on May 17, 1992 at the *Wrestle War '92* Pay-Per-View. It was me, Rick Rude, Arn Anderson, Bobby Eaton and Larry Zbyszko against Sting, Nikita Koloff, Dustin Rhodes, Ricky Steamboat and Barry Windham in a Double Steel Cage match. I was the top heel in the stable and in a main event of a big Pay-Per-View show. That was the wildest damn thing I'd ever been in, up to that time.

Most fans think wrestlers use "blood capsules" to bleed in the ring. We don't. Sometimes you get hit "hard way" and bleed for real, or you can nick yourself with a razor blade and get it going that way.

Some guys don't like to do that, but it's one of those "time-honored traditions" that's always been a part of our business. One thing about my character is that I've never been leery about getting color—bleeding—if the situation calls for it. Obviously, it adds a lot of drama to the match.

I remember at that *Wrestle War '92*, I tackled Dustin Rhodes. I was beating on him and he looked up at me and said, "Good color."

I said, "Thanks." We both had gushers that night. That was a bonding moment.

Another time, Dustin and I were working together in Phoenix. It was a bad house with slow ticket sales and the WCW agent, Grizzly Smith, was running the show. Dustin and I had a great feud going and were just terrorizing each other that whole tour. I said, "Hey, man, whaddaya think, want to get some color tonight?"

And Dustin said, "Yeah!"

So we went over and asked Grizzly Smith. Dustin said, "Hey Griz, what do you think about me and Steve getting some color tonight?"

And Griz went, "Well, yeah, I think that might help your match."

So we went out there and we both hit gushers, and we both came

back bleeding like stuck pigs. I remember we both walked back together through the door, and there was Lex Luger, all oiled up and ready to go out and flex. And he looked at us with horror in his eyes. He didn't understand what we were trying to do.

Whether what we did was right or wrong didn't matter. We were just busting our asses and giving people a helluva show, and we got some color to do it. Lex was visibly shocked. But then he's a damn idiot, in my opinion, and has never understood our business.

I don't think Ric Flair was on the card that night, which is why it was okay to get color. The Nature Boy's matches usually ended with his blond hair turned red. So usually the option of getting color was reserved for Ric Flair.

After Paul E. got fired by WCW and they broke up the Dangerous Alliance, I had a one-time-only match with the other *real* Steve Williams, "Dr. Death." One night, Dr. Death's normal tag partner, "Bam-Bam" Terry Gordy, couldn't show up for his match. It was October 25, 1992, and we were doing a Pay-Per-View called *Halloween Havoc*.

I wasn't originally booked on the card, but they wanted me to wrestle. It would have been fine except for the fact that I was supposed to be enjoying a long-overdue day off.

I was living in Douglasville, Georgia, in a log home on ten acres. I was in my basement, opening up my garage door so I could wheel out my YZ-490 dirt bike and go dirt biking when my phone rang. It was "Cowboy" Bill Watts. He was booking WCW at the time, which made him my boss.

"Steve, Bill Watts," he said. "We're in Philadelphia," or wherever the hell they were that night for the Pay-Per-View. "Terry Gordy didn't show tonight. We need you to come up and fill in for Gordy and be Doc's partner against Barry and Dustin for the tag-team title."

He heard this silence on the phone, because I was thinking, Damn, I was just fixin' to go dirt biking. But instead I said, "Okay, I'll go to the airport."

So it was Steve Williams and Steve Williams, for all intents and purposes, versus Dustin Rhodes and Barry Windham. Unfortunately, it

turned out to be only an average match, at best. After thirty minutes, it ended up in a draw. But then, it was really just thrown together at the last minute. It was a one time deal.

Steve "Dr. Death" Williams is okay in my book. Hell of a worker, and a big star when he was with Bill Watts's shows and WCW. He wrestled in Japan for most of his career.

I'm really proud of how solid a worker I was back in WCW—more so than I was when I finished up. But you wouldn't necessarily know it by watching my matches. It was just something that I knew and the crowds didn't.

MOM: That steel chair thing, I still can't stand it. The very first wrestling match we went to see Steve in was at the Sam Houston Coliseum in Houston. That's when he was in WCW. It was awful and I had to leave. It was just a bunch of hollering and tossing those steel chairs. I said, "I'm sorry, I've got to go." We had a bunch of friends from home that went to the show. I went downstairs to the concession stand and sat there. They picked me up on their way out.

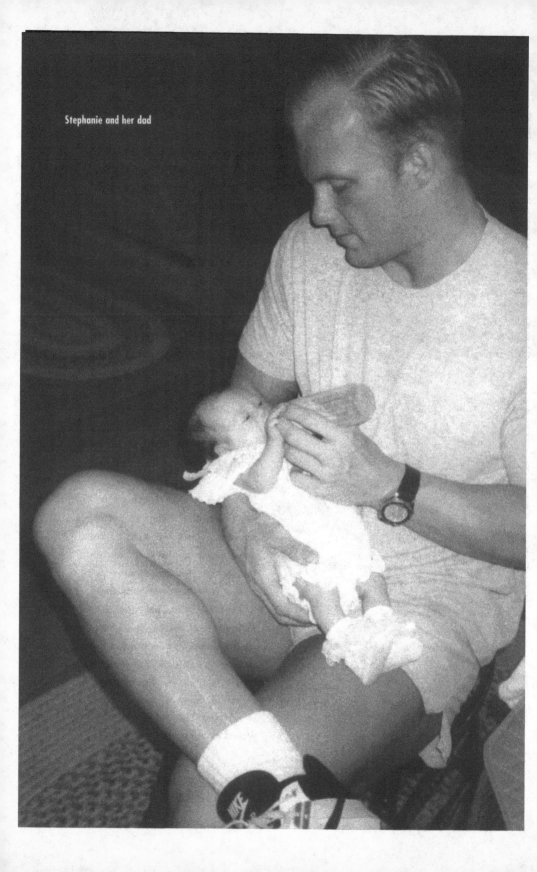

Stephanie and her dad

Stone Cold Becomes a Father

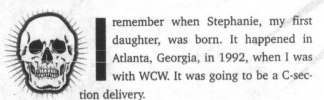 remember when Stephanie, my first daughter, was born. It happened in Atlanta, Georgia, in 1992, when I was with WCW. It was going to be a C-section delivery.

I was right there, I had a Polaroid camera around my neck and I had a movie camera and a 35-mm camera

too, because I was going to document the whole damn thing. Everything came out fine. The baby and Jeannie were completely healthy. Everything went great and we all got lucky.

Afterward, Jeannie was all drugged up and there wasn't a whole lot I could do for her or the baby. They took Stephanie and put her in the baby nursery. There she was, behind the glass. I could see her, but she didn't know who the hell I was.

And I couldn't talk to Jeannie, because she was still out of it. So I called up Rick Rude. Then I put all my guns in my car and we went down to the shooting range, and shot pistols for a couple of hours.

That's what I did after Stephanie was born—went and shot pistols for a couple of hours with Rick Rude. After that, I went back to the hospital and checked up on everybody. They were fine.

That was when they let me hold our baby, and that was really

Holding Cassidy, just after she was born.

cool. I was someone who never, *ever* wanted to have kids. I love kids, but I didn't want to have any of my own. I was sure wrong in that regard. But it was cool holding my daughter, one of the absolute best days of my life.

Some people are a little squeamish about changing diapers and all that. I did it all. I remember when Cassidy, my second daughter, was born in 1996, I was in the New York area on tour with WWE. All of a sudden, I got the call that Jeannie's water had broke. The next morning I was on the first flight back to Georgia. I got to the hospital and twenty minutes later, Cassie was born. It's like she was waiting on me. I was there for only twenty minutes and it was like, "Okay, she's ready." and Cassie came into the world.

This time it was a natural birth, and everything happened as smoothly as anyone could ask. The baby was perfect and Jeannie was fine. We had gotten lucky again. We took Cassie back into the room and I fed her first bottle to her, and handed her back. Another great day in my life. My girls are my greatest blessings.

My next-door neighbor from over in Douglasville was there with me, and I said, "I gotta go, man. I gotta wrestle in Pittsburgh tonight."

I caught a flight out and wrestled in Pittsburgh a few hours later. I was red-eyed and tired, but I wasn't going to miss a show. I only miss shows if I'm injured. So I worked in New York, then flew to Atlanta and watched Cassie get born, flew back up to Pittsburgh and worked that night and never missed a shot. That was cool. That's the old-school wrestling business.

Now, with the divorce, Jeannie has unfortunately moved the kids to England. That part sucks. I try to be the best father I can. It's not like I've seen them lately, but I enjoy being a dad.

Jeannie wasn't supposed to leave a fifty-mile radius area from where I live, much less leave the country completely, so she broke the divorce decree. However, we're on good terms and working on the situation. Maybe one of these days Jeannie will move back to the States. It would be nice. I'd love more than anything in the world to see my girls grow up. I really love those girls.

Not too long ago, my daughter Stephanie gave me a call. I had just talked to her a couple of weeks earlier, but I was happy to hear from her again. Then all of a sudden I realized that she had a British accent! She had always talked the same way I do, with the same Texas accent, and all of a sudden she had a British accent!

I remember that when I hung up the phone, I started crying. It broke my heart that Stephanie had this new accent. She wasn't supposed to be from there! But I talk to my girls all the time and we e-mail each other regularly.

The funny thing is Stephanie has a real normal-sounding, nice girl's voice. She's ten. But Cassie, she's got my raspy-sounding voice. Oh, my God, it's the funniest damn thing to listen to her talk, because now she's got that English accent too.

When I first heard it, she was a little shy on the phone, because it was so long since I'd seen her. She started out real quiet, and then as she started talking more and more, this real raspy voice with this British accent came out. It was funny as hell.

I really love both my girls. They are the best things to happen in my life.

I also adopted Jeannie's daughter, Jade, who she had with Chris Adams. Jade was fifteen at the time I adopted her, so she was at an age where I wasn't really going to be her dad. I was a stepdad, and besides that I was usually on the road.

Jade's a lot like Chris Adams—a headstrong girl, if sometimes in the wrong ways. But I'm always there for her if she wants my opinion or someone to talk to.

Some friends have asked me if I would let my girls get into the wrestling business. The answer is I'd let my girls do whatever they wanted to do, and I'd support them to the Nth degree. I'd rather they *not* get into pro wrestling. But if that was their dream, to get into pro wrestling, I'd stand behind them one hundred percent.

That's kind of what my folks did with me. They didn't really understand the wrestling business or have any friends or family in the wrestling business, but that's what I wanted to do. They said even when I was sending those postcards about not having any money and eating

potatoes every day. I'm sure they were worried, but they never discouraged me. I thought that was pretty good. Sometimes you see parents who want to live their kids' lives for them or live vicariously through them. "I want my boy to be a doctor." And you ask the kid, "Why do you want to be a doctor?" and he says, "Well, that's what Dad wants."

Then you ask them, "Well, what do *you* want to do?" and they say, "I'd really rather be a cop."

DAD: Steve really misses his girls. He loves his daughters very much. Hopefully, they can spend some time together in the future.

The Hollywood Blonds

In February 1993, I was promised a big singles push from WCW, with Harley Race as my manager.

Harley was a legendary, seven-time NWA World Champion, which was a record for many years (Lou Thesz had held the title only six times). Race was a legit tough guy and had wrestled all

over the world, including Japan, for the NWA, and for WWE as "the King" Harley Race (this was before Jerry Lawler came to WWE).

Then Harley suffered a serious injury in a boating accident. He returned a few years later in WCW—this time as a manager, and a damned good one. He quickly got Lex Luger to the WCW World Championship. Later on, Big Van Vader won the title as well, with Harley as his manager.

Harley Race was real popular with the young WCW talent, and I was no exception. I *could* have learned a lot from him.

I was still flying high about having Harley as my manager when I showed up in Columbus, Georgia, for a TV taping. Suddenly I saw Brian Pillman, who I barely knew, walking up to me.

Brian said, "Hey, Steve, how's it going?"

I said, "Hey, what's going on, Brian?"

He said, "We need to think of a finishing move since we're a tag team now." I said, "What are you talking about?"

He said, "Yeah, Dusty just made us a tag-team."

And I went, "Damn!"

So I went and harassed Dusty Rhodes, the booker, telling him, "I was going to be with Harley Race—you know, a World Champion manager."

Dusty said, "Yeah, baby, we changed our mind. Now we're going to make you and Brian a tag team. Just trust me, baby. This tag has legs."

So I just said, "All right." In all reality, what choice did I have?

I didn't argue. And that's how Brian and I got together.

We started out wearing different color trunks, using our old attire. Then we began coming up with some ideas for our team while we were out riding on the road.

Brian said, "God dang, kid, if we're going to be a tag team, we gotta have a name. Every good tag team has a cool name and some matching outfits and stuff like that." We had to at least "look" like a team. Scotty Flamingo, aka Raven, was traveling with us and was real creative about this stuff. We started kicking around names and ideas for trunks and jackets, and things like that.

That's when we came up with the Hollywood Blonds idea. I think

Raven came up with that name for us first. J.R. told me that in the early seventies there was another Hollywood Blonds tag team consisting of a veteran wrestler named Jerry Brown, who once swore he'd shoot "Cowboy" Bill Watts, and Buddy Roberts, who was to become known as a member of the Fabulous Freebirds. Those guys had some good heat going with the fans. J.R. thought we were a good update on that concept.

I had just ordered a hundred and fifty dollars' worth of new ring wear, which I could barely afford, from a lady in Texas . . . and Brian wanted to order all new stuff? Damn! I was a cheap bastard back then, and for good reason.

But we *were* in desperate need of a look. Brian had his little Bengal-print trunks on and I was wearing these horrible-looking red-and-black trunks that looked like an independent worker's hand-me-downs. We didn't look like a tag team. We looked like we were just two guys thrown together.

So we came up with some designs for our trunks that showed off the name. We had the star and HOLLYWOOD BLONDS on the back, and three stars on the front. We had a black pair and a red pair. Then Brian had the jackets made—a silver leather jacket and a black-and-red jacket.

Brian said, "We gotta wear some chains," and he got me a deal on one. It's got more sentimental value than anything I own. It's just a gold chain, but it's the chain that Brian got for me when we were the Hollywood Blonds.

I had it ripped off one time in a fight and thrown a pretty good distance into the bushes, and wondered if I was going to lose it. But I looked real hard and found it. I wear that chain all the time. That's the one you see around my neck on WWE television and in many photos, and Brian is right there with me.

About the same time, we came up with all the stupid little camera stuff and the "Brush with Greatness." That was when Brian would do a comedy pantomime like he was filming me while I put a power move on a guy. We got a little bit more interview time and the fans were getting into what we were doing. We were different, and we listened to the fans to gauge what they were buying from us.

The Hollywood Blonds. Brian Pillman was my best friend in the business.

Then we started making fun of the legendary Ric Flair. We figured that would get us some heat from the crowd. It did, because we were so damn cocky, especially Pillman. He was the Hollywood Blonds' guiding force.

The "Flair for the Old" segment got over real big. This was a parody that the Hollywood Blonds did on Ric Flair and Arn Anderson in WCW.

Every week, Flair had a televised segment called "A Flair for the Gold" with Arn Anderson as his cohost, and he'd feature himself or one of his friends in some kind of cheesy interview segment. Brian and I would rag on those guys in our promos and refer to that segment as "Flair for the Old" to get heat on us being wise-asses and not respecting the legends, whom we actually admired greatly.

It was all ad-libbed. We just went out there and did it. They turned out to be some very entertaining segments and the fans started cheering us. That got us legit heat with the office because it was turning us baby-face.

Brian always got more interview time than I did, because Brian could really run at the mouth. He had a very good command of the English language, so when they stuck the microphone in front of his mouth, he'd just start going. He was real good at making a point, and not like everybody else, and it was real well thought out. Just by hanging with him, I was forced to try and keep up on the mic. He was instrumental in getting my gears going, thinking about how to cut promos.

While Brian would be talking, I'd do "Arn Anderson" by just standing behind him like a statue, rubbing my chin and nodding in agreement with whatever he was saying. Yeah. That was some funny stuff we did. But we were put together as an interim tag team to put someone *else* over.

We ended up getting over ourselves. Pillman and I became a hot team.

They shut us down. They buried us. They didn't want us to become popular. That was bogus and not good business, because the fans wanted to see us, and there was an opportunity for the company to make money.

Pay outs to "Steve Austin," see
what a difference a year of hard
work makes.

Looking back at it now, I can see the fans were changing, what they liked was changing. WCW just couldn't see that. Office politics suck, especially in the pro wrestling business.

When we went on road trips, I would always drive. Raven would talk and Brian would be laying in the back, reading words to us from his power vocabulary book. Brian had an unbelievable vocabulary as it was,

but he'd buy and pore through these vocabulary power books to learn ridiculous new words and their meanings, so he could turn around and use them in TV promos.

After Brian learned some new words, he would try them out on us in some of the most outrageous promos you ever heard. As I said, I always drove, because Raven had convinced us it was better for everyone's health.

We called ourselves "The Comedy Trio." We were three funny guys who traveled together. And we had our own Comedy League within the company, with a Comedy League Heavyweight Champion, as voted by his peers.

The Comedy League Heavyweight Champion at the time was Kevin Nash. We had a tournament to crown the champion, which consisted of Brian Raven and myself, Nash, Cactus Jack, Tex Slazinger (Mideon), Shanghai Pierce (Henry Godwinn) and Dan Spivey (Waylon Mercy). Spivey was a dark horse candidate for champion. He had a real dry sense of humor. Shanghai Pierce was our traveling secretary and head of security.

One time Brian, Raven and I were driving around the Cobo Hall in Detroit; we couldn't figure out where we should park, and couldn't find the back entrance. We saw Kevin Nash walking in the parking lot and asked him to find a security guy. Nash blew us off, so we voted to strip him of the title of Comedy League Champion. "Big Grouchy" was having a bad day.

I had wanted to be a singles wrestler and Scotty—Raven—wanted to be the tag-team wrestler with Brian. They would have been hilarious together! But the bookers at WCW put Brian and I together as a tag and ended up letting Scotty go, and he went up to WWE and wrestled as Johnny Polo.

Harley Race, who I had originally been given as a manager, was put with Lex Luger. I wish I would have had the opportunity to be with Harley, but it wasn't in the cards. Luger never really took advantage of being with Harley Race, one of the game's all-time great in-ring talents. Lex wasn't blessed with a ton of common sense, in my opinion, though he did look good in an 8-by-10.

Harley Race, by the way, was a legitimately tough son of a gun. He had done it all, which was why I had so much respect for him. We would have been great together, I always thought. He was a great champion, an unbelievable worker and he cut a hell of a promo in the days when shows weren't based on promos.

Back in WCW, when he was managing Luger, Harley Race was always doing something to torture the other wrestlers backstage and have some fun. He'd walk around with one of those stun guns in his pocket, sneak up behind one of the boys and take out the zapper. Then he would lay it right on the guy's leg or on his ass and press that trigger button . . . and innocently keep walking!

People would jump and then look around! He never did it to me, I'm happy to report, but a lot of boys tasted that stun gun. I heard Theodore Long actually wet his pants thanks to Harley's stun gun. The "playa" peed his pants!

Brian Pillman and I remained friends through the years. When I got to WWE and Stone Cold was "on fire" and shooting to the top, Brian Pillman came to WWE too. He had been doing "the loose cannon" deal at WCW and was acting like a crazy person, working both companies, the boys, the kayfabe sheets and the fans.

No one knew what Brian was doing. I didn't know what he was doing. His own booker didn't know what Brian was doing. There was so much "buzz" about Pillman that,

Me and Brian Pillman;
he's going to discover
the meaning of D.T.A.

out of the blue, he got himself a contract up at WWE—even though he had just had his Hummer accident and his leg was all banged up. Sometime before that, either his WCW contract had run out or he got out of it using a loophole. I'm not sure about those details, but there he was joining WWE.

I talked to him a little bit at that time, but I didn't ask him about the "loose cannon" stuff because I didn't want to come off like a mark. It was one of those deals where he figured I knew all about it, but I wasn't going to ask him and he wasn't going to ask me if I knew for sure. It was something I just stayed away from, as a professional courtesy. I think if I had asked him about it, I would have gotten some sort of sideways answer from him, and that's not the answer I would have wanted from a friend.

I respected what he was doing, and he was breaking new ground. It was cutting edge. I just remember watching it and saying, "Damn, whatever this is, that sumbitch is off." It was great. Brian was really talented.

When Bret Hart put his Canadian heel group together, Brian's the one who made it work with his gift for gab. Whereas Bret would cut this straightforward logical promo, here was this trash-talking, raspy-voiced sumbitch who, everybody knew, could kick their ass. He always had a mouthful of words to spew at you, and he could do it with some real heavy sarcasm. When it came to cutting promos, he paved the way for a lot of guys, and certainly inspired me.

Brian and I didn't talk much about his personal life or his problems. I knew that the guy was in a lot of pain from getting knocked around so much, but I didn't know how many painkillers he was taking, and I didn't know about any of the other stuff he was said to be taking. Around me, he never did any of that. At WCW and later at WWE, we always went our separate ways once we checked in at the hotel.

When I hooked up with Brian as the Hollywood Blonds in WCW, I remember sitting there at the bar one night and hearing him say, "I've stopped drinking."

Maybe he started again later on in WWE, but here he was saying

Working a tag team
match back in WCW.

he had stopped. I gave him hell over it, just like he gave me hell in WWE when I was trying to be a heel and was getting cheered instead.

I was sitting there and pounding them down, and I was thinking, This is Flyin' Brian. This is supposed to be one of the wildest guys there ever was. He ain't drinking nothin'.

The other stuff people talk about? Maybe I saw him take a couple of Vicodin pain pills here and there, but I didn't know how many he was eating. Cocaine? I never saw that. HGH or steroid injections? I never saw him do those either. I certainly never saw Brian smoke dope. It wouldn't have jelled with his personality, I think.

But I wasn't concerned about him because I didn't think he had a problem. I really didn't.

One night I saw him dragging his little suitcase behind him in Minnesota and I became worried about him then. To me, that wasn't Brian Pillman. Here was a guy who was one of the smartest guys in the business, who was a hell of an athlete and had a great career and a beautiful wife and kids at home.

Just hours before the WWE *In Your House* Pay-Per-View on October 5, 1997, where Brian was to have wrestled, his body was found in his hotel room. At first, many thought that it was Brian's use of drugs and alcohol that led to a fatal overdose. It was later established that he suffered from a rare genetic heart imperfection, which not only caused the early death of his father, but ultimately his own. There is no question, however, that Brian's lifestyle and use of drugs aggravated his heart condition.

I never figured that Brian was going to die, at least not at the age of thirty-five years old. He was Brian Pillman and he was going to keep doing whatever he was doing. And he was going to make it, because he was that strong.

Now, when I look back and look at where Brian was, I can see some of the signs that he was in a little deep. But I certainly didn't know what he was on. I wish not only that I'd talked to him, but that I'd tied him up with a rope and said, "Damn it, you're going to a place to get clean," and then been forceful about it.

I got a chance to talk to someone several months ago who was hav-

ing some of the same problems, and I didn't hold back when I voiced my concerns. I'll never, ever lay back and think a guy's too strong to die again. After what happened to Brian Pillman, I'm always going to voice my opinion and let the sumbitch know straight up what I think and what he ought to be doing about it. It might not be my business to speak with someone like that, but I'll make it my business.

It would have been nice if Brian could have stayed around and hit a big chunk of change. He made decent money, but he never got to hit the big money. I haven't seen Brian Jr. in two or three years now. He's a real cute kid. He looks like he's going to be just like his dad. He's definitely carrying some of Brian's genes. He may turn out to be a helluva football player, or maybe he'll be the guy who turns the business on its head one of these days.

Brian had a helluva "Pillman Hall of Fame" down in his basement, all of his college and pro football accomplishments, which were numerous. It was well put together, one helluva cool room. I never knew the guy was such a big football star. God dang, he had all kind of awards down there. I hope his widow, Melanie, has maintained it for all of Brian's kids to see.

Brian had throat cancer as a child. It took thirty operations before he was three years old to get him over it. Pretty tough kid.

That's why it's so important to me to wear the gold chain that Brian gave me. If I'm wearing it, then Brian is right there with me. I sure miss that raspy-voiced hell-raiser. He was a great friend.

J.R.: When WCW teamed the combustible and charismatic Brian Pillman with the wrestling machine named "Stunning" Steve Austin, I thought that there was finally some sanity on the twelfth floor of the CNN Center, and that perhaps the company was going to actually build for the future and develop some new stars. Pillman and Austin felt like money to me. Both had athletic skills, passion, a thirst to get over and both were not "dumb jocks." But this duo never really got the opportunity I feel they should have. I can't tell you exactly why, other than the normal wrestling politics that many of us have seen and personally experienced over the years. It is not a flattering side

of our business, though I'm pretty sure office politics exist in most business environments. For whatever reason, the "office" half-assed it with the Hollywood Blonds, which resulted in Brian and Steve falling off the main event level where the money is. Perhaps management didn't know how to manage these two new-generation talents. This was a very frustrating time for Steve, and I am sure many guys in his position would have said to hell with it. But he didn't. He hung in there and persevered. He would not quit. But that didn't keep him from getting fired by WCW.

How Eric Bischoff Fired Me from WCW

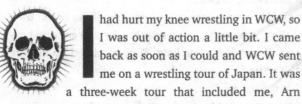

You said you didn't suck.

Who sucks now, you bastard?

—Austin to Pat Patterson on *Raw*

had hurt my knee wrestling in WCW, so I was out of action a little bit. I came back as soon as I could and WCW sent me on a wrestling tour of Japan. It was a three-week tour that included me, Arn Anderson, Ron Simmons (Faarooq), Chris Benoit, Eddie Guerrero, Dean Malenko and a couple of other guys, all great workers.

On the third night of the three-week tour I jumped off the ropes to give a guy a splash. A simple, stupid splash! Unfortunately, he moved and I landed wrong on my right arm and tore my right tricep muscle off my elbow.

I ended up wrestling for two and a half weeks with a torn tricep and a sore knee, which I don't recommend to anyone, and didn't miss a single show. After I got back to the U.S. and went and got the medical exams, the doctors told me how bad it was. The next day I was in surgery getting my tricep reattached to my elbow. While my elbow was healing, I went to a WCW TV taping every now and then, just to see the boys and to watch the matches.

I remember seeing Kevin Sullivan, the booker, in the hallway. He said, "Hey, how's it going, Steve?"

I said, "Oh, pretty good. I'm rehabbing and hope to be back soon."

Sullivan was short, well under six feet, had been around the world with the wrestling business, was a good "office politician" and had one helluva Napoleon complex. I don't think he liked me a whole lot for some reason.

Looking back, I think Sullivan had a hand in what was about to happen to me.

Soon afterward, I got a phone call from Janie Engle, who worked as Eric Bischoff's assistant. Bischoff, a former announcer, was running WCW for Ted Turner at the time.

Janie said, "Hey Steve, give Eric a call when you get a chance."

Now, Janie was a good person. You talk about someone who knows all the dirt on the old WCW and where all the skeletons are buried, she does. Before WCW, Janie had worked for NWA promoter Jim Crockett Jr. and UWF owner Bill Watts, in Dallas.

I was at my buddy's pawn shop when I got the call, so I went back to my house. To tell you the truth, I knew exactly what was going to happen. I gave Eric a call and got put on hold. Then he picked up the line and said, "Steve, it's Eric."

I said, "What's going on, Eric?"

He said, "I just wanted to let you know that, based on the amount that we're paying you and based on the number of days you've been

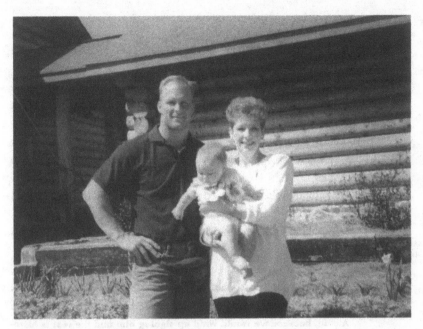

Me, Steph and mom at my house in Douglasville, GA.

incapacitated, we're going to exercise our right to terminate the agreement."

I thought about it for a second and said, "Well, basically you're telling me I'm fired, right?" Fired from my contract, which was bringing me $300,000 a year at the time!

And he said. "Yeah."

I said, "Okay, are you going to send me something in writing?"

He said, "Yeah, it'll be there tomorrow."

And that's how I got fired by WCW.

To this day, I don't know exactly why they did it. Maybe they thought I was an injury problem. I wasn't—I was working my ass off.

But the thing that really pissed me off was the *way* I was fired. You know, I only lived thirty miles from CNN Center in Atlanta. It wasn't like I was going to kick Bischoff's ass for firing me. I mean, treat me like a damn decent human being and invite me down there and say, "Steve, we know you're hurt and we're sorry about that. But we ain't got nothing for you."

In other words, I thought he should have fired me to my face. The way it went down was totally disrespectful.

On the other hand, I shouldn't have been surprised. Some time before, Bischoff had actually said to me, "You know, Steve, you might need to find something else to do for a living, or somewhere else to go—maybe New Japan or ECW—because you go out there in those black trunks and black boots, and there's not a whole lot of ways for me to market that."

He actually told me that I'd never amount to anything, and then he fired me. I'll never forget that day. At the time, it wasn't much fun.

But looking back, it actually turned out to be one of the best days in my career.

J.R.: I have told Eric Bischoff several times since he joined WWE that one of the best things he ever did while he ran WCW was to fire Austin, because we would wind up signing him and the rest is history. Eric did many good things managing WCW, especially when you consider the success of Monday Nitro. That was great competition, which made both companies work smarter and more aggressively. Actually, Eric was not the first boss to fire a talent who went on to become a star, and he will not be the last. I'm just happy that Bischoff pulled the trigger prematurely on the "unmarketable" guy with the short black boots and black tights.

ECW! ECW!
"SuperStar" Steve Austin Debuts

14

What you have just proved beyond a
shadow of a doubt, is that you are the
world's dumbest SON OF A BITCH.

—AUSTIN TO VINCE MCMAHON RIGHT
BEFORE MCMAHON WAS ARRESTED
FOR ASSAULTING AUSTIN

After I was fired by Eric Bischoff, just about the time that my tricep was getting well enough for me to think about doing some things, Paul E. Dangerously (or Paul Heyman)—the guy who had managed me in WCW—called me up out of the blue.

He was running ECW, Extreme Championship Wrestling, a small but popular group in Philadelphia. It

had a cult-type following that loved ECW's violent and hardcore style.

I always got along well with Paul, even though he's one of the best, world-class BSers I ever ran across. He's a guy who's my age, or maybe a little older, but he's been in the business forever and knows a lot about it. I respect a lot of his opinions. I just wouldn't want him doing my taxes or answering my phone.

Anyway, he called me and said, "Hey, man, why don't you come up here and work for us?"

I said, "Paul, my arm's still messed up. I can't wrestle just yet."

He said, "That doesn't matter. Come on up and we can cut some promos. You'll just talk. I'll pay you five hundred dollars a show."

I was thinking, *He's going to pay me five hundred bucks a night to just cut promos? Hell, man, I'm in.* I had just lost a job making almost six thousand dollars a week, and any money coming in was going to be of help to me and my family.

So Paul flew me up to Philadelphia. There was someone there to pick me up and they took me right to the building.

I got there and Paul said, "I want you to do an in-ring interview."

I said, "Sure. What do you want me to talk about?"

He said, "Hell, anything. Whatever you want. What about getting fired? What about WCW? Talk about that. We'll just sit down, Steve, and talk about how you feel, for real."

So I cut about an eight- or ten-minute promo talking about what had happened down in WCW. And I started doing the Bischoff impressions. And Heyman just let me go off. He'd throw out a scenario or ask me if I had any ideas, and I started to do these impressions of Hulk Hogan or Bischoff or whoever else I was doing, and most of these interviews were done between three and five in the morning.

Other guys were doing their promos and vignettes at that time. Everything always ran late because it was only a one- or two-man crew with one camera. Of course, Paul was doing everything and directing everybody. And he gave me an opportunity and a platform to vent all the years of frustration that had been built up from WCW. The interview skills I later used in WWE were actually developed and refined during my short stint with ECW.

"Stunning" Steve Austin with Paul Heyman.

In my first appearance with ECW, I did a shoot promo—in other words, a serious one—that aired prior to ECW's weekly program. I talked about my termination from WCW, the political games backstage and my future in the business. It was the start of a whole new attitude for me.

I said, "Four weeks ago, Eric Bischoff told his secretary to tell her secretary to leave a message on my answering machine for me to call Eric Bischoff. And when I called Eric Bischoff back, he proceeded to fire me over the phone. "They say you are what you eat. In WCW they didn't feed me nothing but garbage, so I let myself become garbage. I became complacent with everything that they said, as long as big Ted kept sending in the checks. Maybe I wasn't happy with what was going on, but I became complacent. Then, they send me to Japan, the big injury. Bischoff delivers the shot heard around the damn world. Steve Austin's out of a high-paying job.

"All of a sudden the phone starts ringing off the hook. It's ECW, it's WWE, it's All Japan, it's New Japan. They're all calling. And all Steve Austin's gotta do is make a decision. For the last two years all I've heard about, anywhere in wrestling, is the famous ECW Arena. So I strolled into the ECW Arena. It's the biggest piece of crap I've ever seen. Debut night, I roll in. You've got a bunch of damn misfits running around thinking they can actually wrestle. All I've seen in ECW is a bunch of violent crap. And that's exactly what I call it, because that's what it is.

"Steve Austin is here to wrestle. It's what I do best. It's what I do better than anybody in the world.

"There's no Hulk Hogans here. There's no Ric Flairs here. There's not a Dusty Rhodes, and there damn sure isn't an Eric Bischoff here. There's no one that can hold back Steve Austin now. 'Stunning?' I tossed it out the damn window. It never was meant to be.

"ECW's gonna find out firsthand what Steve Austin can do. And I'm gonna show everybody here exactly what a true superstar is supposed to do. What a true superstar is suppose to be. Because no one here can hold me back. Not Hulk Hogan, not Eric Bischoff . . . nobody. I'm gonna be the

superstar that I always knew that I could be. Because there is no one here that can stop me."

ECW might have found their fan base by trashing the other two major companies, but for me, it wasn't really about trashing them. It was about finally getting a platform for something I really had a reason to talk about. That was stuff from my heart. It was stuff that I felt. Those turned out to be some of my best interviews. The way I see it, if WWE ever gets back to allowing talent to speak from their heart and not from memory, our product and business would improve dramatically.

That's what really taught me to properly cut a promo—having something to talk about and getting the chance to do it. I owe Paul Heyman for that opportunity, because he was the guy who let me do it. And he's the guy who gave me feedback. He'd tell me what I might want to talk about, but he didn't tell me how to say it.

He'd just say, "Talk about this."

I'd say, "Well . . ."

And he'd say, "Just talk about how you really feel."

Man, once he said that, there I was. So I have to give Paul E. a lot of credit for my learning how to cut a promo.

I wasn't "Stunning Steve" anymore. I had cut my hair off when I was in WCW. I was in the process of growing it back. It was medium length, almost on my red neck again. My gimmick there was I was coming out of WCW, which was a much bigger organization than ECW, so I was, of course, a superstar. They called me, "The Extreme SuperStar Steve Austin."

And Paul even picked the perfect music for me to come out to, "Jesus Christ Superstar." I'll tell you one thing about Paul E.—the guy's volatile, but he's got a lot of ideas.

One time Paul wanted me to wrestle a match against Mikey Whipwreck, a cruiser-weight-size, homegrown ECW babyface, and Paul wanted me to take the belt off him.

I said, "Okay, Paul, I'll do that, but damn, let him beat me one time." If you just put me in there with a Mikey Whipwreck–type guy,

everybody knows I'm going to beat him. Why not surprise everybody and let him beat me, and then we'll do another one and *then* I'll take the belt off him? We did that and it seemed to work.

I also did one match with the Sandman. It was a Kendo Stick match or something crazy like that. I don't remember a whole lot about my matches in ECW. They weren't what you'd call classic wrestling. I know Mikey Whipwreck beat me with my trunks pulled way up. But that was my idea. I was there to talk trash and cut promos and raise the heat level at the ECW Arena in South Philadelphia.

I used to love to watch Cactus Jack and Raven do promos on each other when they were both in ECW. Those were some brilliant promos and I learned from them too. It just goes to show how smart Cactus Jack is, and also Raven, at turning bull crap into something that is legendary. Those guys were magic. Cactus, Mick Foley, became a huge star in WWE while Raven never did. WWE may have missed the boat on Raven.

People were watching that ECW stuff and seeing what I was doing since I was fired from WCW. It was outrageous stuff and a lot of fun to do while I was healing up. I was only there a few months. I cut scathing, sarcastic promos on WCW and on Bischoff. I also did bad impersonations of Hulk Hogan. It was a lot of funny stuff, but I was learning how to cut promos and my character became more defined.

So there I was, cutting promos in ECW. My old friend Kevin Nash liked them and told me he was talking to WWE about me. Kevin and I used to travel together back in WCW, and he was instrumental in getting WWE to call me up.

Kevin asked Vince, "Hey, what are you guys doing about Steve Austin?

Vince said, "Nothing."

I had spoken with Vince once before. It was when I was negotiating with WCW and my contract was almost up. I was flown up to meet with Vince and Bruce Prichard at Vince's house. I didn't see that they really had a whole lot for me, so I went back to WCW.

Another time, I was flown up to talk to Bill Watts, when he was helping Vince out at WWE and acting as Vince's assistant. But again, there wasn't a whole lot there for me, so I flew back home.

After Bill Watts was gone, Kevin Nash asked Vince McMahon again, "What are you guys doing about Steve Austin?"

Vince said, "What do you mean?"

Kevin said, "Well, hell, he's the hottest free agent out there. You guys ain't trying to sign him?"

J.R., who was watching my stuff in ECW late Saturday night on the MSG Network from his home in Connecticut, was just getting started in the WWE Talent Relations Department. He was also a major factor in getting Vince to think about me in a positive way.

Sure enough, not too many days later, my kitchen phone rang. I was still in an arm cast, living in a log house in Georgia. It was Vince McMahon, the most powerful figure on the face of the wrestling planet.

Vince had an idea for me.

J.R.: I used to stay up late on Saturday nights in Connecticut and watch Paul Heyman's ECW Wrestling on the MSG Network. When Paul picked Steve up for a few shots after Steve was canned from WCW, I saw a side of Steve that I had not seen on TV before. He was cutting promos that were unbelievably entertaining and thought provoking. It was as if he meant every word he said and for the most part, at that time, he did. Steve was angry about being fired. He was injured. He had a family to take care of and he was only making about five hundred dollars a week instead of the six thousand or so that he was pulling down with WCW. He was wounded in a variety of ways and he began expressing it. Paul Heyman gave Austin the forum to speak his mind on ECW television and Eric Bischoff provided Steve with the motivation. Interesting what has to happen in someone's life to allow him to get to where he wants to be. Both Kevin Nash and I spoke to Vince McMahon about Steve. Steve was looked at as a very solid in-ring hand, but lacking in charisma. That was the book on Austin at that point in time. Obviously, not enough people in our office were watching Steve raise hell on ECW television programming. Steve was hired by WWE because he could wrestle, because he could work with anyone and have a good, solid match. He was hired to be a mechanic, which meant he would never go higher than the Intercontinental Title.

Jim "J.R." Ross

I want to say something at this point about my good buddy Jim "J.R." Ross. Ever since he helped bring me to Vince McMahon's attention and opened a door for me at WWE, he has been one of my best friends.

I remember J.R. from WCW. I used to talk to him back then, but we weren't really friends the way we are

now. I always thought he knew I was a hard worker and that he appreciated that. But he had different duties back then.

When I came up north, J.R. knew I could help WWE. And because of the Oklahoma–Texas connection, we just started talking more and more, and became real close. We were two southern boys up there in the North, so we hit it off. And he's the guy I would always ask when I wanted advice, because the guy has been a million different places and in many different situations involving talent.

I could ask his advice as a brother, father or friend, whatever. He's just like family to me. If I want an honest opinion concerning anything in life, man, that damn J.R. has always got a good answer, whether I like the answer or not.

When I was going through my second divorce, WWE flew me around on private jets so I could bring my kids with me to Pay-Per-Views. My friend Ricky Fisher's wife, Sandra, would come with me on the jet so she could watch my girls, while I would work with Vince or whoever. It was J.R. who lined all that up with me, getting it okayed by Vince.

J.R.'s helped me a lot with my character too. He doesn't put sugar on everything. He tells it like it is. If he agreed with everything I want to do, his opinion would not be worth so much to me.

In my opinion, he is the best damn announcer in the history of pro wrestling. I grew up watching Houston wrestling and they'd have stuff with J.R. from *Mid-South Wrestling* and *Power Pro Wrestling,* so I was always a fan of his work. And then I saw him announce on TV from Atlanta.

That's another reason I gravitated toward him, because I respected the guy for what he had accomplished in this business. J.R.'s a guy every WWE wrestler should have a good relationship with. He has led the way in assembling a hell of a talent roster.

J.R. is also the biggest John Wayne fan in the world. He can explain the plot of any John Wayne movie in wrestling terms. And it's funny to hear to him do it, because he's so passionate about it.

It's like when he was crawling up the ropes on the WWE show *Raw*

after Eric Bischoff busted him open with a cinder block. Before the show, he was telling Vince McMahon about the John Wayne movie *The Cowboys*, when Bruce Dern was beating up John Wayne. And boy, he had Vince's attention hook, line and sinker.

"Well, what'd he do then?" Vince asked.

When you've got the Duke down and Bruce Dern's the ultimate heel, that is heat that's "real." It's plausible. That makes Wayne a hell of a hot babyface. Bruce Dern ended up shooting John Wayne. J.R. has never forgiven Bruce Dern for doing that to this very day. Seriously.

Anytime I'm in Stamford, I have an automatic invite over to J.R.'s house for a home-cooked meal. Jim and his wife, Jan, are both Grade A cooks. It's better than going to a restaurant. Hell, they've written two successful cookbooks! Jan even lets me use her washer and dryer.

J.R. was to be very instrumental in my career after I got to WWE, and I sure do appreciate it. I just wish the hard-headed Okie would slow down a little and smell the BBQ sauce.

I joined him at the Oklahoma University Sooner team hotel after the 2003 Rose Bowl and he looked to be stress-free. J.R. needs more days like that, and let me tell you, Oklahoma football has no bigger fan than Jim Ross.

I appreciate my good friend J.R. It's just too bad he's Sooner-bred.

J.R.: The first time I saw Steve in person after his unscheduled hiatus of eight months or so from WWE was on January 2, 2003, in Los Angeles after the Sooners won the Rose Bowl. I had called Steve and let him know I was going to the game and he told me he was going to be in L.A. at the same time, so we decided to get together. A few hours after the game my wife and our friends the Wilsons from Tahlequah, Oklahoma, arrived back at our hotel, which happened to be the same hotel where the OU team and staff, along with a ton of Oklahoma fans, were staying as well. Steve arrived wearing an old Las Vegas Outlaw XFL football jersey and a customary cap someone had given him. The OU players and fans flocked to him like crazy. I think it made Steve feel real good. Here these kids are after just winning the

"granddaddy of 'em all," the Rose Bowl, and all they want to talk about is when is Stone Cold coming back. He must have signed a hundred autographs standing outside the hotel while we were talking. The players also got camcorders from the Rose Bowl folks, so I can assure you that Stone Cold is on a bunch of videotapes that the Oklahoma Sooner football players will cherish forever.

Here I am with the Million Dollar Championship and my manager Ted DiBiase.

The Ringmaster 16

"Hello?"

"Steve, how ya doing? It's Vince McMahon."

"Hi, Vince. How're you doing?"

"Good, pal. Listen, I got an idea for you. Tell me what you think. I want to bring you into WWE as somebody called 'The Ringmaster'—you know, like the master of the ring. Ted DiBiase is going to be your

manager. We're going to make you The Million Dollar Champion."

I was thinking that it sounded like a damned circus act! Ringmaster . . . ? But remember, I had been fired from WCW by Eric Bischoff and I hadn't worked in several months—other than making my five hundred dollars a night, one night a week. That five hundred dollars was much appreciated, but it didn't go real far. I had saved my money from WCW, but I was more than ready to go back to work again. I needed a steady job.

So I said, "Well, okay," trying not to sound reluctant or apprehensive.

A couple weeks later, I told Paul E. that I was finishing up and going to WWE. I wrapped up my business with him and ECW, and a few days later I went to a WWE TV taping and signed all the papers.

Then Vince flew me to see the WWE seamstresses, Terry and Julie. They said, "Okay, the office wants you to wear emerald green."

I said, "What do you mean, emerald green? I wear black."

They said, "You can't wear black because Diesel (Kevin Nash) wears black. They want you to wear an emerald green singlet."

I said, "A singlet? This is the WWE system? They're telling me what to wear? This is their concept for what I'm going to be?" That's what they did back then.

But I said, "I'll tell you right now, I'm not going to wear no singlet. I just don't do that. I wear black trunks."

They said, "You can't wear black trunks because that's Diesel's color."

So I said, "Okay," and they made me a pair of emerald green trunks, but absolutely no singlet!

Later on, I was talking to Vince and I said, "Well, what about a vest?"

He said, "Ah, you don't need a vest."

I said, "Well, what about boots?"

He answered, "Ah, just wear your old boots."

I'm thinking, What the hell kind of plans do these guys have for me, man? I'm wearing old white boots with a black star on them and I got green trunks, because that's the color of money. What the hell?

Right away I knew they didn't have any serious plans for me. They just needed another body out there, a mechanic, another guy on the roster who could work a match. Anyway, things went on, and I became The Ringmaster. Hey, I had to start somewhere, didn't I?

One of the guys who helped me when I started wrestling for WWE was Jack Lanza, a road agent for the company. A road agent is a guy who helps run a show and helps the talent come up with interesting ways to entertain the crowd. They're also there to help newer talent learn the business. Road agents in the WWE report to either J.R. or Vince. Some agents specialize in different things, so being a road agent can mean many things, but they all help do something backstage with the talent. Since they are all ex-wrestlers, they have knowledge and experience to pass on. They've been in almost every situation. These are all guys Vince can trust with his business.

Anyway, I remembered Jack Lanza from television as "Black Jack" Lanza, one of the greatest tag heel workers in the business. He was in a tag team, with Black Jack Mulligan, called the Blackjacks.

When I was wrestling as The Ringmaster, I was a very physical worker. Scotty 2 Hotty was doing the honors for me in my first WWE match, and I just pounded the guy. I was working my punches, but I was very physical.

Jack saw that and he told me to keep doing what I was doing. Pat Patterson and Jerry Brisco, who I knew from watching Houston wrestling when I was a kid, said the same thing—to just keep doing what I was doing.

They said, "It's going to take you longer to get over, because of these other guys with gimmicks that they're really pushing. But when you get over, you're going to stay over, mark our words."

So Jack Lanza was with me from the word "go."

At the time, I was wrestling a lot against Savio Vega. I loved working with him. We were having some real bad-ass matches. But I was blown up because I was out of ring-style shape.

I told the company and the agents, "Bear with me, I'll make it. I'll be okay. I'm sorry to drag you down."

Jack Lanza, who loved the business and recognized when some-

body was busting his ass, told me I was doing good. He said not to worry about it.

We got to be pretty good friends. We'd see each other at the hotel bars, lounges, whatever, kicking back a few drinks and so on. We are a lot alike, and we both love the business so damn much we'd just talk. He kind of took me under his wing.

When I got hot later in my career with WWE, Jack would be one of the guys I'd turn to for advice. Nine times out of ten he'd be the agent for my matches. And he's another guy who I'd go to if I had a problem. He was a father figure to me. Jack had done it all and he had great advice when it came to ring psychology and stuff like that.

Pat Patterson gave me advice too. He was (and still is) one of the greatest finish guys ever in the business. He's always thought of the ways a match should end that was interesting, made sense and left the fans wanting to see more. He had a lot more experience in finishes than I did, and Pat laid out a couple of good finishes for me that were helpful in getting me up the company ladder.

Jack was my guy in the locker room when I started with WWE, but so was Jerry Brisco. I was a big Brisco brothers fan and he was from Oklahoma, so I was always ribbing him about Texas–OU stuff.

In May 1996 we were in Kuwait holding a tournament and I was wrestling Marty Jannetty. There was this red carpet that went all the way around the ring and all the way up to the entrance, probably a hundred yards long. When the match was over, Jerry walked out to ringside and I was kind of bent over, catching my breath. He chicken-winged me and over-the-head suplexed me onto the carpet.

There was nothing I could do about it! I was just chicken-wing suplexed in Kuwait!

Then Jerry and the referee ran to the back, leaving me there. There was no explanation why he just suplexed me and I was left lying out there on the floor. I guess with me bending over, he just thought it would be funny.

So I rolled all the way to the back up that long red carpet as a ha-ha for the boys in the back. I rolled like a tumbleweed and the people

With Jerry Brisco. The only agent to get away with suplexing me.

booed me out of the building. They don't know what the hell they saw that day, but it was unusual and entertaining.

When I got to the back, I said to Brisco, "Are you all blown up?"— asking if he was winded from suplexing me. The former Oklahoma State University wrestler immediately put an amateur wrestling hold on an unlucky wrestler who happened to be standing nearby, where the guy couldn't breath.

My stuff was fake, but not Brisco's. I don't care how old he was, Gerald Brisco was still double tough. He'll be the toughest man in the AARP someday.

But Brisco wasn't the only one with a sense of humor. Jack Lanza had one too. I used to do this bit in the back where when somebody said something stupid I'd take my hat off and throw it against the wall. It was like I was all mad. But I wouldn't be mad at all. It was a rib, you know? Something funny.

One day we were in the dressing room watching a TV show, and one of those goofy infomercials came on about people who were losing their hair on top. They were selling that black spray paint stuff you could spray the top of your head with. It was a little uncomfortable because Jack, who is follicly challenged, was standing right next to me.

All of a sudden, he reached over, grabbed my hat off my head and threw it against the wall.

We laughed our asses off. I wonder if Jack ever called that phone number on the infomercial . . . ?

After six or eight months, things were going okay. Then we went on a tour of Germany and I was working in the main event with Shawn Michaels every night. They needed someone he could have a good match with, and I can have a good match with anybody. Even though the fans might not have known who I was, they knew I was working the main event.

The Heartbreak Kid, back when he was on fire, was a big name for me to be working with. J.R. was doing the booking. Being a mark for great wrestling, he wanted to see how HBK and I would do together. It worked. Man, I was out there having classic matches with him.

Now, I wasn't making Shawn Michaels's kind of money, but I was getting good feedback from the road agents. Time was going by, and I started thinking, This Ringmaster name just ain't cutting it. It sucks.

I was getting it done in the ring, but my gimmick was lame as hell. The Ringmaster had no upside. I felt it, but more importantly, the fans felt it too. I had to change my in-ring persona or I would eventually be back at the freight dock in Dallas or selling insurance in Edna, and I wasn't ready for neither.

Something had to give . . . oh, hell yeah!

J.R.: Steve was a wrestling heel, as it is known in the business. A wrestling heel is a great guy to have on your cards, a guy who can work with virtually anyone and will always give you a great effort. In the old days of WWE, Steve would have been a setup man. In other words, he would have lost to babyfaces who were going to wrestle in the main event the next time the group was in town. The setup man historically lacked the proper amount of charisma to propel himself to the next level, the main events. I think this was how Steve was viewed when he wrestled as The Ringmaster. I booked Steve with the incomparable Shawn Michaels because I wanted to see how Steve would do in a main event–level match with a world-class opponent. I can remember road agent Jack Lanza telling me that the matches Shawn and Steve had were priceless, and had to be seen to be believed. I think that series of matches helped get Steve noticed as the feedback to Vince was positive and intriguing. Maybe we were on to something, after all.

The Origin of Stone Cold Steve Austin

I got nothing to say to you. Just park
my damn truck and if you scratch it, you
are going to get your ass whipped.

—Austin to WWE announcer
Michael Cole, as he arrived at the
Royal Rumble 1998

I was still living in Atlanta while I was
working with WWE, and I was watch-
ing HBO one night. This HBO docu-
mentary about the *Iceman,* a serial
killer-for-hire named Richard Kuklinski, came
on. He used to put his victims in freezers to keep the bod-
ies preserved, then he'd finally dump them out a year
later. Man, I watched that show and it got my gears spin-

ning, because I was a heel, and here was this cold-blooded guy who didn't give a damn about anybody.

Not that I approved of what he did. It was just that cold, "I don't have a conscience" attitude that attracted me. I saw something in this psycho that I could use in my in-ring presentation. I could, as perverse as it sounds, relate to this animal.

I pitched my concept to Debbie Bonnanzio, senior vice president of WWE Creative Services. She was in charge of gimmick characterization, and they started faxing me pages and pages of names. But the names just weren't working. They were all temperature-based things like "Fang McFrost," "Ivan the Terrible," "Ice Dagger," names like that. The names were horrible. Our creative group did not "feel" my new character idea.

I was thinking, Man, they don't understand where I'm coming from on this. I could just hear Howard Finkel, the ring announcer, saying, *"Ice Dagger . . . accompanied by his famous sled dog, Nantucket!"* More non-reality-based horse manure . . .

I told a few guys about all this and damn, they ribbed me terribly about it. I got frustrated as hell. Then, one day, I was just sitting there in the kitchen, thinking about the name thing.

Jeannie, my wife, who's English, drank tea all the time. Knowing how frustrated I was, she made me a cup.

"Ah," she said, putting the tea down in front of me, "don't worry about it. Just go ahead and drink your tea before it gets stone cold." Then she paused, with this light in her eyes, and said, "That's your new name . . . Stone Cold Steve Austin."

I raised my eyes up from the cup of tea and said, "Yeah . . ." After I'd had a chance to think about it, I wondered if it might not be too long. "Stone Cold Steve Austin. That's four words," I said.

But I liked it. It had a ring to it, those four words together. Originally I was thinking about using the Iceman name, but Iceman King Parsons had done that in Dallas in World Class Wrestling, so I couldn't just take his name.

Anyway, I pitched the Stone Cold idea to someone at TV. They told me to call Jerry Brisco and J.R.

I called Jerry, explained the concept and finished up by saying, "I

want to be this guy and I want to call him 'Stone Cold Steve Austin.'"

Jerry said, "Okay, let me check through the normal channels."

He called somebody else, and they put it through legal to see if it wasn't trademarked or something. Eventually, Jerry called me back and said, "You're cleared. You're Stone Cold Steve Austin."

I was thinking, Oh, hell yeah!

And they just started introducing me that way. There was no big buildup or explanation or anything like that. There were no vignettes or interviews, to provide some background on this cold-blooded guy. The name just started catching on, and I was Stone Cold Steve Austin from Victoria, Texas.

But I still wasn't really going anywhere. I had the name, but no one knew how I had gotten so cold-blooded. I had to get this thing kick-started somehow.

Beating Jake Roberts at the *King of the Ring 1996*. Jake was one of my favorites of all time.

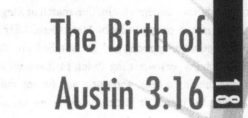

The Birth of Austin 3:16

18

"Austin 3:16" all came about at the *King of the Ring* Pay-Per-View on June 23, 1996, when WWE announcer Dok Hendrix (Michael P.S. Hayes, a former "Fabulous Freebird") told me in the locker room that Jake "The Snake" Roberts was going to cut a religious promo on me.

Jake, who had a string of personal issues, had been preaching in the ring lately about how he turned his life around. That got me to thinking about how I would respond after the show was over.

In my first tournament elimination match at *King of the Ring,* I got kicked in the mouth pretty badly by Marc Mero. After I beat him, I had to go to the emergency room and get stitched up. This was going on while Jake Roberts was wrestling Vader. I came back to the arena right away, never missing a beat, and got ready for my match against Jake, who had won his match. It just made me more intense, because I was booked to win the thing, but I had to be there to do it.

When I did my infamous "3:16" promo after winning the *King of the Ring,* that was a strong-ass promo and none of that stuff was scripted. At the time that Dok Hendrix stuck that mic in my face, he had no idea what I was going to say and neither did Vince, J.R. or the guys in the TV truck. It all just came out.

> I said, "The first thing I want to be done is to get that piece of crap [Jake Roberts] out of my ring! Don't just get him out of the ring, get him out of WWE, because I've proven, son, without a shadow of a doubt, you ain't got what it takes anymore. You sit there and you thump your Bible and you say your prayers, and it didn't get you anywhere. You talk about John 3:16 . . . Austin 3:16 says, I've just whipped your ass!! All he's got to do is buy him a cheap bottle of Thunderbird and try to dig back some of that courage he had in his prime. As the King of the Ring, I'm serving notice to every one of the WWE Superstars . . . I don't give a damn who they are, they are all on the list, and that is Stone Cold's list, and I'm fixing to start running through all of them. Steve Austin's time has come, and when I get the shot, you are looking at the next WWE Champion, and that's the bottom line . . . 'cause Stone Cold said so!"

That started off two of my trademark sayings, "AUSTIN 3:16" and " 'Cause Stone Cold Said So." It all happened that night at *King of the Ring*.

By the next night, AUSTIN 3:16 signs and posters had already started showing up in the crowd. When WWE came to me with the idea of doing a Stone Cold Steve Austin T-shirt, I said, "Just print a black T-shirt with plain white lettering. Put AUSTIN 3:16 on the front and a skull on the back, with 'Stone Cold' written on it."

That shirt probably outsold any shirt in the history of wrestling.

That's why I think we need to get back to the way it used to be, with guys spitting out their own ideas and learning how to develop a character, because Austin 3:16 would never have happened or even come up if I was waiting for writers to tell me what to say. It all came from my heart as soon as I learned what Jake Roberts did in his prematch promo.

Wrestlers are not trained actors. To be successful, a wrestler must truly feel and understand who he is as a performer. If he really feels it, he can deliver a promo that is both believable and entertaining. If he's simply memorizing his lines, the promo fails, much more often than not.

I do have to say that even after I did my 3:16 promo at *King of the Ring* and I introduced my new catchphrases, Vince still didn't listen to all my ideas. I don't think he had ever pushed anybody like me before. I'm not saying I was the best. I was just a different breed of cat. I was trying to be a heel, but I was accepted universally as a babyface. This was new ground—for me too. I was just kind of working my way through it, but it was new to me.

I kept my hair short at that time, but I wasn't happy with it thinning out more as time went on. I did my 3:16 debut with Jake Roberts at *King of the Ring* with very short hair, but the sudden change in my demeanor called for a few adjustments in the way I looked. Stone Cold Steve Austin needed some new visuals.

I really liked that Bruce Willis had a buzz cut in *Pulp Fiction*. I thought he looked very cool for a guy who's been losing his hair, and very cold-blooded at the same time, so I got a buzz cut. Then I saw

Woody Harrelson with his shaved head in *Natural Born Killers* and that was it! I decided to just completely shave my head smooth. I grew a beard and mustache and re-created myself as a whole new persona. I looked "Stone Cold" and felt "Stone Cold."

All of a sudden, I was getting more promo time. But a new problem reared its ugly head. Some of my best stuff was getting edited out.

I remember running down Aldo Montoya (Justin Credible) on one of our TV shows. He had that yellow mask on his face and I called it a jockstrap. I just cut him and cut him and cut him. Then, later on when I watched the show, I noticed that some of these good things I'd said weren't on the air. I was like, "Man, what the hell?"

We were in a real snowy town in the Northeast, at the old building in Lowell, Massachusetts, and I called Vince aside. I said, "Vince, can I talk to you?"

He said, "Yeah."

I said, "Man, what's going on? It seems like every time I say something, y'all take it back to the shop and chop all my stuff out."

He said, "Well, Steve, your stuff is making the people laugh back in the studio. We are concerned because, as a heel, we want the fans to *not* like you."

I said, "Well, Vince, let me tell you something. I'm six-two, two hundred and fifty pounds. I got a bald head and a goatee. I got black trunks and black boots and a big mouth. Man, if you take my personality away from me, I can't compete with anybody here. You got guys here six-ten, seven feet, three hundred and fifty pounds or whatever. But if you give me my personality, I can compete with anybody. I guarantee it."

Vince listened to me and said, "Okay," and walked off. We left it at that. But Vince had gotten the message. He started letting me just go, and stopped editing a lot of my lines out of the show. Vince was beginning to "feel" and understand the Stone Cold character, which was essential in the development of my in-ring persona.

I tell young wrestlers that they must always be thinking about their TV character, and wear down the WWE creative team with their ideas for that character. And, above all else, they have to develop a positive working relationship with Vince.

Vince is the engine that runs the WWE machine. If he doesn't understand or "feel" your character, you might as well do something else for a living.

Vince was raised as a true North Carolina redneck, and I think the Stone Cold character took him back to his roots and to people he had run across. He was giving the character his support.

And Austin 3:16 was about to explode.

J.R.: Even after Steve Austin slapped us in the face with his controversial persona after defeating Jake Roberts to become the King of the Ring, I still don't think we really knew what we had. He was essentially slated to be the wrestling heel who could work with anyone and make them look good, but it was thought that he lacked the verbal skills to connect with the audience. Well, that changed when Steve did his promo with Michael Hayes [Dok Hendrix]. A new star was born. The "merchandise king" had arrived, complete with his seemingly endless string of catchphrases that did nothing but make money for all involved. These phrases were just natural extensions of Steve's basic personality. He isn't an actor. He is a wrestler with passion.

Michael Hayes and the Stone Cold Stunner

When I was attending college and going down to the Sportatorium or Reunion Arena in Dallas to watch professional wrestling, Michael P.S. Hayes was one of my favorite wrestlers. He was a badass heel with a big mouth, who could be a coward when the moment called for it.

Hayes knew his role. And he wasn't a great wrestler, but he could cut a hell of a promo and he could really make you hate his guts. I enjoyed watching him and understand now how much of an influence he had on my career.

Hayes was one of the Fabulous Freebirds, along with "Bam-Bam" Terry Gordy (who was the badass muscle of the group) and Buddy Roberts, who was a pile-of-trash heel. I remember Michael Hayes getting up on the turnbuckle with that Rebel robe on and he'd dance and shake his hips, flipping his long hair. And I was just thinking, Damn . . . that's cool as hell.

Of course, as a mark I hated Hayes's guts. But that was his job as a heel, to make me hate him.

Then, once I got into the business, I got to know the guy in person and he was entertaining as all hell. More importantly, Michael P.S. Hayes is the guy who gave me the Stunner finish to my matches.

As The Ringmaster, my finishing hold had been the Million-Dollar Dream, which was my manager Ted DiBiase's finish—a submission-type hold also known in the business as the cobra clutch. After I came up with the Stone Cold Steve Austin gimmick, I was still using that finish.

It was okay. It was starting to get over with the fans. But one day at a TV in Fayetteville, North Carolina, I remember Michael Hayes came walking up to me and said, "Hey, kid, come here. You got a second?"

I said, "Yeah."

He said, "I've been trying to think of a good finish for you. You know, that cobra clutch deal is okay, but if you do this other finish, it would be better," and he showed me what he was talking about.

Wrestler Johnny Ace, who now works with J.R. in Talent Relations, was doing a version of it in Japan, called an Ace Crusher. Hayes said, "It's different from Ace's finish, because you put the guy's chin on your shoulder, jump up and then you land on your ass."

We got some of the local wrestlers together in the ring and said, "Hey, do you guys mind helping us with this?"

So I started practicing the Stunner that day. I did it about six times, and Hayes said, "Pretty cool, huh?"

I said, "Yeah, I like it."

Here are two guys that look totally different now. My very first match in WWE was against Scotty 2 Hotty.

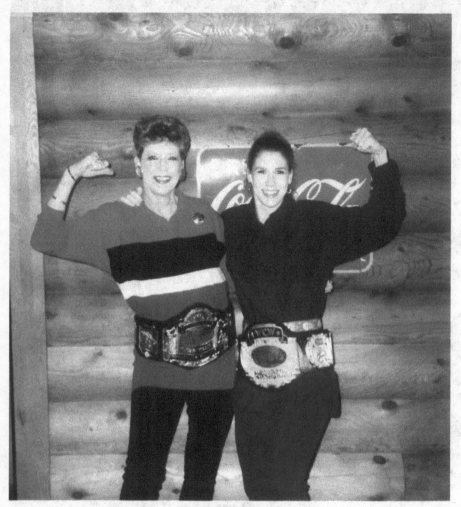

I told you not to mess with Stone Cold's mom. My mom and sister Jenny wearing my old WCW belts. COURTESY OF THE WILLIAMS FAMILY.

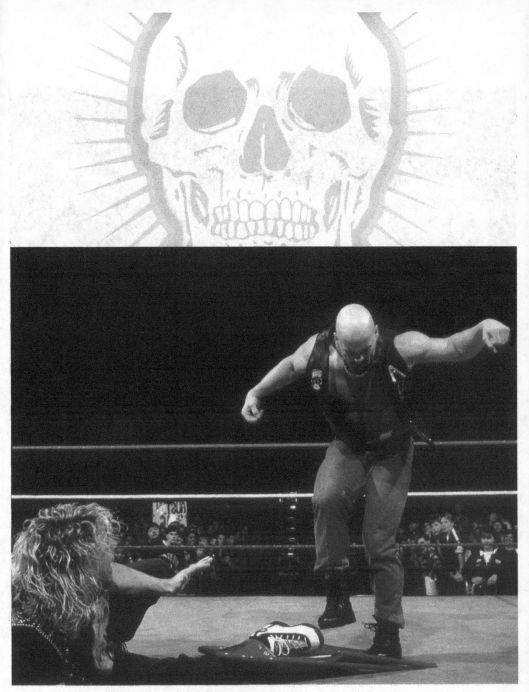

It was great to work with Brain Pillman in WWE.

Some of my favorite matches were with Bret Hart. I really enjoyed my run with him.

After taking care of some business, a Stone Cold salute for the fans.

AUSTIN 3:16

Austin 3:16

STONE

Here I calmly explain to Undertaker "what the bottom line is."

A double helping of whoop-ass for Triple H and Shane McMahon. Shane sold my Stunner better than just anyone in the business.

You'd think by now they'd move the Spanish announcer's table.

Giving The Rock a gut shot to set up the Stone Cold Stunner at *WrestleMania X-Seven.*

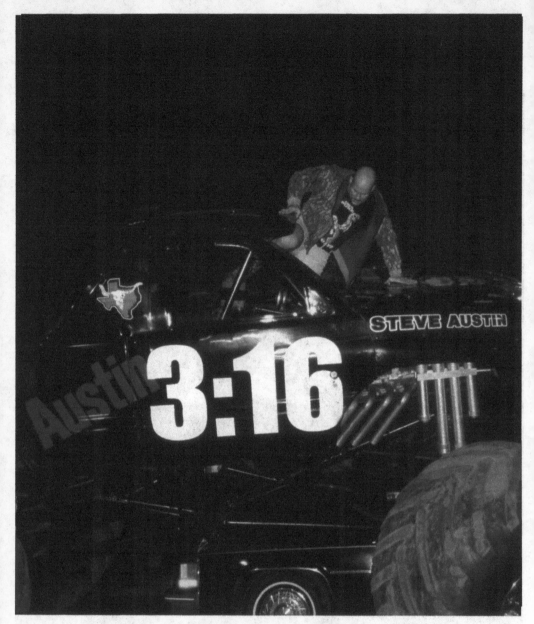

Man, every kid's dream—I get paid to wreck stuff. Here I am crushing The Rock's car.

Running Dude Love into the buckle.

I let Mr. McMahon and his stooges know exactly what I think of them.

WrestleMania XIX,
knowing this could be my last match.

WrestleMania XIX I give The Rock and the fans my best.

I started using the Stunner as my finishing hold that day, and J.R. called it the "Stone Cold Stunner." I was thinking of something else, but that was a perfect name for my new finisher. It said it all. Thanks, J.R.

A few months later, in one of my first few Pay-Per-View shows using that finish, *King of the Ring*, I was going to go straight for the Stunner. We needed a setup thing, so that's when I started with the foot in the gut as a setup, the "gut shot."

It happened so fast, out of the blue, that you couldn't anticipate it. I'd kick you in the gut, and you'd bend over in pain and sell the gut shot. And then I'd put the Stunner on you and drop you, one-two-three.

It was Michael Hayes who helped me come up with the gut shot and then the Stunner. Thanks, P.S. And by the way, the old Freebird still has the number one mullet in WWE!

DTA—Don't Trust Anybody

0

've always been real shy. I don't know why. I get along well with people and am polite to everyone, but to this day I'm extremely private. I have very few true friends. I have acquaintances or whatever, but there aren't a whole lot of people I hang out with, even if I've lived somewhere a long time.

Here in San Antonio, I have my beer-drinking buddy, Ricky Fisher, my personal doctor, Jimmy Baros and Skyler Craig, my training partner. That's it. There are people I talk to at the gym, but I don't really know them. I'm just a little leery about trusting people. You always wonder if people are just coming up to you and saying things because you're Stone Cold Steve Austin.

I say to myself, *Okay, what do you want?* That type of thing.

I'm usually good at reading people. The people I end up hanging out with are people pretty much like me. We just like to have fun, and we have a helluva sense of humor. I just want to laugh all day—just rib on people and laugh, that's what I like to do.

One of the catchphrases I used in WWE in the late nineties was "Don't Trust Anyone." That comes from my experience in the wrestling business, and from being shafted along the way. It comes from being manipulated, watching the political scenes and not being part of certain circles. It's like that in the wrestling business, and in life in general.

You can always find another reason not to trust someone. That's just the way things are. I mean, how many people do *you* really trust? So that whole deal was pretty much the way I truly feel.

But it did add to the mystique of Stone Cold's character. My character's personality was as solid as stone—which was more than I could say for my personal life . . .

Stone Cold, Lady Blossom, the IRS and Howard Stern

hen I first met Jeannie in Dallas, I was dirt poor. We used to go for Chinese food together and she would spring for the bill every time. She even bought me my first pair of wrestling boots.

A few years after Jeannie and I started in WCW, she got pregnant with our older daughter, Stephanie.

Jeannie and I weren't married at the time. One Christmas I gave her a beautiful bracelet. I thought she would be excited as hell about the bracelet, but what she really wanted was a wedding ring.

I did love her, so I thought, Why not? So we got married in a church outside of Douglasville, Georgia, near Atlanta. I married Jeannie, we had two wonderful daughters and we were together for almost eight years—many good, some not so good.

We moved into a log cabin house—a beautiful little house—on ten acres in Atlanta. But because I wasn't working for WCW in Atlanta anymore, and because I was on the road so damn much, I decided I wanted to live back in Texas. I didn't want to live in Houston because I had grown up a hundred miles south of there and Houston is a monster, traffic-wise. Dallas was maybe a little preppy for me. Austin is a great town, but it's got a lot of college kids.

My mom said she and Dad always liked going to Boerne, right outside San Antonio. It's a nice small Texas town with a lot of antique shops. So Jeannie and I flew into San Antonio and my mom picked us up at the airport, and we drove down to Boerne. We stayed at a hotel and drove around and I liked it. We found a place to rent.

About this time, I got a call from the government telling me that they had audited my back taxes for some reason. It turned out that Jeannie had turned me on to some incompetent accountant, and I was $360,000 in debt to the U.S. government for back taxes! I never, ever did anything wrong. I never tried to screw the IRS. Everything I did was on time and I never even had to file an extension.

I just sent the tax guys my forms and stuff like that, and I didn't know he was making up these bogus figures. But all of a sudden, Steve Williams owed the IRS $360,000.

Hey, when I screw up, I take responsibility for my actions, but for once this wasn't my fault. I had no idea how I was going to pay off that kind of debt. I thought I'd be making payments to Uncle Sam for the rest of my life. I lost a lot of sleep thinking about that.

When I was moving back to Texas and I was going to sell my house in Atlanta, I remember that whatever profit I was going to make was going to go to the U.S. government. It was a frustrating state of affairs.

Anyway, I finally found a house in Boerne that I wanted to buy, but in 1995 I didn't have any credit. I had started with WWE and was already Stone Cold by this time, so I called Vince McMahon up and asked him if he would help me buy me a house if I promised to pay him back.

Without hesitation, Vince said, "Hell, I'll be happy to help you buy a house."

I said, "Well, how much can I spend?"

He said, "I don't know, Steve, I'll leave that up to you."

The house Vince helped me buy was about six miles out of town. Jeannie and I both liked it. But after a while, it turned out to be a tough situation for her.

Because I was on the road with WWE 24/7, Jeannie was in the house by herself most of the time. And when I'd get home, I'd go straight up the hill to the house of my buddy, Ricky Fisher, who lived just eight hundred yards away. Ricky and I would sit there drinking beer and telling stories.

U.K.-born Jeannie never really fit in. She liked Ricky and his wife, Sandra, but she didn't really get the Texas way of life. So the whole time we were living in Boerne, Jeannie and I were growing apart. She missed the Atlanta area we used to live in and felt isolated out there. I should have seen it. I should have been more sensitive about Jeannie feeling so isolated.

Our house in Boerne was on six acres and it cost only $165,000. That was the house I was in the process of paying Vince back for, and it was fine with me.

But I wanted to try and make the marriage work, so I asked Jeannie where she wanted to live. She said she wanted to live in San Antonio. So we settled on this nice gated community in San Antonio. The house was expensive, but she really liked it, so I put $50,000 down on it. It looked like things were going to work out, which is what I was hoping for.

A couple of days later, Jeannie called me and said, "Let's meet at the service station."

I got there and met her, and she said she wanted to get separated.

I said, "I just put fifty grand down on this house. If we're going to get separated, hell, I'll just file for divorce."

I can't remember what she said, but I drove off and started thinking, Well, if I'm getting divorced, the last thing I need is a big, expensive house.

I called the real estate agent and said I wanted to back out of the deal. I couldn't do it for free, so I lost half of the $50,000 deposit. Then I went ahead and reluctantly filed for divorce.

At that point, I went back to the house in Boerne that was down the road from Ricky and Sandra's house, and started to pack my stuff up. I had my taxidermist buddy come over and we loaded my guns, my stereo and my TV into my car. Ricky had another friend who lived about three miles from where I was living. The guy was a homebuilder and he had just built a monster-size house for himself, and he had a double-wide trailer he was living in while he built this house.

Ricky called him up and said, "Todd, Steve's going through a divorce and needs a place to stay."

Todd said that he had just moved out of the double-wide, and that he and his family were living in the big house now. If I wanted to, he said, I could stay in the double-wide out there in the front yard for a few months. So I moved everything in and got the phone hooked up.

I remember that living in that double-wide trailer was one of the happiest times in my life. I had a big ol' fishing cooler as my "entertainment center" with a fourteen-inch color TV and a VCR on top of it. My two little girls would stay there with me when I came home after being on the road with WWE.

I'd get up and take Stephanie to school and Cassidy to day care, then I would work out and do my errands and pick them up at five. When it came time to go back on the road, I'd take them back to Jeannie at the house. During this period of time, I was starting to really get hot as Stone Cold Steve Austin and was going what seemed like a hundred miles an hour.

Jeannie and I were going through mediation, and came to an agreement on a dollar figure and a monthly figure for the kids. Then we signed the paperwork. Two months later I was divorced and I was living

in the double-wide. In the divorce decree, Jeannie was ordered to live within fifty miles of my residence, so she ended up leasing a house in the same gated community where I was going to buy that expensive house for us.

Unfortunately, as I mentioned earlier, Jeannie and the girls have since moved to Jeannie's home in the United Kingdom. My kids are my life, and I can't tell you how much I miss them.

My biological father took off on my family before I ever got a chance to know him. I just want to make sure that my girls know I'm always there for them, and how much I love and miss them.

Shortly after my divorce from Jeannie, I was a guest on *The Howard Stern Show* radio show in New York, and I told Howard I'd probably never get married again. I think the thing that I enjoyed the most about being on the show was being able to laugh about a few things, and maybe get them off my chest. Even at a time when I wasn't so happy

Cassidy and me, Christmas '97.

to go out on national TV, it was very refreshing—kind of like therapy for me.

I always have a good time with Howard because there is no preshow interview. On most other shows, a production assistant calls you a couple of days in advance and asks you a bunch of questions to be talked about on the show. It's so lame. The show day comes and you go on, and you and the host just go through the motions. Oh-how-fun. But with Howard, it's flying by the seat of your pants, the way I like it.

I had a real good time on Howard's show and I liked Howard. I think I could hang out with that guy. We'd just sit there and talk, and he's a different person when he's off the air, like I'm a different person when I'm off the air. Same guy, just turned down a notch. I've always liked going on his show. It ain't like any other radio show in this whole country! I am *so* Texas and he is *so* New York, it just kind of works.

When you go on that show, you have to go in with a self-deprecating sense of humor and be ready, willing and able to laugh at yourself. You know they're going to dump on you a little. That's what the show's about. It's entertainment. I don't mind getting made fun of, because I make fun of people all the time. I'm not going to go on there like, "Hey, I'm Mr. Tough Guy and you're not going to say this or that about me." I had a real good time with Howard and his crew.

Howard Stern is great at what he does. He always treats me like gold too, so I appreciate that. He's paid millions of dollars in FCC fines, and in the process that has made him more money, because people would say, "Hey, he's paying all these fines? Now I'm really going to listen and see what the hell is going on there."

Howard Stern has paved the way for many, many radio personalities to become stars and earn a helluva living. I hope I have been able to do the same in wrestling.

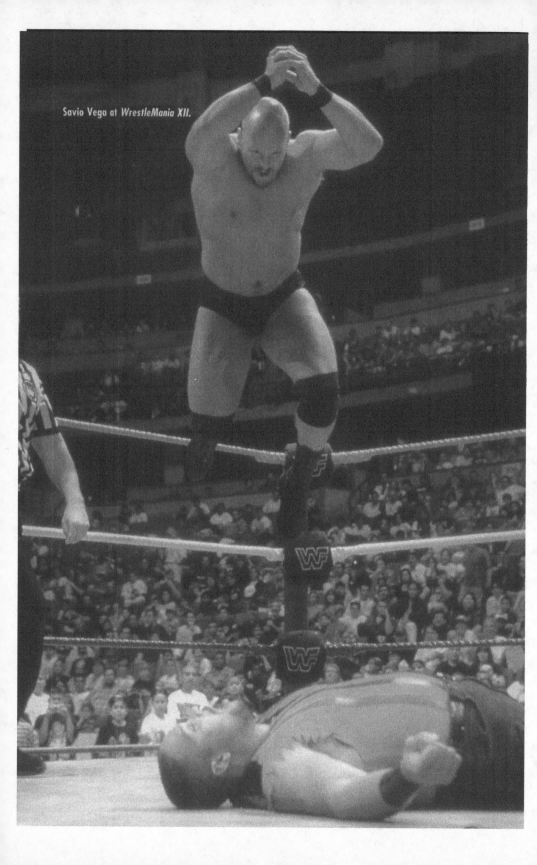

Savio Vega at *WrestleMania XII*.

WrestleManias XII, 13 and XIV

If you put an S in front of HITMAN,

you know what I think of him!

—AUSTIN TALKING ABOUT
BRET HART ON RAW

 remember my first *WrestleMania* with crystal clarity. It was *WrestleMania XII* on March 31, 1996, at the Arrow Head Pond in Anaheim, California.

I had never been to a *WrestleMania* before, so I had never seen anything like it. It was just amazing to be part of such a show—the Super Bowl and the World Series of our business.

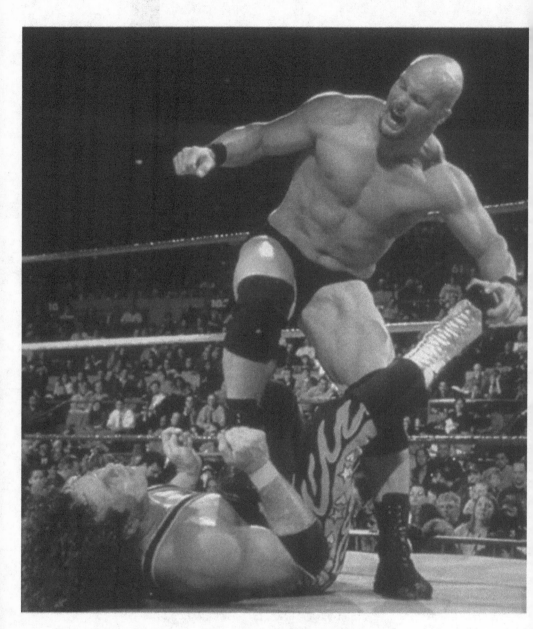

At *WrestleMania 13,* stomping a mudhole in the incomparable Bret "the Hitman" Hart.

I defeated Savio Vega at *WrestleMania XII*, only to drop a Strap match to Savio at the following Pay-Per-View—a loss which meant that Ted DiBiase, my manager, had to leave WWE. That was a good thing for me, as I wasn't allowed to have mic time when DiBiase managed me.

A year later, it was a different story. I was getting a lot better in front of the camera.

I loved doing my programs with Bret Hart in 1996 and 1997 when he made his comeback. I was handpicked by Bret to work with him at Madison Square Garden. I was real proud of that. Then we booked our big match for March 23, 1997 at *WrestleMania 13* at the Rosemont Horizon in Chicago, Illinois. It put him over as a heel for being such a crybaby.

I think that match at *WrestleMania 13* was my favorite ever. I cut some great promos on Bret.

"Bret, you're sitting out there whining and crying, because you are a loser! I tried to come out and help you win the title. It could have been you and me going for it all at *WrestleMania,* but you blew the whole damn thing because you are a loser! Well, Bret, at *WrestleMania 13,* you will say 'I quit,' and someday it will be you and me for the championship, and I will be the next WWE Champion!"

The following week on *Raw,* I said, "A Submission match is not my kinda match, [Bret]. Do I know a whole lot of wrestling holds? HELL NO, I DON'T! But I will beat your ass until you

say 'I quit.' Every week you get on TV saying you been screwed. Well, let me tell you this, son. I ain't bringing a condom to the ring. I'M BRING- ING A HELL OF A CAN OF WHOOP-ASS!!!!"

When that match was being built up for *WrestleMania 13*, I was blind to me becoming a babyface. I didn't see it coming. I wasn't look- ing to be a babyface at all when we had that match. But the fans' cheers were outweighing their boos at the time. Everyone was telling me I'm a babyface.

Brian Pillman came up to me and said, "Hey, man, you're a baby- face now."

I'd say, "No, I'm not."

He grinned and said, "Yeah, you are a babyface," with a smart-ass delivery, as only Brian could deliver. He said, "Steve's a babyface! Steve's a babyface!"

I said, "Screw you. No, I'm not, I'm a damn heel." I was starting to get hot!

And he said, "Listen to the fans, you are a freaking babyface. A damn white-meat babyface!"

So I started listening to the crowd. And at that match, I got almost as loud a cheer as Bret Hart did. That told me something.

I loved working that match. Bret beat me by submission, but I hadn't given up. My face and head were a bloody mess, but I had passed out rather than say "uncle." And when the match was over, everyone was chanting my name, even though I had lost.

I remember that Ken Shamrock was the special referee of that match. It was great. I really enjoyed it and felt honored. Of course, any- time I got to work with Bret it was an honor, because I thought so much of him.

I was hot at the time and "Austin 3:16" and "'Cause Stone Cold Said So" were going strong, but that match at *WrestleMania 13* really locked it in for me. It put Stone Cold Steve Austin square in the middle of the pro wrestling map.

It was a quality wrestling match—a "match of the year," according to some people. I don't think that's an exaggeration either.

MOM: We watched that match on Pay-Per-View. It was so bloody! Somebody was supposed to say "I quit," but it just went on and on. I remember we had some friends over to watch with us. We were in our living room and I was about to die, pacing and pacing, waiting for it to end. We were so exhausted when it was over with. When Steve got that big, bloody face, it was the first time he made all the wrestling magazine covers.

At *WrestleMania XIV*, which was held on March 28, 1998, at the Fleet Center in Boston, I won my first WWE title by defeating Shawn Michaels. A very talented wrestler, Shawn Michaels was another of my favorite guys to work with. But the Heartbreak Kid was pretty beat up at that point. He had some back problems, I remember, and the match wasn't as good as it could have been.

Also, it seemed like he had a real chip on his shoulder for some reason. I don't know why that was. Shawn seemed very egotistical, and it was true that he had been a big success, but he seemed arrogant.

I always had great matches with him and I got along with him, but it wasn't like we hung out together. We weren't buddies. But I learned a lot from him. He was quite a hand.

My relationship with Shawn is a lot better now than it used to be. It's not that he's gone through any real changes, but because it's a different day and age. We're a lot closer friends than we were back then.

Shawn had a lot of issues back then, before *WrestleMania XIV*. He had a lot of demons. He was burning the candle on both ends and wasn't exactly feeling like a million bucks. Man, do I know that feeling.

And then, *wham,* I came along, Stone Cold Steve Austin, getting white-hot and breathing down everybody's neck. I think that was unsettling to him. I think that adversely affected him. He was asked to drop the title belt to me, and at the time I don't think he really wanted to do it.

If it had been anybody else other than me, he probably wouldn't have done it. But he did do it for me. The match wasn't a classic by any stretch, but I did appreciate Shawn Michaels's ability and his timing, which were always impeccable.

Owen Hart 23

I want this put in the contract, Vince. If I can't beat Owen Hart for the

Intercontinental title at *SummerSlam*, after the match when he pins me

one-two-three, if that happens, he can roll down his trunks, pull down his little

panties, bend over and I'll kiss him right on his ass—RIGHT IN FRONT OF THE

WORLD! Vince, put that in the contract! THAT'S THE BOTTOM LINE, I'LL KISS

HIS ASS IF I CAN'T KICK IT, AND THAT'S THE WAY IT'S GONNA BE!!

—STEVE AUSTIN TO VINCE MCMAHON ON HIS MATCH WITH
OWEN HART AT *SUMMERSLAM* 1997

Owen Hart was Bret Hart's brother. I enjoyed Owen's company. But we weren't running buddies.

I was hanging with the people who drank a little bit, and Owen hung out with a lot of the fans and saved his money. He would get rides with pretty much everybody and stay with fans

instead of at hotels, and that enabled him to keep his expenses to a minimum.

One wrestler he hung around with a lot was the "British Bulldog," Davey Boy Smith, they were brothers-in-law and they were both from Calgary. Davey was a drug guy and Owen wasn't. But Owen wasn't an alcohol guy either. Absolutely zero on both those counts.

So, basically, I did my thing and Owen did his. We hung out in different crowds. But Owen was a hell of a hand and I had always enjoyed working with him, just as I had always enjoyed working with his brother Bret, whose style was closer to my own.

My match with Owen was set for *SummerSlam 1997*, on August 3, 1997, at the Meadowlands Continental Airlines Arena in East Rutherford, New Jersey. By then, Stone Cold was really catching fire with the fans.

I was told that I was going to win the Intercontinental belt back from Owen on that night. The stipulation to my challenge was that if I couldn't beat him and win, I was going to have to kiss his ass. We really built that up on TV as a major deal. It was another simple, easy-to-understand story line.

So the day came and I was talking to Owen in the back, and we were throwing a few things together for the finish of the title match.

I said to him, "Well, what about if we do that thing where I come in for the elbow and you rotate your back around and pick me up upside down and give me the Tombstone Piledriver? Then you cover me and I'll kick out right before the three-count." I added, "Now, Owen, I don't trust just *anybody* to do a piledriver to me, but you can do it, right?"

And he said, "Yeah."

I said, "You're going to go to your knees, right?"

And he said, "No, I'm going to drop to my ass."

Then I said, "Well, you need to go to your knees, right?"

And he said, "No, I drop to my ass."

That's two times I said that. And I was thinking, I'm dealing with Owen Hart, brother of Bret Hart and son of Stu Hart. I guess he knows what he's doing. He's ribbing me about dropping to his ass instead of his knees.

Owen was a hell of a technician. When he assured me I'd be okay,

I took his word that I'd be okay. I didn't think twice about it. I had mentioned my concerns to him twice. But in an inverted Tombstone Piledriver, done the way Undertaker does it, it's always knees, not ass.

So I figured, Owen's got it, he knows my concern. I had asked him twice about it, and that was the big spot in the match.

When I came out that night, boy, people were ready to see Stone Cold Steve Austin do the Stone Cold Stunner on Owen for that title belt. The match went along and it was a good match, the right style of match for that year. It was a solid wrestling match. We were going through some things near the end that could be finishes, but they weren't. The crowd was really into all the false finishes. After that we wrestled for another five or six minutes, the idea being to lead into a Stunner.

Eventually, he set up the piledriver spot. I spun Owen around and he landed on his feet. Then he picked me up, upside down, and WHAM—he dropped straight to his ass. There was simply no room for me to protect my head.

If you watch the videotape, my head's about six to eight inches *below* his ass. I weigh 250. He weighed 225 or thereabouts at the time. But with the jump up and the impact down, man, I got spiked headfirst into the mat hard as hell.

That's one of the things that's going to turn you into a quadriplegic quicker than anything, like what happened to Christopher Reeves. It's called axial load. It's not a whiplash thing, but a major impact blow to the spinal chord—*BOOM.*

I remember when it happened, I was going to kick out on two and a half or two and three-quarters. I was going to sell the piledriver, but I was going to kick out of it at the last second. When my head hit the mat, it was as if a big gong went off in my body.

When stuff like that happens, people usually go unconscious or get all groggy. I stayed razor sharp the whole time, and it was like I had super hearing. My legs straightened up, my arms bent up and my hands were frozen.

I remember kind of picking my head up from the mat and telling the referee, Earl Hebner, "Tell him not to fucking touch me, I can't move."

Earl got up and told Owen, "Don't touch him, he can't move."

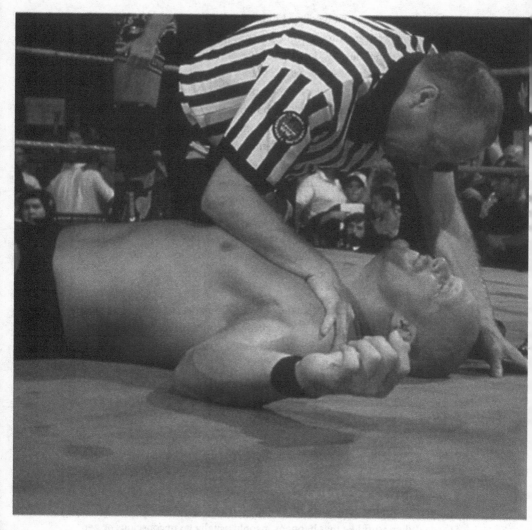

A piledriver gone bad, *Summer Slam 1997*.

I said, "Tell him to buy me some time."

Earl told him that, so Owen started chanting to the crowd, "Now he's going to have to kiss *my* ass!"

He was buying me the time I needed. A minute or a minute and a

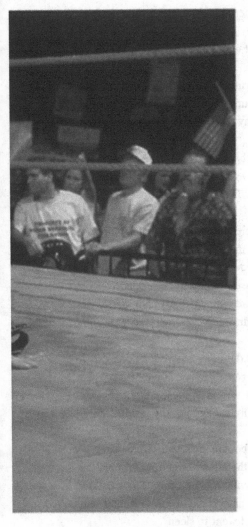

half went by, and I finally started to get a little bit of feeling back in my limbs. My shoulders and my interior delts were on fire. It took everything I had to bend my legs and try to get into a crawl position, but I couldn't crawl on my hands because I couldn't use my hands yet.

Still, we had to get to the finish. And I had to win.

So I was crawling around on my elbows and I told the referee, "Rollup for the win."

He told Owen what I had called, and the next thing that happened was I did the worst-looking rollup in wrestling history, because I couldn't use my limbs. Somehow I managed to hold Owen on his back and get a three-count out of it.

I meant for that to be the end of it, but Owen kicked right out after three. Why? To make himself look strong, like he was barely beat. That kick-out hurt me like hell too, and could easily have injured my neck further.

I should have lain there and gotten medical attention, but it didn't happen that way. It was one of those deals where it was a highly anticipated match. There were a lot of 3:16 shirts out there that night, a whole lot of Stone Cold fans.

Owen rolled out of the ring, defeated, and left. But as I rolled over on my back, I knew that I was completely screwed up.

I had wanted to get the match over with the right way, and the

only reason I called for the rollup rather than just laying there and let him beat me, was because of the kiss-my-ass stipulation. By finishing the match the way it was supposed to go, I was doing everything I could to *be* Stone Cold Steve Austin.

All the referees came out to the ring and it took three of them to pull me to my feet. I got my arms around them and they tried to hold me up and hand me the title belt, but my legs were dragging and I could barely walk.

The feeling was starting to come back in my feet, so I knew that I could walk a little bit. I took my arms away from the refs and held the belt up, and acknowledged the crowd. Then I walked out, but my legs were really dragging.

I got to the back and I was visibly shaken. The whole thing just scared the crap out of me. As they got me onto a stretcher, I just wanted to know what the hell had happened.

I had told Owen, "I don't trust just *anybody* to do a piledriver on me," but I got planted on my head. It had happened. My shoulders were absolutely on fire. My front delts wouldn't stop burning. That goes with the kind of injury I had.

They took me to the hospital and did an X-ray—I don't think they did an MRI that night—but the reports came back negative. Later, when I had further tests done by Dr. Joseph Torg in Philadelphia, it showed that I had a bruised spinal cord. I'm still dealing with the residual damage now, six years later.

Anyway, I left the hospital and bought myself a twelve-pack of beer, and I was kind of starting to feel the effects of getting dropped on my head. I guess it was almost like having a concussion. I was feeling really weird in bed. I probably should have stayed in the hospital, but lying in bed at the hotel drinking beer, I went to sleep.

Despite everything, I got up the next day and drove to Bethlehem, Pennsylvania, to do *Raw* and cut a promo on Owen, because I'm Stone Cold Steve Austin. My delts were burning like crazy and I couldn't wrestle, but I went and covered my ass on TV.

Here's what I said to Owen Hart the next night on *Raw is War;*

"Owen Hart! I'm not going to listen to the doctors. I'm not going

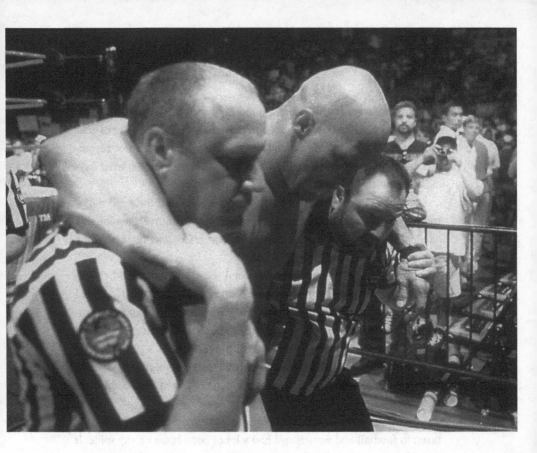

to wear this piece of crap [neck brace] they gave me. The fact that you dropped me on my head don't mean a damn thing to me! The fact of the matter was, you were too stupid to cover me when you had the chance! The bottom line is, you're a loser, Owen Hart. Not because I say you are, but because it runs through your veins, 'cause your mom and dad gave that to you, and I can't do nothin' about that! Tonight I truly will open up a can of whoop-ass and show you exactly what Austin 3:16 means, and that's the bottom line, 'cause Stone Cold said so!"

Over the next few days I went and got a bunch of doctors' reports. Every doctor I went to said to get out of wrestling.

I was out for three or four months after that, and I didn't really think I was going to get back in because my doctor was saying, "No, no, no." He wasn't going to clear me. That was my first experience with an injury of that magnitude. I had all these red flags going, warning me not to get back in the ring.

So I rode my four-wheeler around my ranch all day. I lived out in the country and I had a case of beer in the cooler. I'd drink a case of beer every damn day and ride around on my four-wheeler. I'm not recommending that to anybody, that's just what I did. Over time, I started feeling a little bit better.

I told the doctor that my ring activity could be a little more of a controlled situation. I could avoid certain things. Of course, I avoided all piledrivers after that because that axial load effect was the one thing that was going to screw me up again.

After several long conversations and tests, my doctor said, "Well, okay, if you think you can do it, you can get back in the ring." Then I started easing back, doing tag matches. I did lots of tag matches, slowly getting more and more involved in the matches. And then Stone Cold took off again, and there I was, back off to the races.

But it didn't last, because then I had to have the surgery that would keep me out close to a year. And it all stemmed from that Tombstone Piledriver.

With the injuries and all the physical trauma and the beatings I'd taken in football and wrestling, I had a lot of bone spurs on my spine. If I'd had a normal spinal cord, it wouldn't have been quite so bad, but my spinal cord wasn't normal.

Everyone's spinal cord has a certain amount of room around it. Well, I've got less room than most people. I was born that way—with a congenitally narrow spinal cord. Michael Irvin had to quit the Dallas Cowboys because of that.

But even with all that—the narrow spinal cord and the bone spurs—I would have been all right. It was the axial load from that bad piledriver that got the bone spurs going into my spinal cord and touching the nerves there.

The muscles in my hand were starting to atrophy, and my legs were becoming hyper-reflexive and jumpy, and muscles would start pulsing in my back. The medical name for my condition is central cord compression.

But I was told that I could get some relief from surgery. So I set out to find a doctor who could do it.

That's when I went and saw Dr. Bollman in Ohio, who did Cal Ripken Jr.'s surgery. I was going to let him cut on me. He came very highly recommended. He's an orthopedic surgeon though I felt I needed a neurosurgeon. Besides, I was in his office in Cleveland with a bunch of interns for forty-five minutes. They herded me in and out of there like an animal. They were very professional, but I wasn't comfortable with how that whole deal went.

When I got done there, I came back to Texas. It was during deer-hunting season, and this muscle in my hand was still atrophying real bad. That's when I really noticed it. I told Dr. Jimmy Baros, my friend and personal doctor, "Man, I gotta do something about this. It's not like I can fly to Cleveland every day. It's going to be a three-month waiting process before I can even get my surgery."

Dr. Jimmy said, "I want to send you to see my buddy, Dr. Lloyd Youngblood. He's a neurosurgeon, the best of the best. I think you'll really like him. Just go and get a second opinion. He's right here in San Antonio."

Great! I went to get a second opinion and for three hours, Dr. Youngblood sat with me in his office. I didn't have an appointment, but for three hours he sat there and explained to me in language I could understand everything that was wrong with me. He was just a wealth of information about my problem.

Debra, my third wife, was there with me. I was looking at Dr. Youngblood and looking at Debra, and I turned and said to Debra, "This is the sumbitch who's going to be cutting on my neck."

A week or two later, I was getting cut on. I got the big operation in 1999, a full two years after the piledriver. It was two years of nagging pain. And it wasn't like I had another option besides surgery. I was looking forward to getting cut on because I was in danger and I was having a lot of problems. The only thing that operation was going to do was help me. I wanted it.

At that point, I didn't know if I was going to be able to come back or not. I had no idea if I was ever going to get back in the ring. If I'd had to venture a guess, I would have guessed that my wrestling career was over.

Anyway, I had the surgery and it went fine. I got all fused up. It

took close to a year, but Dr. Youngblood finally gave me clearance to get back in the ring.

Problem was, when I had my surgery done, I was actually a candidate for a three-level fusion. Youngblood's a very conservative doctor and he told me if I had three levels fused, I would be completely done with wrestling, and there'd be a very long healing process of well over a year.

He said, "Let me just fuse this one, but down the road you'll probably have to fuse these two also." So we didn't fuse those two, but now those are the two that are messing me up. That's my problem. So every day that goes by, I'm just working my way closer and closer to another double spinal cord fusion.

All because of that Tombstone Piledriver.

J.R.: After Steve had his neck surgery in San Antonio with Dr. Youngblood, I flew down there to see him in the hospital. I think when I got there, Steve had been able to get a night's sleep and when I walked in he was sitting up in bed eating ice cream. I told him I thought only kids who had their tonsils removed got ice cream in the hospital, but he said he had connections. Boy, did he! You would have thought that it was Elvis or John Wayne himself in the hospital there in Texas, because all the nurses and other personnel were just great and truly felt it was an honor to attend to their homegrown wrestling star. Steve always has been able to connect with his audience and he had already won all the nurses over in the short time he had been hospitalized. There were a bunch of Austin 3:16 fans working in that hospital, let me tell you! He was in amazingly good spirits, because many of the horrible symptoms that he had been experiencing with this neck injury were gone. He had found some significant relief, even though he still had some numbness in his hand and fingers. But Steve knew, and I knew, that he would have to address his wrestling career sooner than later. If Debra had not been there, we probably would have talked about it, but we didn't. That was probably a smart thing. But I could tell by the look in his eyes that he had unfinished business to attend to. The thing was, neither of us knew when it would happen.

MOM: Right after Steve had his neck surgery, I left to visit him and see the girls. I was going to go up and hang out with them for a few days. When I got there, Steve wasn't in the house. He left a note saying, "I'll be out walking up and down the road." Well, I saw this poor, pitiful thing out there walking. He had both of his knee braces on and he had this awful, big brace on his neck. And he had a cane. It just absolutely broke my heart when I looked at him. He looked like this little old man. It just tore me totally up, the way he looked. When he got himself into the house, he could hardly negotiate to sit down, because of all this stuff he had on his body. He couldn't put his shoes on, or tie them. But I was there for the weekend. I was cooking and doing all this stuff. "Well," he said, "Let's take Mom here," or "let's take Mom there." I said, "Oh Steve, you don't have to entertain me! I just came to visit and hang out." He said, "I'm tired of sitting around the house." He wanted to take me somewhere. That was right after the Christmas when he gave his daddy a new pickup truck, and gave me the new Suburban, so I had my Suburban there. I said, "Steve, you get in the front, push that seat back and let me drive." It took all of us to get him in the car. There was this place he wanted to take us to eat, and the people on the streets where we were walking would step back and say, "You're the wrestler who had the surgery, right?" And Steve said, "Yeah." "Well, we been praying for ya." People were just wonderful, backing out of the way. Nobody asked anything of him that day. They were all treating him with respect. They really cared about him. People may be real pushy, and we've had it happen here. They've come to our house and interfered with our family gatherings and stuff. But I was very touched by the feeling that they had for Steve. They really did care about Steve when he was down and out and hurt. The messages, and the things that people said and did, it meant a lot to him. And seeing it firsthand, being with him, I can tell the fans do have a lot of love and respect for Steve.

Owen Hart never called me after he piledrove me and injured me. I heard that his brother Bret kept telling him to call me, but we never connected.

Did I hate Owen? No. That's just the business and we weren't really friends to start with. Did I want to work with him after that? No, I didn't. I didn't want to do business with him again. Right or wrong, that's how I felt.

Sometimes I wonder how it could have happened. As good a technical wrestler as Owen was, he should have known he needed to drop to his knees, not his ass, to protect my neck.

I knew Owen as the consummate all-time ribber. He was always joking with people. I'm not saying this deal was a rib. I'm just saying he was always ribbing people and as good-natured as he was, he never maliciously did anything to hurt anyone. Owen was all about fun, so I couldn't figure out why he did it that way.

When he didn't call me at my house afterward, that kind of upset me a bit. It was like, "Hey, if I damn near paralyzed someone, I'd be calling them every damn day of the week!"

The WWE Merchandise Department came out with a T-shirt that said OWEN 3:16, and on the back it said, I JUST BROKE YOUR NECK. That was pretty damn cheesy. If I was going to get any royalties off that one, maybe I would have liked it better, but if he's going to put the money in his pocket for messing my life up, I wasn't real fond of that.

As I said, I didn't hold any animosity toward Owen. But it was never the same between us. I didn't think he was as funny as I used to think he was.

When we'd pass in the hall or in the back, I'd say hi, but we never really spoke much after I came back. I never could figure that out. J.R. thought that maybe Owen was sorry and ashamed that he screwed the piledriver up, but couldn't, or wouldn't, admit it. I don't know.

Anyway, it was just one of those things, and I'm still paying for it now. That's the way it goes in the wrestling business. It ain't ballet. Things happen, and that time it happened to me. But I ain't gonna sit here and cry about it.

I just deal with it—every day. And I will continue to deal with it for the rest of my life.

Unfortunately, Owen had a freak accident on May 23, 1999, when he accidentally fell over forty feet from an overhead catwalk to the ring

and died immediately from the fall. No one deserves to die like that. That was bad and I felt sad for Owen's family, his wife and his children. I'm really sorry, and was always sorry, that Owen Hart died.

J.R.: Honestly, I was surprised that they were even doing a Tombstone Piledriver, because no one does it better than Undertaker, as it is one of the Deadman's signature moves. Wrestlers usually don't, or shouldn't, use other talents' finishing moves for their own high spots, but that's another story for another time. My take on this incident was this; Owen was a good person and a helluva wrestler. He was born into wrestling royalty in my eyes, as the youngest son of the legendary tough guy and long-time promoter Stu Hart. I always felt that Owen may have thought that he had let down his family, specifically his dad and older brother Bret, with a poorly executed maneuver. It would be like the son of Michael Jordan being cut from his basketball team. It just wasn't supposed to happen. But it did, and I think Owen was so taken aback by what happened, that he never cleared the air with Steve. I will guarantee you one thing—Owen cared and I know he felt bad about what happened, because we used to discuss it often. When Steve was out of commission because of the neck injury, Owen used to ask me about Steve all the time. I would say to him, "Why don't you call him?" Owen's response was always along the lines of, "I'm going to," or, "I will, I just feel so bad about what I did." Those two never had the conversation they needed to have, the conversation both men felt in their hearts before Owen's untimely death. That's one face-to-face meeting I wish I could have orchestrated.

J.R., Debra, me and Jan Ross.

Stone Cold and Debra

24

first met Debra when she came to WWE from WCW.

I had gone out to California to do the CBS series starring Don Johnson called *Nash Bridges*, and Marissa McMahon, Shane's wife, who's both beautiful and intelligent, came with us to help out with PR and stuff. I was telling her about my

woman situation and that I would kind of like to meet someone from the South.

I remember telling her "from the South," and then here comes Debra in WWE. She was born and raised in Tuscaloosa, Alabama, she was gorgeous and I liked a lot of things about her personality—for instance, that she was extremely strong-willed.

I had recently gotten divorced and Debra had been divorced for several years already. I enjoyed meeting her and I enjoyed making her laugh.

I didn't fall in love with her right away though, just like I didn't love Jeannie right away. Sometimes that "DTA" thing of mine can be a pain in the ass. But a mutual attraction formed, and Debra and I eventually turned into a solo item.

During this time, I really started making some big money with WWE—$167,000 in my first year alone. Then it kind of skyrocketed due to the popularity of Stone Cold, with both merchandise and wrestling revenues going up.

I was finally able to write the Internal Revenue Service a check for the $360,000 that I owed them! Other than my daughters being born, paying that debt off to the government was one of the greatest moments of my life. I thought I would be in debt up to my neck for a very long time.

Debra moved in with me in 2000. I had a twenty-foot slide-out camper that I took deer hunting and we lived in my driveway for a few months with my girls. That's when I started looking for a ranch—a real ranch. Hell, this was Texas and I needed a Ponderosa, or so I thought. I eventually bought a 118-acre ranch outside of Boerne.

When I sold my other house there, I think I still owed Vince $30,000 for it, but he said I didn't have to pay him back. Vince has done a lot of cool things for me and I've done a lot for him too. It's been a good partnership, and I'll never forget Vince's generosity. The guy has a good heart, contrary to what many of his jackass critics like to say.

So Debra was living with me in the camper, and then I bought the ranch. We were together for not even a year maybe, and I thought, This is the one. I told Jack Lanza that I was going to ask Debra to marry me.

He said, "Good for you, Steve, congratulations."

I later went on Howard Stern's show and told him I was getting married to Debra. Man, did Howard rag me on that, talking about getting prenups and warning me about what I was getting into.

In attendance at the wedding were Ricky and Sandra, my mom and dad and Jan Ross and her husband, J.R. Debra and I got married at the same chapel in Las Vegas that J.R. and Jan did, the Little White Chapel. I think Michael Jordan got married there too. So did "Brother Love," Bruce Prichard and Frank Sinatra.

I remember the night before we got married, Debra was with some friends at a restaurant, and Ricky and Sandra and I came to the same restaurant. But it was crowded and they didn't have any chairs where she was eating. We had to eat in a different area, but still near them.

I was about to go over and say hi to them when Debra came over to me and cut this scathing "promo" that I didn't come over and sit with her and her friends. I should have known at that moment that Marriage Number Three wasn't such a great idea. Nonetheless, we got married the next day. My gut told me one thing, but my heart was talking a little louder.

Two years later, the incident at the house happened. The police were called and it got national media attention. *You* can talk about it, read about it, and discuss it. I can't—legal reasons. Then we got divorced, which I can't give details on either. There is a gag order. All I can say is I truly regret the whole ordeal.

Because of our strong personalities, Debra and I often argued like cats and dogs, but I loved her to death. I just need my time to myself sometimes. I can be a moody bastard.

I think my walking away from the company was probably one of the key factors in my divorce from Debra. Between that and all the ephedrine and coffee I was putting in my body, it wasn't good. And I've got a short attention span anyway, so I have a hard time sitting still. Debra used to say that I was part Gypsy because I always had to be doing something.

Even when I was home, I wasn't really home. I was just a restless spirit, and that made her a little crazy sometimes. If you tried to stay

around me twenty-four hours a day, seven days a week, maybe you'd have gone crazy too.

If Debra and I had stayed out on the road, we wouldn't have had so much time to be right there under each other's feet all the time. We were damned if we did and damned if we didn't, it seemed.

Every time I turned around at the house, there she was. If I went up to the grocery store, there she was. If I went to the gym, there she was. It was 24/7 constant togetherness. I know a lot of people would treasure that, but some people like the kind of life where the guy is out on the road, like a truck driver or a traveling salesman. You don't get to see your loved ones that much, but it turns out to be a blessing in disguise.

In our case, we were just together too much. It was one of those things where we were too much alike and with two strong personalities, it was just too much. It went haywire. D-i-v-o-r-c-e Number Three. I'm sure as hell not proud of my failed marriages.

But I love Debra, God bless her. I used to drive her nuts sometimes because I don't hear real good out of one of my ears. Sometimes she'd tell me something and I'd say, "What?" She'd repeat it, but I still wouldn't hear her, so I'd say, "What?" And she'd get mad thinking I was doing the "What?" gimmick to her like I use on TV.

That was unintentionally funny. It happened all the time if she didn't talk loud enough at me. What? What? *"STEVE!"* She probably thought I was messing with her, but I honestly can barely hear thunder.

When I bought that prize-winning steer for charity with "Mattress Mac" in Houston a few years ago, it was right before *WrestleMania X-Seven,* which sold out the Astrodome. WWE had a huge fan festival going at the convention center for several days before *WrestleMania* called *Axxess.* They put the steer we bought, Shorty, on display for the fans to see. It had a sign on the pen saying that it was owned by Stone Cold Steve Austin.

The problem was that Debra loves animals (she's always had lots of cats and dogs) and she fell in love with Shorty. He was a pretty cute little steer, but he was sold for charity. Shorty's future was already pre-

arranged and that didn't include coming home with us. Ol' Shorty was earmarked for eatin'.

Anyway, Debra is a sweetheart. It was one of those situations that just didn't work out. We loved each other and neither of us ever cheated on the other one. We still communicate and if she ever needs my help down the road, I would help her in a heartbeat.

In my second marriage with Jeannie, I did cheat on her a few times. They were just a few one-night stands, nothing memorable. It was a payback thing, because I thought she had cheated too. But I never cheated on Debra—not even once. I'm proud of that fact and that's the way a marriage should be. I really wished ours would have worked.

Now, I don't know what's going to happen. Because of the way my last divorce went, I have a hard time trusting women. Hold it—*did I just say that?* I have no animosity toward Debra; we still talk a lot. I have no animosity toward Jeannie either. We still speak to each other—even though when WWE was in the U.K. recently, Jeannie did not let me see my girls. That was like a sledgehammer to the head.

I'm not mad at women, but I've made changes. I don't want to go out and have casual sex with everybody. That's just not a good idea, either from a mental standpoint or a medical one. I prefer to be monogamous.

You can't go out looking for a relationship. It's going to have to be one of those things that one day just happens. I understand that now, so I'm just laid back and I do my thing, and try to make some money and keep busy.

J.R. once told me he *never* thought he would *ever* remarry, being a "two-time loser," but then, *bang,* he met Jan. My Oklahoma friend got lucky. As he says, he "overachieved."

I like being with just one person. I'm not into the hunt—you know, when you're a man on the road, traveling with USWA, WWE, WCW, you have the potential to be with four to seven women a week. For many men, that's a dream lifestyle. For me it's a nightmare. I've always been into the one-person deal.

I was with Kathy for ten years, Jeannie for eight years. And Debra

and I were together for four years. So I've been with essentially three women in twenty-two years, with the exception of a handful of bad judgment calls. I would still like to find that one special woman.

I'm eligible as we speak, but remember, I've got that Dracula cross thing going on. I want a psychological profile on the next person who seems interested in me. What are you, who are you and why are you? What do you want? Do you like Steve Williams, or do you like Stone Cold? Do you want to be with me or with the TV character?

I want to believe that I will be better with my next relationship. My luck with women ain't nothing to brag about, but I keep thinking that someday I might get it right.

On the other hand, I don't see myself ever getting married again—at least not for the next ten years. Anyway, that's how I feel today. But I know that that kind of feeling can change if lightning were to strike.

I was out eating with my friend and personal trainer, Skyler Craig, the other night. This cute little waitress was flirting with me, and of course my natural "charm and wit" were adding to the situation. After the waitress smiled and left, Skyler leaned over and said, "There goes your next ex-wife."

Uh-uh. *Ain't happening.* At least, that's today's story and I'm sticking to it.

> **J.R.:** My wife Jan and I were the only people from WWE who were invited to the wedding. They were married in Vegas in the same place, the Little White Chapel, where my wife Jan and I were married a few years earlier. Unfortunately, the chapel lost the videotape of the wedding. Maybe it will appear some day on eBay or something, who knows? I do remember playing blackjack at the five-dollar table with Steve and his drinking buddy, Ricky, the night before and the night of the wedding at the old Las Vegas Hilton, the one with the statue of Elvis in the entrance way. Steve could have afforded to play at the high-roller table, but he has always been smart with his money and has never lived beyond his means. We played blackjack and drank Crown Royal for several hours while Debra and Jan did some shopping. Everyone seemed to be getting along well and I thought that

this marriage would definitely be Steve's last. And it may be, but I sure wish it would have survived. Steve is a unique guy. He needs space sometimes, and more often than not, he doesn't give you any hints to his moods until it's too late. I wish they would have made it. Long-term relationships in this business are crapshoots, and they fail more often than they succeed.

Does Stone Cold Love to Entertain People? Hell Yeah!

It's always easy to be a smart-ass when you got a microphone in your hand. Hell, son, you're halfway across the building or I'd open a can of whoop-ass on you right here on the Billboard Music Awards! I know you people are looking up here, saying: "Hell, he looks like the toughest SOB on the planet!" Well, guess what? Basically you hit the nail right on the head, because you gotta be one tough SOB to exist in the world of sports entertainment. When I get home, off the road and out of the ring, I like to drink a little beer, drive my pickup truck and do some huntin', but my favorite form of relaxation is to listen to country music. So, I'm real proud to introduce the four finalists of Country's Artist of the Year.

—STEVE AUSTIN PRESENTING AN AWARD AT THE 1998 BILLBOARD MUSIC AWARDS

I appeared in ten episodes of the CBS show *Nash Bridges*, as a character named Jake Cage, in 1999 and 2000. Originally I was supposed to just do a bit part on one episode, but they kept bringing me back in a recurring role.

Don Johnson was really cool to me. You really knew who was in control of the set when he walked on. That

was his set. He was the top babyface and the booker. He laid down the law with a lot of people, but he treated me like gold. If somebody spoke to me in a negative way, he'd get on their ass because you weren't going to talk down to Steve Austin. They were going to be very nice to me, so he took really good care of me and I appreciated that.

The way I got on that show was through Don's bodyguard, who was also his friend and was a big wrestling fan. Sometimes for the show they'd get a football player or a baseball player to do a bit role, so his bodyguard told him, "Hey, man, why don't you get Steve Austin on the show?"

Don said, "Who's that?"

And the bodyguard said, "You know, Stone Cold Steve Austin from WWE! The badass bald guy who gives everyone the finger."

Don said, "Okay, let's get him on."

And hell, I came on the show. I only had a couple of lines at first, and of course I was going crazy running white-hot with WWE. So I was doing this project on my days off. When I went out there, I did it to have some fun, so I'd memorize my lines real fast, and I'd have a couple drinks the night before.

It wasn't like I was really trying to make a name for myself, but I did well at it. So, because I had done well with the limited scenes I had, they started writing more lines for me every day. They kept writing more and more lines for me, and my character kept on coming back.

And, of course, anybody from Texas is a Cheech and Chong fan, so Cheech Marin was real cool to me now. He had a son about fourteen years old who was a big wrestling fan, so I got along great with him. Yasmine Bleeth was also extremely nice to me when she was on the show. I got along fine with her. CBS offered me a series the next year based on the Jake Cage character. But, of course, it wasn't something I could do—I was still hotter than a firecracker with WWE. There wasn't time to get out of this game yet. Plus, what I would make on a TV show wasn't even close to what I was going to make at WWE. Sports entertainment definitely paid me more money than I was going to make playing Jake Cage. But I'll tell you, I enjoyed doing *Nash Bridges*.

I really didn't see too many stars when I was out there, because we

filmed *Nash Bridges* in San Francisco, and not too many people film there. I only went out socially with Don Johnson maybe a couple of times, and he would always have a part of the restaurant sectioned off. It might even have been his restaurant—I don't know.

The other times, I'd just go to the local seafood and fish houses, and drink beer and eat oysters. I was doing the low-key thing anyway. I never did ask Don Johnson if I could drive that Hemi Cuda they used on the show. I got to ride in the car a couple of times, but I never got to drive it. They had three of them on the set and they were on a guarded lot. They gave me a motorcycle and I'd ride that all over the place.

Don bought, or got, those cars, after the show was ended. He auctioned one of them off on a big nationally televised auto auction earlier this year and it went for over $100,000. There is a good chance that it really doesn't have a real 426 Hemi motor in it, and that it was a prop 383 or something, but that didn't seem to matter to the bidders.

> **MOM:** When Steve told us he was going to be on *Nash Bridges,* we had never heard of *Nash Bridges.* We asked, "What channel is it on?" He said it was on CBS, but it was just going to be a bit part. The weekend the episode aired, Steve asked me to come to Boerne and take care of the girls. Well, he's in the whole thing. He is the whole episode! I said, "I thought you told me it was a bit part." He said, "Well, after we got out there and started doing it and they found out I could actually say more than two words, they wrote me a bigger part." On one of the episodes Steve had to speak some French when he ordered from the menu. We loved that one. Everybody here just got the biggest kick out of watching those episodes. They said the nights Steve was on, the ratings were just fantastic.

As far as other forms of entertainment, I've had fans and people in the business ask me, "Why doesn't Stone Cold do movies?" When I was running at my hottest, I probably could have been considered for movies and other TV projects. But I was the horse pulling the WWE wagon, being the main guy, and I wasn't going to go nowhere to do a movie. Maybe down the road though. That door is always open.

Am I interested in being a gigantic movie star? Not really. A bit part here and there to pay the bills and keep up my exposure would be cool though. Even those corny little Lorenzo Lamas–type movies might be cool. I used to hate that guy, but now I sit there and watch his movies, and they're so goofy—if I'm not careful I might actually start to like the guy.

I'm kidding. I enjoy Lorenzo Lamas's movies. Like Mick Foley says, movies on TV are movies for guys who like movies.

I don't have to star in a blockbuster. Just something to entertain my damn brain. And something that doesn't last too long, so I can go onto the next thing or go hunt or something like that. Something to throw some money in the bank. As ol' J.R. says, it sure beats picking up rocks.

I just want to keep my name out there. I'm not interested in going haywire like I went haywire in the wrestling business. I don't entertain thoughts about being Sir Laurence Olivier or Robert DeNiro, or anything like that. All you gotta do is find your niche.

Look at Don Johnson. *Miami Vice, Nash Bridges*—same thing, different clothes. Look at every Joe Pesci deal—wise guy, smart mouth, *My Cousin Vinny, GoodFellas,* whatever. Same deal. Will that thing ever come along for Steve Austin? Who knows?

I kind of did that in *Nash Bridges*—I had a different name, but the guy I played was like Stone Cold. On one of the episodes, when I was walking down the street, you could even hear my entrance music in the background coming out of someone's car.

Regardless of what name I use, I can always be me. I really can't be anything else. It's not like I'm a trained actor. I'm from South Texas and I am who I am. But I'm thirty-eight years old now. That's not prime time to start a movie career. If I were going to do anything, I'd do a hunting show. Stone Cold hunting, fishing, whatever. That would be a lot of fun.

Even though I can't physically get through the rigors of working in the ring very much longer, I can see myself entertaining people in other

ways. I've been told I could do a forty-five-minute stand-up comedy routine at Caesars Palace in Las Vegas: *"What?*—An Evening with Stone Cold Steve Austin."

I'll have to maybe think about that one . . . plenty of F-bombs!

Yeah, I like to think there is a spot for me somewhere in show business. It would be nice. Maybe I should do one of those theater deals in Branson, Missouri. Build my own theater, the Stone Cold Theater. I'd do two or three shows a night, come out, sing some songs, cut some promos and do my deal. I think that would work! Well, that might be a stretch, but you get the picture.

If I worked in a movie, I'd love to play a heel. That's what I wanted to be my whole career in wrestling—it just didn't turn out as well as I wanted. Jenny, my little sister, knew I always wanted to be the bad guy. To me, it's always the best role. When you're a heel, you can do absolutely anything. As a babyface, there are a lot of parameters and boundaries you can't cross.

As a heel, you've got to be aggressive. You gotta be one tough SOB and a little bit of a coward. And you can cheat. To me, that's the easiest way to express myself. That live camera allows me to turn that switch on, and being a heel is so natural to me—being aggressive, outspoken, loud and decisive.

Sounds like Vince McMahon, doesn't it?

Stone Cold
and Vince McMahon 26

Can you speak up, Vince? I can't hear a damn word you're saying because

you've got eighteen thousand people calling you an asshole.

—STONE COLD TO VINCE McMAHON

You think you can beat my ass, Hell No!

Do I think I can beat your ass? Why, Hell Yeah!!!

—STEVE AUSTIN TO VINCE McMAHON

Stone Cold will never be "Employee of the Month."

—J.R. ON *RAW*

The absolute highlight of my wrestling career was an extended three-and-a-half-year feud with my boss, the owner of WWE, Vince McMahon. It is said by many that we had the most-talked-about rivalry in the history of sports entertainment. Based on today's mass media, cable and satellite penetration, that's probably true. We went at each other in so

many bizarre scenarios that newer fans might wonder, How in the world did all that start?

It was a simple formula that started the "era of attitude" at WWE, and shot the ratings sky high. We caught lightning in the bottle on that one, for sure. When Vince threw himself in there as the corporate heel owner, he saw money, even though I might not have seen it. That was Vince's great line drive out of the park, and it generated millions of dollars of revenue for WWE. It was all new to us, but we did have some damn great television! We worked so well off each other, I really enjoyed going at it with Vince week after week.

I was doing things that blue-collar and even white-collar people could identify with. It was stuff they would have liked to do themselves. I was standing up to my boss and doing crap to him and I was getting away with it, which is why I think it was so universally accepted. Our fans could suspend their general disbelief of the product and relate to what we were doing. The best wrestling story lines are the ones that are easy to understand and relate to.

My feud with Vince began on January 18, 1998, when I faced and beat The Rock in the final match of the *Royal Rumble*. That victory guaranteed me a WWE Championship title shot at *WrestleMania XIV.*

So far, so good. As we were building toward *WrestleMania,* Vince did everything he could to screw with me and the fans backed me up all the way. Vince would tell me in the ring, "Austin, I'm the boss and we can do things the easy way or the hard way. Tell me how you want it."

I'd ask the fans, "Do you want to see Stone Cold Steve Austin do things the hard way, give me a Hell Yeah!" Capacity crowds would yell, "Hell Yeah!" so I'd give Vince the Stone Cold Stunner and climb the ropes to celebrate with the fans. They took a lot of pleasure in my physicality toward my boss.

Then the WWE promotional machine really started grinding. Vince always comes up with something way over the top for *WrestleMania,* and he didn't disappoint the fans on this occasion. To make sure the match would be "fair and square," Vince brought in the notorious boxer "Iron" Mike Tyson, who would be the special "enforcer"

My mom's wondering why, if I'm so sick I just
had to wrestle. Because it was the Houston
Summit sold out Austin vs. Mankind, that's why.

referee. Can you imagine that? We got worldwide press coverage. That tie-in with Mike Tyson was a hell of a deal. Yeah, that was a home run, a real grand slam for the company. It was a helluva good idea by the big Irishman.

It was all good working with Mike Tyson. The first time I met Mike, he called me "Cold Stone." He kept calling me that, even though we did several shows together. So I used to make him mad. I'd say to him, "Why you gotta call me 'Cold Stone'? It's damn easy! STONE COLD!"

I'd do it in character, barking at him. He'd say, "Okay, Steve," but sure enough, he'd call me "Cold Stone" the next time. Mike was a big fan and wanted to meet all the wrestlers. He and Shane McMahon seemed to hit it off pretty well.

Mike liked to talk about all sorts of things. I had the usual conversations with him, nothing like solving the world's problems or anything like that. The guy I met was intelligent. I think it's a case of him sometimes being in the wrong place at the wrong time.

But you got to give the guy credit. He hasn't made the greatest decisions in his life, but hey, he's owned up to all of them too. I enjoyed the guy. I'm not going to hold him under a microscope. Everyone's made mistakes and he's made his share. Big deal, so have I.

And he did well for our company. That whole issue with Stone Cold, or "Cold Stone," as he'd say, was good stuff. The Austin–Tyson story line was super for our business, and Tyson came out of there a huge babyface at the end of the day.

"I am sick and tired of seeing Mike Tyson. He comes in, he's shaking everybody's hands, making friends with all the WWE Superstars. It made me so damn sick that I've been in the back throwing up." (Stone Cold on *Raw* before *WrestleMania XIV*)

"Everybody's calling you the baddest man on the planet, but right now you got your beady little eyes locked on the eyes of THE world's toughest son of a bitch!" (Austin to Mike Tyson on *Raw* from Fresno, California, before *WrestleMania XIV*)

"Do I think you can beat my ass? Hell no! Do you I think I can beat your ass? Why, hell yeah! I don't know how good your hearing is, but if you don't understand what I'm saying, I always got a little bit of sign language, so here's to ya!" [Steve gives Mike Tyson the double-middle-finger Stone Cold salute] (Austin confronting special enforcer Mike Tyson before *WrestleMania XIV*)

At the press conference before WrestleMania, being able to sit there with Mike Tyson was really fun, and he brought in a lot of outside people. Everybody knows who Mike Tyson is. There was a tremendous crossover appeal when he came to WWE. I'm a big boxing fan and he's a big wrestling fan, so it was cool.

At one point in the press conference, he shoved me. *Hard.* I shoved him back, and everybody just started shoving everybody else. There were hundred-dollar bills shooting out of Mike's pockets. There was just money everywhere. He had a lot of money on him that night, thousands of dollars in cash. It was just a great piece of business. I never got one of those loose hundred-dollar bills though.

Wrestlemania XIV finally arrived. It was an absolutely *huge* event that sold out Boston's Fleet Center. Despite Triple H's and Chyna's best attempts to help Shawn Michaels win, I beat the current WWE champion, with some help from Tyson. He ended up turning on HBK, which allowed me to win the WWE title for the first time.

J.R.: I have had the privilege of sitting at ringside and doing play-by-play for wrestling since the seventies and I have been to a ton of big-time sporting events, but I have never experienced anything like the night that Stone Cold and Mike Tyson confronted each other in Fresno, California, on *Raw.* Mike was, and is to this day, one of the most controversial figures ever in boxing. Mike's public image has taken a beating, much of it deserved and some certainly not. I found Mike Tyson to be a very cooperative professional who dearly loved the wrestling business and could give you chapter and verse on many of the business' most significant matches and stars. Mike was a huge

fan as a kid growing up in the Bronx, and I would assume he is still a fan to this day. When "Iron" Mike Tyson, the baddest man on the planet, shoved the toughest SOB at WWE, Stone Cold Steve Austin, it was magic—animalistic magic that I had never felt before sitting at ringside. I will always feel that night was a real launching pad for our company, and did it ever get folks talking! On a side note, Shane McMahon became Tyson's closest confidant within WWE, and I always thought and even suggested that if the McMahons had been able to promote Mike in that period of Mike's career that Mike would have been very well served. Mike needed to surround himself with people who actually cared about him and not his money, and I feel that Vince and Shane would have done that.

In the context of the story line, Vince McMahon was not pleased at all with me as the new WWE Champion. He did not like the way I made the company look with my beer drinking and colorful language and finger motions, so he did everything possible over the next year to cause me problems and to try to pry the title away from me.

Stone Cold wasn't a "corporate" enough image, is how it all began. Vince told the fans that if I won the WWE Championship, it would be a corporate nightmare. That angle had more people watching wrestling than had ever watched before. We did some great television and some things that were very cutting edge. Everybody wanted to know what Stone Cold was going to do to that bastard Mr. McMahon the next Monday night on *Raw*.

I represented the classic "working man" and Vince played the evil owner of the company, who was trying to manipulate his employees like a puppet master. It was a universal story that everyone could identify with.

I was getting back at my boss.

Vince McMahon: "Steve, for once in your life, please listen to reason and don't react in a physical and violent way."
Stone Cold: (to the audience) "If ya want me to react in a physical and violent way, give me a HELL YEAH!!!!"

"*Hell yeah!*" the crowd roared, and Vince is stunned once again, to the delight of everybody.

Every week Vince would try to screw me, and I'd come right back with something really wild that would shock the fans and keep them coming back for more. It was super-ego versus super-ego. Vince tried to screw Stone Cold at every turn, but I got my revenge in some very creative ways. Nobody tells Stone Cold what to do, and that's the bottom line.

I filled up Vince's classic Corvette convertible with tons of concrete from a cement mixer I drove into the Nassau Coliseum. I crushed his limo with the 3:16 Monster Truck. I drove a beer truck into the arena, and hosed him and his stooges down with thousands of gallons of beer. I attacked him while he was in the hospital and zapped him with those heart paddles. I brained him with a bedpan and jammed an enema gimmick up his backside.

The next week, I filled up his corporate office at WWE headquar-

ters with cow manure. I also hit him with steel chairs and kicked him in the testicles many, many times. I'm not doing that on purpose, by the way. What I'm trying to do is kick him in his gut to set him up for the Stunner. The idea is to kick him in the gut, but sometimes my shorts or jeans were too tight, depending on my weight situation, and I couldn't lift my leg high enough. Anytime I kicked him below the belt, it was not intentional. It's just the way it happened. That's my story and I'm sticking to it.

But Vince has never bitched about it, not even once. For a rich guy

who takes a limo to get a haircut in New York City twice a month, don't kid yourself. Vince is a tough SOB.

He's also whacked me with steel chairs and made me bleed a few times himself. I have a scar on the back of my head that's a permanent souvenir from one of Vince's chair shots. But I loved working with the man.

A big part of my WWE career was working with Vince. For a guy who's north of fifty, the chairman of WWE is a physical freak. Vince has his share of critics and I've personally butted heads with him, as has been documented. But bottom line, there is nothing Vince won't do for our business.

Ever since day one, I've listened to everything that comes out of his mouth because I know how smart he is. Anything he says I can learn from. There's a lot of things I've learned in the course of my life and my career I've forgotten about, but I can recall every conversation I've ever had with Vince McMahon—what I said and what he said in return.

I think the guy is a genius and a shark. He's gutsy and he goes by his instincts. He's made his mistakes, yeah, but he's a winner.

And so is his family. The thing I always appreciated about the McMahon family was they didn't tell you to work hard. You worked hard by following their example. They all work their butts off. That impresses me. I like those people. Sometimes that can be a double-edged sword, but I've enjoyed working for them.

I mean, Vince is the boss, but I also consider him a friend. He's someone who I think I could pretty much ask anything from, and get it. And he could ask anything from me. Anything I could do for him and his family, I would do. I think that much of that whole family.

It's been a real education. I've learned more from Vince than I think I could have learned at any college. Not about all kinds of subjects, but about life in general, how to entertain people and how to handle yourself. Working here is like a college education in life, business and success.

When I got more and more involved in the top mix, which is the top four guys or so, I was the new guy. Vince usually gravitates toward

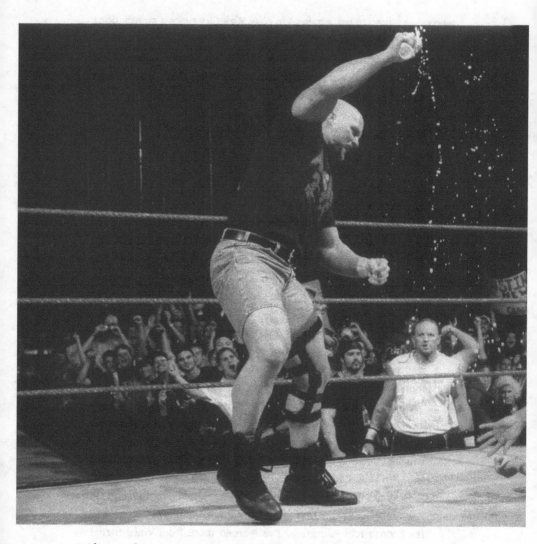

the number one guy. For a long time it was Bret Hart, then Shawn Michaels, then Undertaker and then it was me.

Then I got injured and it was The Rock. Then The Rock left, so it was Triple H. Before all of us, it was Hulk Hogan, and that's kind of the way it goes. Vince trusts those people because they are "in the spot." So he's going to listen to them, and of course they're going to listen to Vince.

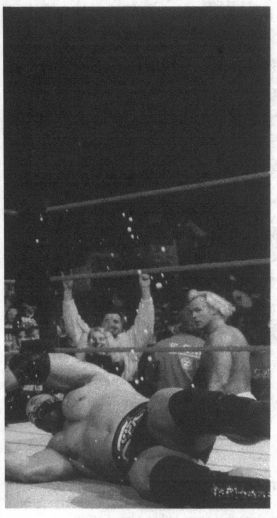

Vince is still the boss, but if I have a good idea, he'll hear me out. He's always been open to listening to me. And the fact is, he's always open to listen to anybody. As smart as he is, he knows that you can always learn something from somebody else. Even if it's a damn idiot talking, he might say something you can put to good use.

Vince will do anything for his product. He's put himself on the line in the ring against me many times. I think he always wanted to be a wrestler, but I don't think his dad, the successful wrestling promoter Vincent J. McMahon, wanted him to be a wrestler. So that was that. Vince couldn't be a wrestler. His dad flat out wouldn't allow it.

Now, Vince can do anything he wants. When the situation calls for it or the card needs something, Vince can throw himself in there and have a damn entertaining match. Like that Cage match main event Vince and I had at *St. Valentine's Day Massacre* on February 14, 1999, where he took that big bump off the cage onto the announcer's table.

He didn't have to take that bump. We didn't need that bump. But he did it to make the match special and get Stone Cold over more with the fans.

Vince had a bad neck on top of it and his head went down hard. I wouldn't have taken that bump. And there probably aren't too many guys on the crew who would have done that bump either. I know Mick Foley would have, Shane McMahon would have . . . but other than that, I mean, come on!

Vince is a multi-multimillionaire and he doesn't have to do a damn thing other than use his pencil and his brain, but that guy is unbelievable. I think he still feeds off the adrenaline. I think he's still got a wild hair. He likes to go out there and get into it.

You see what kind of shape he's in. He's in his fifties now and I'm thirty-eight. He's in twice the shape I'm in, so you can do the math on that deal. Probably the funniest thing we did was when Vince was in a hospital bed. Vince was lying there with a thermometer in his mouth, bitching and moaning. And Mick Foley and I are in the bathroom, giggling like a couple of kids 'cause we're listening to Vince and talking about all the stuff we're going to do to him.

We were laughing so hard, the TV crew had to keep coming in and telling us to be quiet so they could tape Vince. I always had a good time with Mick. Then I went into the room to torture my boss. Vince's foot was all wrapped up, so that was the first thing I was going after. I pounded on that damn foot and he sold it like crazy! I loved it. It's just what Stone Cold would do—go right for the weakest part and make the guy scream like a little girl—and Vince squealed like a pig stuck under a gate.

Everyone seems to remember that bedpan shot. Of course, I whacked him pretty hard in the head with it.

The story on the bedpan was that he wanted me to beat him up. We talked about me beating up on his foot, but he wanted to know what was next. So Vince came up with the idea of me hitting him in the head with the bedpan while he was lying there in bed.

I said, "Man, Vince, these things are pretty hard. They're solid stainless-steel bedpans. I don't know how to hit you with it and have it not hurt."

He said, "Hit me with the bedpan. And make it look good."

So I said, "Okay, if you want me to."

I spent five or ten minutes on the other side of the room, testing the damn thing on my own head, trying to see where the best acoustic sound spots were versus the best places to receive the blow. I did it out of respect for Vince.

It was going to be one take only, and we needed a hell of a bang.

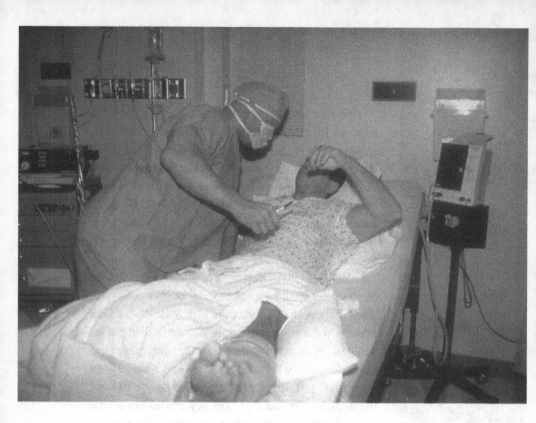

I wanted it to sound good, but I didn't want to hurt him. So I tested the damn bedpan over and over again.

Then we did the take and I thought I clocked him pretty good. And he sold it so damn well. Maybe he didn't have a choice in the matter, but everyone seems to remember that moment. It's always good for a laugh, no matter how many times you've seen it. I can watch it ten times in a row.

I heard that the day after they shot that vignette, one of the writers brought the video to the WWE Publications Department and had everybody watch it. All the guys loved it. But three women in the department said the ending was too violent, with me zapping Vince with the heart paddles, and then ramming that enema gimmick up Vince's butt.

Of course, the vignette stayed in—unaltered and unedited.

Vince McMahon is the owner of the company, but he's also "one of the boys." So what are you gonna do, other than go out and have fun with it?

"Hey Vince, from now on, it's open season on Vince McMahon, so what that means is any time you show up on a *Monday Night Raw,* as soon as you step out of that car, Stone Cold Steve Austin can punch you right in the mouth and the only thing you can do about it, Vince, is reach down, pick up your little teeth, put 'em in your shirt pocket and go on about your business. If you decide *not* to come to work, that means Stone Cold can drive to Greenwich, Connecticut, knock on your little front door and when you answer that front door I can punch you right in your mouth. And the only thing you can do about it is pick up your little teeth, put 'em in your shirt pocket and say 'Hey, Linda, Stone Cold knocked out some more of my teeth.'" (Austin to Mr. McMahon on *Raw* after *King of the Ring 1999)*

Vince McMahon is extremely close to being the Mr. McMahon television character, just as I'm extremely close to being the Stone Cold character. They're both one and the same, they're just turned down a few notches. But they can be turned up at the flip of a switch.

Vince McMahon's best traits are his work ethic and his passion for this business. The guy loves making money, but I think he loves the wrestling business even more than that. At this point he's got so much money, it really doesn't matter. I think the guy just loves the business. A lot of money just happens to be the by-product of all his hard work and his passion for wrestling.

His leadership abilities and his ability to make decisions are right there. I've also seen Vince McMahon with his eyes kind of watered up a few times. I know the guy gives a damn. But I think that's not a side he likes anyone to really see. I think it's just something that happens every now and then, because he can be a pretty emotional guy. But again, you just look at the exterior and you see one tough, heartless promoter who will work you to death.

Vince likes to be in control so much that he hates even sneezing, because it's an uncontrollable reflex. I've seen him cuss a blue streak after a healthy sneeze or two. He even gets POed when he yawns.

At one time, the wrestling business was cutthroat and run by ex-wrestlers who still had massive egos to feed. Even though they weren't the top babyface or the top heel, they were the owner of the territory. They were also the booker. They had all the power, the omnipotent power.

I don't know if Vince could have gotten to where he is if he wasn't tough. I think Vince had to show a cold veneer. I don't think that sumbitch could have shown any weakness or any remorse. Take no prisoners—I'm coming. I'm going to run your territory. I almost think he had to do that to survive in that world.

He showed a good side of himself when he helped me buy that house. I wrote him a check and I remember him asking me, "What do you owe on that house?" It was thirty-five grand, and he said, "Ah, the hell with it. It's all right." Not many bosses would have done that.

Vince has got a good heart, no doubt about it. But he's been conditioned not to show it. And the way he grew up, with abusive stepfathers beating the hell out of him—and I mean beating the holy crap out of him—I'm talking about fistfighting, drunken stuff. Abuse. I think he did that to survive.

So I look at him differently than most people do. I've been in too many one-on-one meetings with the guy and I've seen the sumbitch just break down and cry about things.

J.R. told me that he said to Vince one day, "You've got to call Steve and talk to him, because his health situation is eating him up. He needs to hear from you. Vince, I can take it so far, but he needs to hear from you. Steve's physical problems are much more serious than we thought."

Of course, Vince didn't know what all my problems were. It wasn't like he didn't want to call. To J.R., he was like, "Oh, okay, I didn't know."

J.R. told me that later in the day, Vince called him on the intercom and said, "Can you come in here for a minute?" J.R. went into Vince's office and Vince's eyes were red, and he was wiping the tears from his eyes. He said, "I just talked to Steve and he's really screwed up. Not screwed up in the head, but physically."

He really cared. That's what pisses Vince off. He's so combative,

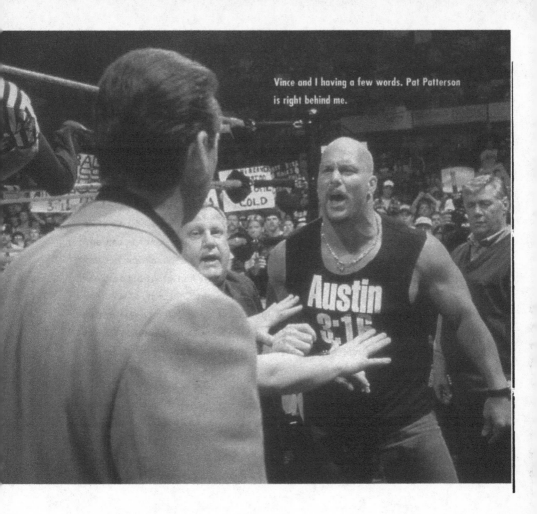

Vince and I having a few words. Pat Patterson is right behind me.

just out of his instinct to survive, that when somebody implies that he's evil incarnate and doesn't care about the boys, I think it eats him right up.

I think if he had fewer inhibitions, he'd be like basketball coach Roy Williams when he went from Kansas to North Carolina. He'd talk about the kids he was leaving in Kansas, and he'd cry like a baby right in front of everyone. It was almost embarrassing. I think if Vince had the opportunity sometimes, he'd break down and cry and say, "Yeah, I'm human."

But he won't allow himself to show any weakness—just like Stone Cold won't. Vince McMahon is a name that millions of our fans world-wide boo and call an asshole, but he's also a man I greatly respect.

J.R.: It was Vince's vision and Steve's talent and passion that made their rivalry work so well. This was classic, old-school wrestling in my eyes. The hero who the fans believed in and supported passionately and the villain who the fans loved to hate, and who the fans would pay good money to see get his ass kicked. Simple booking, Wrestling 101, but, man, did it work! The defiant hero and the dictatorlike boss battled it out seemingly every Monday night. It was episodic TV at its finest. Vince's dad was a great man who did not want his son and namesake to even get into the wrestling business, much less become an in-ring performer. But I think Vince always had a burning desire to perform. When he became Mr. McMahon, the Chairman of WWE, he found his true calling, in my opinion. As great as Steve was during his run, there is no way he would have been as successful as he was without a great heel to play off—and Mr. McMahon filled the bill perfectly.

Here's Mick as Mankind going up against Stone Cold. One of the toughest human beings I know.

Mick Foley **27**

DTA, you stupid piece of trash. Don't ever trust anybody. You ain't gonna be

my partner . . . never! 'Cause you are a longhair freak, and you suck!

—AUSTIN TO MANKIND, AFTER GIVING HIM THE STONE COLD STUNNER

For a while, Dude Love and then Mick Foley was my tag-team partner. When he wrestled as Mick Foley, he had this great gimmick. Mick had a little sock puppet on his hand, and "the puppet" would choke his opponents.

The first time I saw Mick Foley was in the mid-to-late eighties, when he was wrestling as Cactus Jack

Manson. It was usually the Von Erichs and the Freebirds who drew me to the Dallas Sportatorium, but this time it was Cactus Jack.

His promo was amazing. When they showed the footage of Cactus Jack coming to town, I was thinking, Damn, this sumbitch is crazy! So even before I saw him wrestle, I became a total mark for his stuff. And of course, I had to go down to the Sportatorium to see him, because his match wasn't going to be televised.

First I saw the Freebirds and the Von Erichs battle, and the Freebirds cheated and won that night. Great heat! Finally it was time for the main event and the TV cameras had been turned off.

Cactus Jack Manson came out with that wild hair, and he's dropping elbows off the apron onto the floor, killing guys. I took notice of him back then. When I worked in the Sportatorium, Cactus Jack had already left for WCW. Then when I came to WCW, I got to know Mick quite a bit. And later on, we worked together at WWE.

Mick has never been a great athlete, but he's always had his style and understood crowd psychology. That came out in his promos, which were always riveting, and it came out in his work in the ring.

I remember when I first went to ECW and they gave me the opportunity to start talking a little bit. It was Paul Heyman who gave me my platform about getting fired by WCW. But when it came to how to express myself, I always looked to Mick's example.

Mick was a guy who was always on time, always there, a guy who worked hard and didn't complain about a damn thing. And anytime you got him in the ring, he gave you absolutely everything he had. That's what I remember about him.

He's also one of the smartest guys in the business. If I have a conversation going, or a question about something in the ring, or even a movie, I'd always go to Mick for his opinion on the matter.

Of course, Mick and I have similar twisted senses of humor. And man, we used to have so much fun. We used to travel together when we were with WCW, and he was as cheap as I was. Maybe more so.

Sometimes we'd travel with Diamond Dallas Page. When we'd travel with Page, we'd just sit there and rib him to death, to see who could crack him first.

My tag team partner Mick as Dude Love.

Let's just say that DDP might not do too well under intense interrogation. Page is easily cracked.

I always liked working with Mick. It didn't matter which of his characters he was using at the time—Cactus Jack, Dude Love, Mankind or Mick Foley. He was so intelligent; he had four different characters wrapped up in one body. And each one had his own signature stuff, and he could keep them separated in his mind.

Now, if he wanted to interplay all of them he could do that too. But for a long time he kept it all separate.

In WWE, Mick (who was Dude Love at the time) and I were tag champs together. I loved the deal where I was doing the "DTA" (Don't

Trust Anyone) gimmick, insisting on being a loner, and this guy wanted to be my tag partner.

I gave him the Stone Cold Stunner and told him, "DTA—you stupid piece of trash! Don't ever trust anybody! You ain't gonna be my partner, never! 'Cause you are a long-haired freak and you suck!"

But after enough of him badgering me, I let him be my partner. That was fun. It made no sense, but it was fun.

It's hard for me to say, but I'd guess that Mick is probably done with wrestling at this point. He's been enjoying his time as a family man, writing and all that stuff, which is good. But that guy—man, you never can tell. I know he probably hurts a lot, but if anybody can pull off a comeback, Mick can.

Thrifty Mick Foley is a helluva talent.

Getting Paid to Drink Beer and Crush Cars

28

I used to tell my buddies near the end of my wrestling career that I was drinking beer for a living and wrestling on the side. I cannot remember where the beer first made its appearance. Mark Yeaton, who works on our ring crew, is my designated "beer tosser." I'm pretty good at catching those cans when he tosses them right, which Mark does more often than not.

I can catch beer better than anyone in the world.

The beer deal was the end of my act. It was how I finished what I was doing in the ring. Once fans saw the beer-drinking finale, they knew the show was over.

It helped me bond with the crowd. And when I did it with other talent, like The Rock or Vince, it helped me bond with *them*. Of course, sometimes I stunned them afterward, but that was the beauty of Stone Cold.

Some of my favorite over-the-top bits on *Raw* involved Stone Cold driving and smashing different kinds of vehicles. The fans remember those and always ask me about them. They were pretty wild television, especially when you consider they were on a live show.

Probably the one that started the trend was when I filled up Mr. McMahon's nice classic Corvette with tons of fresh concrete from a cement truck at Nassau Coliseum. I was looking for major ways to PO Vince and figured this might do it.

There aren't too many times when you get to wreck a Corvette on purpose. When I saw that car, I said I would just as soon take it home as destroy it. It was a nice car that WWE had purchased out of the newspaper for this stunt.

This was live TV, and I'd never driven a cement truck before. There was a mechanism you had to use, with buttons and levers to make the chute work and the cement go. I was out there learning how to drive it just twenty minutes before the show started.

There are a lot of things that can go wrong on live TV, but this little piece of business turned out to be a blast! The window glass of the Corvette shattered as the car filled up to the top with cement, so that was cool. Then it was running out the windows. That car must weigh ten tons or more now! They still have it and haul it around the country to each *WrestleMania* for the fans to see.

My personal favorite vignette was "the Beer Truck" on *Raw*, in Albany, New York. That deal was tough to beat. I rolled into that damn building with a beer truck, drove it into the packed arena and parked it butted right up to the ring. I got out to a tremendous cheer, and the crowd went crazy when I broke out the hose. I was blasting everybody in the ring, including Vince, with beer from a high-pressure beer hose.

They were selling it like crazy and slipping and sliding all over the place. Anytime you get to blast people with a beer truck, that's gonna open some eyes.

Then I climbed up on top of the truck and was doing all the Stone Cold stuff, shooting fingers, the whole deal. People were just going out of their minds, because you don't get a chance to see that every day. It was truly an electric moment.

Another fun thing I did with a vehicle was when Stone Cold crushed The Rock's brand-new Lincoln Continental with the Stone Cold 3:16 Monster Truck. This was about a month after the beer truck incident, on *Raw*, from Grand Rapids, Michigan.

While they were shooting the beginning of this, I was sitting in the monster truck in a holding garage for two full minutes, and the fumes from that thing were burning my eyes. My eyes were watering really badly and I could hardly breathe. I thought I was going to choke to death.

Then I got the green light to go. I gassed it so hard that all four wheels spun out. The truck was on a carpet, and the sudden acceleration shot the carpet out from under it.

If you're watching the *Hell Yeah* video, you can see that the cameraman went flying. He was standing on the carpet and fifty feet worth of it shot out from under the guy, and he just went flying.

But I did drive the thing, and I crushed that brand-new Lincoln Continental that was purchased that very morning. Hard to believe, but Vince McMahon bought a brand, spanking-new Lincoln Continental that day at a local dealership just to have me destroy it! A $40,000 investment for a few seconds of entertaining television, but fans still talk about it.

Another time, just to shake things up, I drove a Zamboni—another vehicle I had no experience with—into the Joe Louis Arena. I ran over a few light stands on the way to the ring. That got a pretty good pop, as who doesn't like a Zamboni driven by a madman?

My car-crashing career was capped off when I smashed and blew up the DX luxury bus on the April 27, 2000, *SmackDown!* taped in Charlotte, North Carolina. That was pretty cool, but since it was

SmackDown!, a pretaped show, we had special effects. But crashing into the bus was pretty cool. DX had been a little bit too proud of that damn bus. Yeah, I torched it pretty good.

When I attacked Booker T in a supermarket on *SmackDown!,* December 13, 2001, in Bakersfield, California, that was pretty wild too. I needed a little shot right there in my career, and that was something very different—but it was also something Stone Cold would have done to someone who pissed him off that much.

We fought all over that store! We tore the hell out of it. It was classic Stone Cold, with Booker T being a fantastic comedic accomplice. Actually, both of us laughed our asses off and had a good time. And we also had a good time doing spots on each other with the food. There's no telling what the damage cost WWE. Vince had to write another check in the name of entertaining our fans, but it was a very memorable episode of *Raw.*

The expression on that fan's face says it all; I throw in with Mr. McMahon.

Turning Heel !2.9

You come out here claiming you're a
gorilla, yet you hee-haw like a jackass.

—Austin to Gorilla Monsoon

My running battle with Vince McMahon ran from 1998 right through *WrestleMania X-Seven* in Houston's Astrodome on April 1, 2001. Even though I was not the prototype for what you'd call the classic fan favorite, since I was going against the evil, pompous WWE owner Mr. McMahon, I was tremendously popular with the fans.

It was a hell of a run. But I remember when I wanted to turn heel against The Rock at *WrestleMania X-Seven*, I was looking for something big to come out of the match. I was feeling a little stale as a babyface. I felt like the Stone Cold character wasn't running on all cylinders. The story lines for me seemed to be a little weak.

I wanted to shock people, which has pretty much become a tradition at *WrestleMania*. I wanted to do something they would talk about for a long time to come.

Then it came to me. I would turn on The Rock. And better still, I would accept the help of my enemy Vince McMahon in beating him. All of a sudden, I would become a heel.

A lot of guys like to work as heels. It's more fun, even though you sell less merchandise as a rule. Of course, if I could go back in a time machine knowing what I know now, I'd never have turned heel at *WrestleMania X-Seven*.

But back then I said, "Okay, I want to try something different. I want to challenge myself in a different way."

That's the reason you turn heel—to switch gears. I thought it would be entertaining for the fans to have an opportunity to hate me for a while. I thought it was going to be good for business.

I had been so white-hot as a hero. Now that I was starting to level off, I wanted a different type of ride.

I remember going into *WrestleMania X-Seven* in Houston, and cutting my promos against The Rock. I thought I out-promoed the guy, even though Rock's stuff was awesome. My stuff was just more intense. I felt it—it was real.

Anything I say or do on TV—I mean, it may be a work—but if it's Stone Cold Steve Austin, it's real to me. I believe it one hundred percent. I *am* that guy when I'm cutting a serious promo.

Going into that event, it's in the Houston Astrodome and it's two top babyfaces, but clearly I was the favorite with that crowd because I lived only a hundred miles from there. It was home. It was Texas.

I remember the end of that match. I was whaling on Rock with a steel chair and then, after a hell of a series of false finishes, I pinned him one-two-three. Vince was the one who came out there and handed me

that steel chair. I was about to make an audible call right there in the middle of the ring because that crowd was so hot, and I was going to turn heel that night with Mr. McMahon. I damn near just said, "Hey, we're not going to drink a beer together, but . . ." and then give him a Stone Cold Stunner. The fans would have really liked that, I think, and our feud would have continued.

When I look back, that's a call I wish I had made in the ring. I wish I had told Vince, "Never mind" when he offered me that beer in the ring. Because I had gained so much of my edge back by the end of that match, the fans didn't give a damn about me beating the hell out of Rock with that steel chair.

It was a no-disqualification match, so the fans didn't care. It was a legal move. When I got the win there was a hell of a pop. There were over 67,000 people yelling for me. What I was feeling right then was, *Don't turn heel!*

But hey, that was what we carved into stone, what we had agreed upon. So Vince and I shook hands and drank beer together in front of the fans at the Astrodome, making a lot of them mad at me.

I wish I had called it all off right there in the ring. From that point, I wouldn't have been so much a "tweener." It would have been back to, "Hey, there's that edgy Stone Cold. Whether he's a good guy or a bad guy, or whatever, he's going to do exactly what it takes to get the job done. No friends." DTA, remember?

I never did "feel it" as a heel. I thought we had built a franchise and a character that was everything that the average Joe would aspire to be, an overachiever. My own man. Someone who lived by no one's rules but his own. I go on my instincts and my guts, and I do what I believe is right. I like that guy.

And then J.R. told me a story about John Wayne. Why was John Wayne never a heel? The Duke was always the top babyface and everyone always knew that. J.R. never felt the heel turn was right for me either, and told me so more than once, but I guess I had to try it.

Normally, the time when babyfaces turned heel in the wrestling business is when they are at their hottest, when they are at the peak of their popularity. That's when it would make the most impact.

But it seemed like the Stone Cold character transcended that logic. The fans didn't want to hate me. It just didn't work. Just like the fans really didn't hate Rock at the last *WrestleMania,* even though he was supposed to be the heel.

The next night we were going to be broadcasting *Raw* from Fort Worth, still in Texas, and the fans there almost turned Vince babyface more than they turned me heel. It was almost like the fans were thinking, Vince is saying you can't beat Austin, so if you can't beat him, join him. He's still from Texas, he's still one of us, he whipped Rock's ass in a no-disqualification match, so anything goes. Steve got the draw on Rock and hit him with a chair. But Rock wouldn't have hit Steve with a chair if he'd gotten the chance. Don't think he wouldn't have. I don't know what the hell Steve's done that was so bad.

The Texas fans justified everything that had happened in their minds and I was not a heel to them. We had some work to do on this concept. We needed to do something shocking.

The next night we did *SmackDown!* in Oklahoma City and I simply used the old Oklahoma–Texas rivalry, and the fact that good ol' J.R.'s a beloved hometown boy made good. We knew we had to take that sumbitch up to a drastic level, so I beat up J.R. in front of his family, friends and hometown crowd. When we did that, yeah, there was a little rise in the heat that night in Oklahoma City. They didn't like it. But it still wasn't that white-hot heat that you want as a heel.

I was thinking, Damn, if it's not going to be white-hot heat in Oklahoma City when good ol' J.R.'s busted open like a butchered hog by his buddy—the guy he's loyally stood up for through thick and thin— what's it going to be like next week in Boston and New York?

It never caught on. It was one of those deals where everything went sideways. If it had worked, it would have been great. But the people didn't like it. They were taken completely off-guard by it.

It was like, "Oh, no."

The irony of that is I was still selling more merchandise than anybody else, even though I was supposedly the top villain in the company. Heroes always sell more merchandise than heels. That was some "mar-

ket research" we didn't listen to, and that's more my fault than anyone else's.

The fans were saying, "Okay, we're going to buy his stuff. He's a heel, but he's going to come back around. So I want to go ahead and have his stuff." And I was kind of taking pride in being a heel and still selling a lot of merchandise. Naturally, I didn't want my merchandise sales to drop off, because I didn't want to make less money. But those things really don't work out together. It was kind of like Bret Hart wanting to be a heel in America and a babyface in Canada. It didn't work as well in reality as it does on paper.

After I turned heel at WrestleMania X-Seven, WWE put a picture of me and the quote, "Why, Stone Cold, Why?" on the cover of Raw magazine and sold truckloads of magazines. That was a quote from J.R., but I started impersonating J.R. and making it real whiney sounding—"Why, Stone Cold, Why?"—just to piss people off.

To pour fuel on the fire, when we did Raw in Oklahoma City, we did a live interview in the ring and J.R. asked me that question. I couldn't be his friend anymore, so I had to beat him up. I remember the moment I cut him with that blade, blood was running down his face and I was pounding the living hell out of him for real.

Afterward, backstage, he had a headache and knots all over his head and he said to me, "Damn Steve, how come after you cut me you were hitting me so damn hard? Wasn't I bleeding enough?"

And I said, "No, that was fine, I just wanted it to look good for TV."

J.R. said, "Well, hellfire, I guess it did." The doctors wanted to give J.R. a few stitches after the angle, but he opted to have the cut glued shut. Ol' J.R. wears that battle scar with pride to this very day.

I think his daughters were backstage after the show. They didn't come up and say anything to me like they usually did. Maybe it was because I beat the hell out of their dad pretty good that night in front of all his friends and family. My business with J.R. in Oklahoma City worked, at least more than it did anywhere else, in my ill-fated heel turn. Everyone was asking why I had turned on my good friend, J.R.: "Why, Stone Cold, Why?"

I enjoyed being a heel, but I didn't really have the success that I was used to having. So eventually I became a babyface again. But looking back, if I hadn't turned heel back then, I would never have come up with "What?"

So it all works out in the end, I guess.

J.R.: I never thought Steve's heel turn would succeed, no matter how hard all of us worked to get it over. We had jointly built a wrestling franchise in Stone Cold that was extraordinary. This was not your typical star babyface who at his hottest turns to being a bad guy and it gets over. This was Stone Cold Steve Austin and short of Steve's kidnapping a school bus load of kids, I did not think that there was anything we could do to get the twelve to seventeen and eighteen to thirty-four male demographic to hate Austin. Our fans never disliked Steve to the point to where they would pay their hard-earned cash to see him get his ass kicked. If fans will not pay to see a heel get thumped, then the heel isn't "over." It was like attempting to make John Wayne a Nazi. Ain't gonna work.

Boy, did that stiff, big-knuckled son of a gun kick my ass good in Oklahoma City on day three of the ill-fated heel turn of Stone Cold. My home state did not like it one bit. They could see Stone Cold beating the barbecue sauce out of good ol' J.R., but they still couldn't understand why. That is not what they wanted to see, in my opinion. I thought I knew what to expect in the beatdown, as I have been hammered by wrestlers several times over the years and it seemed like I always got beat up in Oklahoma, but let me tell you, I was not ready for what I received. Steve also forgot to take off that damn skull-and-crossbones ring he wears and it left knots all over my head. I had attempted to warn my kids, who were in attendance, and my wife, who would see it on *SmackDown!* a couple of days later, but I sort of undersold what I thought it was going to be like. I have been in real fights in my life with less physicality than the angle we did on *SmackDown!* from Oklahoma City. It was one hundred percent old school.

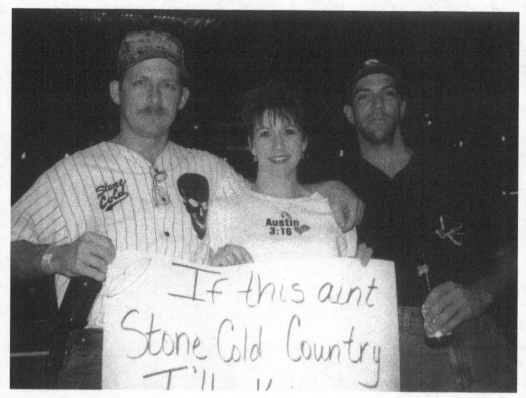

"Crazy Kevin," Jenny and Jeff

Astrodome Fever 30

I'm gonna check myself into the
Smackdown Hotel, roll right up to room
3:16 and burn that sumbitch
to the ground!!!!

—AUSTIN TO ROCK ON THE *RAW* BEFORE
WRESTLEMANIA XV

Funny thing about the match between
The Rock and me at the Astrodome at
WrestleMania X-Seven . . . the conflict
between Stone Cold and The Rock
wasn't limited to the ring. It became a family
affair.

Because it was in Texas, I had gotten seats with the
WWE family members for my brother Kevin, my sister,

Jenny, and my good friend Dr. Jimmy Baros and his wife, Debbie. They were sitting right behind The Rock's mother, who is just as fanatical as my brother. Kevin was yelling and screaming like an idiot for Stone Cold to kick Rock's ass, even though he knew that the outcome was predetermined.

All of a sudden, The Rock's mother turned around and gave Kevin a dirty look. He was so carried away by then, he said to her, "What're you looking at? Turn around and watch the damn match."

That's my emotional brother Kevin.

Of course, everyone had a great time. Then I took them all to the big post-*WrestleMania* party and they got to meet everybody, and vice versa. Naturally, Rock's mom was there too.

But she and my crazy brother Kevin got along just fine at the party. Luckily for all of us.

WHAT? 31

When I started doing the "What?" gimmick, I was preparing to wrestle Kurt Angle at *SummerSlam* on August 19, 2001.

I'd been off from work because I got three broken vertebrae in my back when Booker T clocked me on the announcers' table over at Continental Airlines Arena during his debut. So I was out of shape

and I was working with Kurt, who was an Olympic gold medalist and a badass, to get back to fighting form.

But it wasn't enough to get in gym shape. I had to get in ring shape, so I got myself booked in a couple of house shows. I was driving by myself to these shows and I was bored, so I called ol' Christian on the phone.

Christian's one of the younger guys in WWE, and he's done real well. He's always early, he works hard and he shows good drive and determination.

Christian was in the gym, so I got his voicemail. I start talking to it, and I was just going on and on and on.

I said, "You know, Christian, why do we have to be professional wrestlers? Why can't we just be . . . *what?* Why do we have to fight each other all the time? *What?* Why can't we all just get along? *What?* I'm stopping for gas now. *What?*"

I was just saying stuff like that, because we were doing this thing where out of boredom we were leaving all these long-winded messages for each other all the time, just to entertain each other. But on this one particular promo, at the end of each sentence I'd just say *"What? What?"*

I was riding down the road and I was a heel at the time, so I started thinking, You know, that would be a pretty good deal to start doing in my promos. It's real intimidating to ask a guy a question and just cut him off before he can answer it. It's heat. It's to disrespect him and stick it up his ass.

I first started saying *"What?"* with Scotty 2 Hotty, and I was playing like he was Kurt Angle. I was right next to his mouth with the microphone, and every time he'd go to open his mouth I'd go, *"What? What?"* I was doing it to bully and belittle people and intimidate them and make them look like shit.

It worked too. But shortly thereafter I decided, Hey, man, this ain't workin' the way I want. Nobody really wants to hate me that much, so let's go back to being a babyface. I'll make *"What"* entertaining, not intimidating.

Boom, people started picking up on it and said, "Okay, if he gives us a space here, we'll say 'What?'"

After I'd ask the question and say *"What?"* the fans put two and two together and then they said *"What?"* They all did it together. Crowd participation is always good. So now, anytime I talk, if I give them that space there, I get the big *"What?"* chant from the audience. I love it and they love doing it.

It's amazing. I did a fifteen-minute promo in the ring on what I ordered from Whataburger for lunch and the crowd was with me all the way.

"I went to Whataburger for lunch today . . ."

Crowd goes, *"What?"*

"I ordered a Whataburger with cheese . . ."

Crowd goes, *"What?"*

"Small fries . . ."

Crowd goes, *"What?"*

"A large Diet Coke . . ."

Crowd goes, *"What?"*

"Large coffee . . ."

Crowd goes, *"What?"*

Will Sasso, of MadTV, as the fan reaction of "What?s" build to the only conclusion of someone who mocks Stone Cold.

"I had a beer . . ."

Crowd goes, *"What?"*

"Then I had another beer . . ."

Crowd goes, *"What?"*

"I ordered a Whatachicken . . ."

Crowd goes, *"What?"*

"Apple pie . . ."

Crowd goes, *"What?"*

I had a lot of fun with that and so did the fans. It made it hard on the other guys, especially Kurt Angle. After it caught on, when somebody would be in the ring cutting a promo and they paused for a second, the crowd would yell, *"What?"*

It threw off their timing. At the peak of its popularity, the fans chanted *"What?"* while Lilian Garcia, our very talented ring announcer, was singing the National Anthem. I'm not proud of that one.

But Kurt learned to work with it. He's completely endorsed it. At first he said he was mad about it, but you can see right through Kurt and you could tell he was having fun with it. He used it to his advantage. He's great. He's smart, he gets it.

And I could use that gimmick to move onto the next thing. I remember when I got thrown out of that last *Royal Rumble 2002* we had in Atlanta. I had already told all the fans on TV that I was going to win. That was when I cut the Whataburger promo. I did Whataburger, Whatafries, Whatacatch and all that other stuff. Now I had lost that match and needed to move on, without losing my momentum.

I came up with the idea for that next promo while I was driving to Tuscaloosa, Alabama, to pick up Debra because someone in her family had died. I was sitting there with a lot of idle time on my hands after the Pay-Per-View, and I was thinking, I didn't win the PPV. I had said I was going to win that match and I didn't, so I needed to cover my ass. I needed to cut a promo to erase that fact in people's minds that I had just lost.

After mulling on it for a while, something popped into my head. I said, "I got a concept. I got an idea about the Beverly Hillbillies."

Then I told somebody about it and they said, "What's this about a Beverly Hillbillies promo?"

I said, "You know what, it's either going to work like a charm or the people are going to completely crap all over me."

I pitched the idea to Vince. It wasn't like a three-hour process explaining it to him. It was like a two-minute deal. I don't think he really understood it, but he trusts my judgment on things like this. It was one of those deals where it was either going to be a complete success or a complete flop. But he let me go with it and it turned out to be a complete success. Vince went with my instincts and it paid off.

I went out there and cut that story about the Beverly Hillbillies. I basically sang the whole theme song, pausing at the end of each line for the fans to say *"What?"*

I walked to the ring, put the mic to my mouth and said, "I don't want to keep you guys too long, but I want to tell you a story. This isn't a story about a man named Jed."

"What?"

"Poor mountaineer barely kept his family fed."

"What?"

I went through the whole deal about the Beverly Hillbillies, and then I said, "Well, that's not the story I'm gonna tell you." I said, "Right now, I'm officially entering myself in the next *Royal Rumble,*" the one I should have been in 2003 had I not been out from neck surgery.

When I cut that Beverly Hillbillies promo, the audience completely forgot that I just got my ass tossed over the top rope. They didn't care. Everybody remembers the promo though.

I had them thinking, Damn, it doesn't matter if Stone Cold won or not, I like the Beverly Hillbillies and Steve Austin's in *Royal Rumble 2003,* so that's all I really care about."

I'm always thinking about stuff like that when I go out there. I've always thought you should promote ticket sales, which is why I have a problem with people doing infomercials on themselves today, rather than trying to sell tickets.

But never in a million years did I intend for one word like that to get over like it did. Who the hell would have thought that?

What?

Edmonton, Canada, wrestling
hometown boy Chris Benoit.
An awesome wrestler.

Stone Cold and the Canadian Crippler

32

Don't take this
ass-whoopin' personally, son.
—STONE COLD TO BENOIT

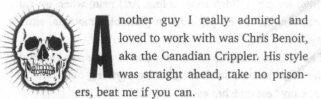

A nother guy I really admired and loved to work with was Chris Benoit, aka the Canadian Crippler. His style was straight ahead, take no prisoners, beat me if you can.

Like me, he overcame a neck injury, and his surgery was done by Dr. Youngblood, who did my surgery too.

Chris had to take a year off and the whole nine yards, just like I did.

My favorite match with Chris was at *SmackDown!* on May 31, 2001, in Edmonton, Canada. It was a match that I needed as a heel, as I was having a hard time getting people to hate me. Edmonton was Chris Benoit's hometown and he was over like gangbusters, so it was a great place for me to try to get the fans to hate me. He's vicious, and he's very believable, but so am I. I wanted to go out and have a great wrestling match with him because I knew we could do it. Before the match, I said to Chris, "How much time?"

And he said, "I don't know, sixteen minutes? What do you want to do?"

I remember telling our road agent, Jack Lanza, "We're just going to wrestle. Here's the finish. After he gives me ten German suplexes, here comes Vince."

I think we worked close to twenty-seven minutes, and I think twenty-four made it to TV. I said, "I don't care how long it is, we're just going to keep wrestling. We're just going to have a kick-ass match."

We had a set of ten German suplexes, a dive off the top into the belt and a reason for me to go up to the top rope and him to start chopping the crap out of me. We had four or five things lined up. We had laid out the simplest skeleton of a match ever. We went out there and just let it happen.

There was true, natural, raw emotion in that match. The bald-headed, foul-mouth American who had aligned himself with "Satan" (Mr. McMahon) and the born-and-bred Canadian. There were all these great, plausibly real elements. Even though we weren't in the middle of a hot program, all the elements were there. All the emotion was there. It wasn't written for me. I didn't recite a line. And man, when we can find those personal issues and put guys in plausible emotional situations, it's magic.

I could have theoretically done less and gotten a comparable result because of the stage that was set. But I gave it everything, and it wound up being one of my best matches ever.

And I feel like it put Chris Benoit on the map. As amazing a work-

er as he is, he needed that type of match on TV, and that's what I gave him. And he gave it to me also.

The deal with Chris, and I love him to death, is that he's an eight-cylinder motor running on seven cylinders. He doesn't have the promo or the persona part of it down just yet, but he's one of the best wrestlers in the world. He just needs that other cylinder, which is a little bigger personality, to be a top, top guy, because he can flat out work his ass off.

It would also be to Chris's advantage to slow down. Sometimes he goes through those kicks and chops so fast and it's like . . . what the hell just happened? Which move do you sell, the second one or the sixth?

But Benoit's an awesome talent. He's one of those guys who if you ever get in a fight, you want Chris to be with you. If you want to hang out, you want Chris with you. If you're going to be in this business, you want Chris with you.

He's the type of guy where if you say, "I've gotta go work and I've got last week's payoff in my wallet. Would you mind holding my wallet for me while I go to the ring?" you know that when you get your wallet back, you don't need to count your money. He's an honorable man and he knows everything that's going on. He watches. He doesn't say a lot, but he watches.

When he gets the persona part of his game going, watch out. I think Chris can make himself a true superstar in our business. He's a wrestler's wrestler and he should be a champion many times over in the course of his WWE career.

Vince McMahon loves to see guys kick and scratch and fight to get to the top, because that's what this damn business is all about, and Chris Benoit is capable of doing that.

Have I Had Lots of Fun with Other Gimmicks? *Hell Yeah!* 33

Oh, isn't that special? Why don't you

kiss his ass while he's bent over?

—STONE COLD TO GERALD BRISCO, WHO IS

HOLDING THE ROPES OPEN FOR VINCE

MCMAHON ON *Raw* IN AUGUST 1998

The ridiculousness of Stone Cold Steve Austin singing on *Raw* was one of those things I came up with while I was injured. I had those broken vertebrae in my back and Kurt Angle was beat up too, so neither one of us could wrestle—but we could still go on television and entertain the fans.

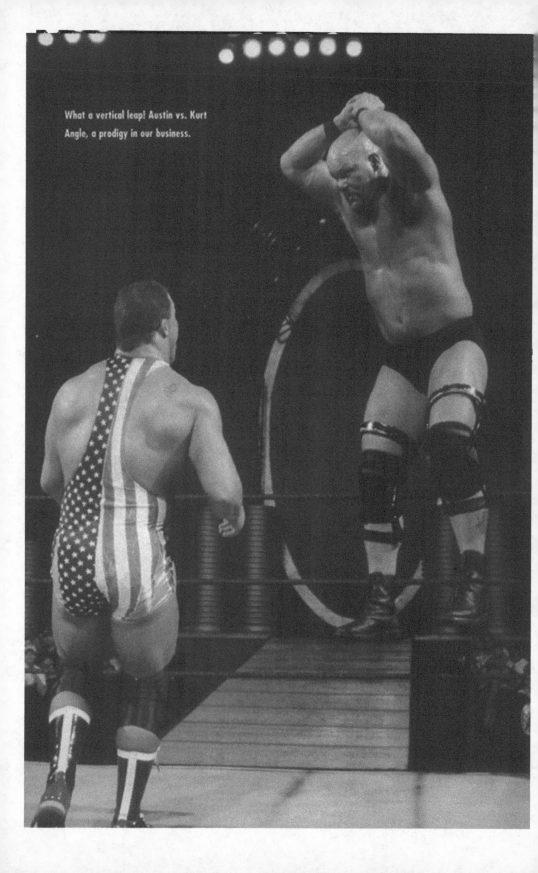

What a vertical leap! Austin vs. Kurt Angle, a prodigy in our business.

The singing was my idea. I figured, I'm a horrible singer, but I'm a heel so I can get away with it. As a heel you could show your ass and get away with it. Coming from my "musical background," I always wanted to play the guitar, but I was never able to learn to play it.

I went up to Vince and said, "I've got some ideas for next week. With all the stuff going on, I figure maybe I'll sing a couple of songs to you on the guitar and try to cheer you up."

Of course, he fell in love with the idea. He didn't know what I was going to sing. I was going to surprise him. We were going to pretape it that afternoon at the arena. We did it almost in one take, but too many people started laughing. Then we did a second take, but we ended up laughing our asses off and had to start again.

It was one of those extreme "laugh out loud" moments where everybody, talent and crew, wants to just roar, but they can't because it's time to get this thing done because of the time constraint.

So I sang "Kumbaya" to Vince to calm him down, while badly strumming an out-of-tune guitar. Then Kurt moved in on the action, doing the exact same thing and acting like a complete idiot because that's how good and quick-witted he is. He sang

"Jimmy Crack Corn" for Vince and that pissed off Stone Cold, because it was Stone Cold's idea to sing to Vince, not Kurt's.

Most of that was ad-libbed and it was so much fun. I was just doing my part to be entertaining. I couldn't get in the ring and wrestle, so it wasn't heat, but I didn't want to be totally flat as a heel. Anger for the sake of anger with no direction and no chance to do anything about it just makes you a steaming pile of cow dung.

That's when we started doing all the comedy stuff with me and Kurt and Vince. We did some real funny things together that people seem to enjoy and remember.

Then I came up with the hugging idea. I had just turned heel, so the fans didn't really know what I was thinking. They thought maybe I had lost it.

On *Raw*, I came out of a limousine and there was Vince, and I got this really psychotic look on my face. Vince looked at me like he was scared. So what did I do? I grabbed him and hugged him, keeping that crazed look on my face the whole time, just staring real hard as we went off the air. I knew if I hugged Vince, it would make the fans do something. It would command a reaction of some sort.

And it did. They fans went, "What the hell is this?" as we went off the air. And they tuned in next week to see what was going on with Stone Cold.

Kurt and I did a live deal in the ring on *Raw* where we were trying to lure Vince over to each of us so we could grab him and hug him. It was classic stuff, for sure, with Vince being bounced back and forth between us like a pinball. Kurt is such a talented hand and Vince sold it so well, plus the fans were wondering, What the hell is Stone Cold up to? Has he lost too many brain cells? We were both so serious about wanting to hug Mr. McMahon.

Then we turned it into an ass-kissing thing, with me and Kurt each trying to impress Vince the most and be his "favorite." And of course Kurt's right there, because he can be as cheesy as the next person. I mean, the guy's a genuine Olympic gold medalist and he's so quick and funny. He's amazing.

The little cowboy hats were my idea too. At the San Antonio air-

port, Debra and I spotted a little-bitty cowboy hat in a store window, so we bought it for Kurt and laughed the whole plane ride thinking how funny it was going to turn out.

Kurt was nice enough and goofy enough, pro enough, to wear the damn thing. Again, an Olympic gold medalist wearing this stupid little kid's hat. My God. He wore it the entire show and looked like the biggest, most moronic goof in the world. But it was so damn funny and entertaining, it was great. Just thinking about that big, strong guy in that stupid little hat still makes me laugh, because Kurt was so straight-faced when he wore it.

"Badges? We don't need no stinking badges."

That was a completely ad-libbed response on my part when Kurt tried to give Vince, Debra and me some cheap toy sheriff's badges.

So while Kurt and I healed up, we did some damn entertaining TV and we didn't sit at home. And our characters were still on television and we were still contributing to the show.

Kurt has a chance to become one of the all-time greats in our business. The guy is pure gold.

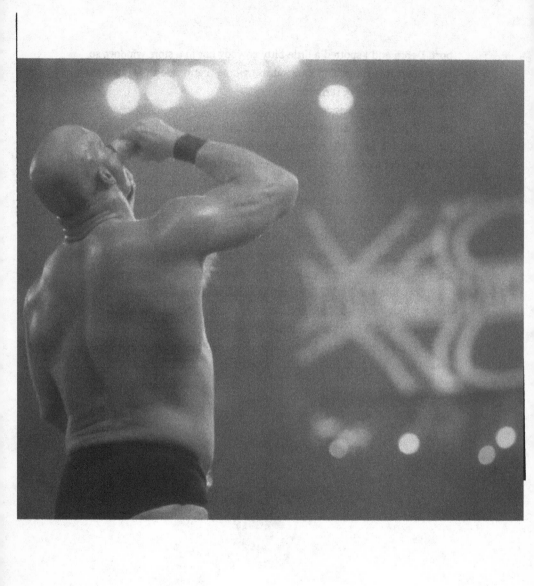

The Real Reason Why I Left WWE (Why I Took My Ball and Went Home)

Why did I walk out on WWE on June 10, 2002? It wasn't a spur-of-the-moment decision. It had been building up for some time.

There were clues beforehand that I was not happy. On March 15, 2002, I did an interview with WWE.com where I said, "I ain't real excited about some of the direction the company is taking, and the way busi-

ness is being conducted from a writing standpoint. I've got no problems with any individual talent, but I'm just watching and being very patient, waiting to see what happens, the reasons that everything happens and that it's done for the right reasons. I think a lot of things are done for the wrong reasons now, and there's guys being sacrificed. Hopefully everything will work out. I'll leave it at that."

At *WrestleMania X8*, I was in the third or fourth match—it wasn't even the main event. It was just some match on the card, the way I looked at it. And I wasn't happy with that at all. You can tell me this business goes in cycles, and sometimes you're not as hot as you want to be, but where I was on that card didn't make sense to me. The match wasn't promoted properly, it wasn't built properly, nothing.

People said I had heat with Scott Hall, or Scott Hall had heat with me. I didn't have heat with Scott Hall. I like the guy. He's had problems, or whatever; that's stuff he's got to deal with. As far as getting in the ring with him, I like working with the guy. But you can't expect him to come in here and get over in a couple of months and be in a *WrestleMania* match.

So I wanted to work with somebody different. I have no animosity toward Scott Hall. He's as good as gold with me in the ring.

After 'Mania, I was fried. I was burned-out and frustrated. Debra and I did not even attend the traditional post-*WrestleMania* party. One day later, before the Montréal *Raw* in March 2002, I left and was gone for two weeks.

Then, on May 31, I appeared on WWE.com's online webcast, Byte This! In the two and a half months since my previous interview, things had gotten worse. On the live show I said, "The bottom line is that everything sucks. I'm not happy with the way Stone Cold Steve Austin is going. I'm not happy with the way the whole company is going. The writing has been pretty substandard. I'll go one better than that. It's been piss poor. I guess if that pisses some people off, then that's just the way it is. I think it could have been a whole hell of a lot better creatively than what it's been. It's been pretty shitty. I wasn't happy before *WrestleMania X8* and I wasn't happy after *WrestleMania X8*, as we speak presently."

I said that I still loved my job, but by then feathers had been ruf-
fled once too often. Vince had to respond with his own Byte This!
appearance, where he said that I was "the most demanding Superstar he
had ever worked with."

Quite frankly, that's why our relationship worked and we drew
money together. I "demanded" great creative and Vince "demanded"
that I carry the ball and get results.

We were about to do a show in Columbus, Georgia, and we were
going to drive up I-85 to Atlanta for *Raw* the next night. Debra, with
whom I'd had a big, damn argument, was already in Atlanta, waiting on
me.

So I was in Columbus, lying around in the hotel room all by myself
before the show, and J.R. gave me a phone call. We talked about what
Creative wanted for Monday night. They wanted Brock Lesnar to slip
over me real quick (an out-of-nowhere win) in an unadvertised match
with no buildup or promotion or meaning, in a tournament-style deal.
There would be a screw job and he'd catch me for a three-count.

I thought that was complete crap. I told J.R., "They're going to
have to change that. I ain't doing it."

J.R. said, "Well, that's what Vince wants to do."

I said, "If they don't change it, I ain't gonna fucking be there." To
me this wasn't business.

J.R. said okay and said he'd called Vince.

I worked the house show that night, wrestling Ric Flair in a cage.
In the meantime, Vince called me back and left a message on my hotel
voicemail, saying, "Steve, this is Vince. Give me a call no matter what
time it is. Give me a call so we can talk about that Creative for tomor-
row's show."

I checked out in Columbus and drove to Atlanta and made a point
of not calling Vince back until I got all checked in at my hotel room in
Atlanta. My cell phone rang a few times in the car, but I didn't answer
it. When I got to Atlanta and got checked into my hotel room, I called
Vince. It was around two in the morning.

"Hey, Vince," I said, "It's Steve. I'm just calling you back."

He ran the same scenario by me. Brock goes over me with no

buildup in a surprise situation in a tournament-type match. He laid all that shit by me and I sat there and listened, and said, "Okay."

Vince was thinking I was saying okay because I agreed to do it. But I was saying, "*Okay,* I'm fucking fed up. *Okay,* this is bullshit."

Something similar had happened not so long before that. When we were over in England, they wanted me to do a job for the Big Show in another no-buildup, no-story match.

Now they wanted me to do a job for Brock with zero buildup. I started seeing the writing on the wall. That was when I decided to walk, right or wrong. It had nothing to do with the fact that it was Brock. It could have been any of a dozen other guys. I love Brock to death. He's a great kid and he's going to be a big Superstar in this business.

But here's the bottom line: I'm Stone Cold Steve Austin. I've drawn more money than anybody in the business. I've reportedly sold more merchandise than anybody in the business, and I've sold more Pay-Per-Views than anybody in the business, so Stone Cold is not the first in line to do a job to Brock Lesnar.

I'm happy to do a job for anybody—when it's time to do business. If you know the business, and you know what *is* business, then I'm the last one to job to Brock. That's the money match, the ones the fans are supposed to be dying to see.

His catching a quick win over me in a TV tournament-style situation with no buildup, no advertisement, no story line . . . that was just wrong. It wasted a situation where money could be made.

If there was a buildup and a reason to beat me, it would have been different. If it had meant something, I would have been willing to listen.

I had no problem with putting him over. But I should have been the last in line, not the first. It made no sense to me. I thought it was poor planning.

This stuff—what I thought were stupid creative decisions—set me off. It was the fuse that lit the dynamite. But the fact was that I had a lot of other problems going on at the same time.

My health had been failing for the last six to eight months. My serious neck and back problems were getting worse, and so was the problem I had with the reflexes in my legs. Of course, I wouldn't admit that

any of it was happening. I kayfabed it—I didn't say anything about it. But these were ongoing problems, and I could tell my body had had enough. I couldn't perform the way I wanted to.

I was frustrated and I was scared. In my mind, I was feeling like less of a man than what I wanted to be—less of a man than I had been.

And while I was going through all the frustrations of my health issues, I was also dealing with the problem of my marriage to Debra and the problem of my kids moving to England. I was completely stressed out with so many things going on. The BS just kept piling up on me.

Finally, I'd had enough. As far as I was concerned, it was a done deal—I was *gone*.

I had already told J.R. I wasn't going to be there in Atlanta, and I wasn't going to argue with Vince on the phone. And I wasn't going to show up the next day and try to hammer it out at TV. They had screwed with me to the Nth degree.

As soon as I hung up the phone with Vince, I looked at Debra and I said, "We're going home tomorrow."

She said, "No, no, no."

I told her what they wanted me to do. Then I called WWE Travel and changed my flights. That was the wrong thing to do, because they call their bosses to see if it's okay that you're making the changes. I should have made them on my own.

That's how J.R. knew I was on the airplane when he called me. Also, I learned that Debra called someone at the office from the plane, freaking out that we were on our way home and saying that's why she wouldn't be at *Raw*—basically covering her ass.

So that's how it ended with me and Vince and WWE. On June 10, 2002, I walked out on the greatest job I've ever had.

Everybody thought I left because I was mad about creative decisions. But that wasn't the real reason. That was just the straw that broke the camel's back.

I can see where people would say, "Oh, this guy got pissed off at the company because he didn't want to do a job, or because he thought he was treated badly." In that light, I looked like I was just bitter.

But the bottom line was, I was just overwhelmed, mostly by my

health problems. You don't know how it feels to have those kinds of problems unless you're actually physically going through it. They just weigh you down. They change your whole outlook.

The stuff that was going on at WWE was only part of the picture. It was a tough time in my life because I was standing on the sidelines, people were throwing rocks at me, my body was quitting on me and I didn't have any recourse but to try to get out of it.

Back on that *WWE Confidential* episode that aired the week after I left, the one where Vince and J.R. explained why I had screwed myself and walked out, they speculated on why I wouldn't meet face-to-face with Vince in Atlanta that day at *Raw*—why I instead "took my ball" and went home.

J.R. told the audience that someday the real truth might come out. When, he didn't know. The attack on me was typical of the type of smear campaigns a company carries out when a valued employee leaves on bad terms. Or maybe that's just in the wrestling business.

I've seen it plenty of times before, so it wasn't a surprise. I expected it. But some of the comments made by some of the talent surprised me. Others, I knew, were just saying what they were told to say. But as I said, I understood the game that was being played.

Everybody thought, Oh, he left because he was mad. No, I left because my health was failing miserably. No one else really knew what was going on with me. I was feeling all these crazy things going on with my reflexes. I didn't know how to handle it. I wouldn't talk about it to anyone. It's not like I was going to sit there and call Vince and say, "Hey, Vince, my health's gone south."

You don't do that as an athlete or as a performer. You don't just go up to your boss and say, "You know what? I've got this big bunch of limitations I want to drop on you now." I was hiding it and hiding it, and I finally got tired of hiding it. And because of all the situations that kept presenting themselves, it gave me an excuse in my own mind to get out.

I walked out. I took myself out of the business. That was a hard thing to do. WWE had given me a great opportunity. But I had held up my end of the bargain. I had provided them with lots of entertainment. I got paid for it, the company got paid for it and the fans had gotten their money's worth.

You know, it's funny, when WWE did that damn "anti-Austin" campaign on me, and they did a pretty good job on it, I didn't say anything. I just sort of sat back and took it. I mean, they owed it to me and I deserved something like that for leaving like I did. But, man, it wasn't fun. It was brutal.

So I went home for seven or eight months and stayed in shape and continued seeing my doctors. Vince left me a message once, but I was still mad at him and didn't call him back.

I wasn't going to call *anybody*. I was going to sit at the house, stubborn as a mule, because I truly felt like I'd been messed with time and time again. And I was going to stay just where I was until something moved me off high center.

One day, that something happened. I got a card in the mail from J.R. He sent me a nice hand-written note that said, *I'm here. If you need anything, don't hesitate to call me. J.R.*

That's when I picked up the phone and called Jim Ross and we talked for two hours, because I know I went through two cell phones. We talked for two straight hours about what was going on and where my life was.

Finally he said, "Is there any way you'd want to meet with Vince and talk about how things got all screwed up at the end? I know that's not how you would have wanted to finish up."

I said, "Yeah, I'd love to talk to him and find out why everything happened like it did, and he can ask me the same thing."

J.R. said, "I'll talk to him and see if I can set it up, and I'll call you later." So he set up the meeting.

It took place about a month later, when *Raw* was in Houston. The WWE office set us up in the penthouse at the Westin Hotel, at the Galleria in Houston.

It was a big-ass suite and I got there early, as usual. I was just waiting around watching ESPN and Vince walked in. You can imagine it was a little uncomfortable for me, seven or eight months after doing a "walkout" job.

But we hugged and we shook hands, and he asked how I was doing. It was one of those weird deals where he was beating around the

bush a little bit. Then we started talking about current story lines and where I thought they might go.

Finally he was sitting on one couch and I was sitting on the other and he said, "What happened?"

And that's when I opened up to him all my frustrations about what they wanted to do to my character and how it was bullshit. But I didn't clue him into what I was going through with my health. He asked me if I would consider coming back, and I said, "I'd consider coming back, but not in an active role in the ring."

He said, "Well, that's how Creative works, they get you back in a story line and then you're back in the ring."

He didn't know where I was coming from and I wasn't ready to tell him about my recent health diagnosis.

I told him I was sorry, but that I did what I did. Vince and I have that relationship where I'd do anything for the guy. On a personal level, I love that guy to death. But when it comes to business, he has to understand that. I don't like to brag, but I do know what I've done in this business and I got a pretty big freakin' ego just like he does.

This was a case of J.R., the outside referee, making the match and putting us together. We hugged, we talked about what was wrong and in the end, we buried the hatchet.

I said to him, "Hey, Vince, I've been thinking about doing some personal appearances; I didn't want to go behind your back, so I put them off. Is it okay if I do them?"

He said, "Sure! Let us know if we can help promote them. No problem at all. If there's anything I can do, let me know, I will."

So we shook hands and I wished him a good show. They went on to do *Raw* and I watched it on television.

It was an unreal relief. Damn, I love Vince in a strange sort of way. He's given me a lot of knowledge and wisdom. It's been a great job. I've had so much fun doing it.

I trust that guy hitting me in the head with a steel chair and vice versa. I've given him stitches, he's given me stitches. He's not afraid to do anything that he'd ask me or anyone else to do. It's like a fifty-fifty partnership. He's my boss, but we're fifty-fifty. Well, fifty-one-forty-nine.

It was more personal than professional, because I knew I was going to be limited coming back. And like I said, Vince treated me like gold.

I think that same attitude Stone Cold has on TV is the attitude that Vince has in real life. I think that's the reason we got along so well and the chemistry has been so good between us. Vince is a headstrong, go-forward guy who takes the bull by the horns and does what he wants. He's very shrewd. I'd rather have Vince on my side than against me, any day of the week.

At the end, there was that animosity and friction, and things fell apart. But even if I never went back to work for WWE again, Vince McMahon and I would have remained friends. He would still have respected me and I would still have respected him.

When I came back to WWE it was because I didn't like the way I left. I don't like quitting anything. I wanted to fulfill my obligation—more because of my personal loyalty to Vince than because of my legacy as Stone Cold. I just wanted to wrap it all up the right way, rather than think I had disappointed Vince or the fans.

I didn't want to screw Vince. That's the bottom line.

That's why I met with him, after J.R. sent me that note, and it looked like we were going to work out my return. *Raw* magazine did a cover feature story on "Why Stone Cold Quit." I hear it was the biggest-selling issue of the magazine in years. Everything I said in that interview was true.

I finally got to tell my side of the story. And I haven't had one person come up to me and say, "Hey, that article sucked." Everybody liked it.

But I didn't talk about the serious issues with my neck and my back, or my personal problems, the way I'm talking about them now. Taken together, they were really the deciding factor in my leaving.

I hadn't left the business solely because I thought the story lines were not up to par, as most folks seemed to think. It wasn't about losing. The creative part was just the icing on the cake.

When I came back to *Raw* the first time, I went up to each one of the boys—even those who said unkind things about me in the magazines and on *Confidential* and *Raw*. I looked every one of them in the eye

and shook their hands. Most of the boys in the locker room welcomed me and were glad to see me.

A few guys didn't want to respond to me, and that was their prerogative. I don't want to name names, because I don't want to put any heat on anybody. But when it came to those guys, I met with them privately and we talked about it.

In general, I seemed to get a fine reception. And I did the same thing on the first Pay-Per-View after my return, where I saw the SmackDown! talent for the first time in about eight months.

There were a couple of people who I pulled aside, or who pulled me aside, and we buried the hatchet with regard to the stuff that had gone on. In the cases of the guys I had referenced in the Raw article, I got them alone and said, "Hey, it wasn't my time. I was going through some personal problems. Professionally, I was running into a brick wall."

I've always had a good relationship with Chris Jericho. We had stayed in touch. The same with Chris Benoit, Eddie Guerrero . . . guys who know what it's like to be jerked around by the system like we all were in WCW. I knew I'd get no heat from those guys.

The bottom line is I did what I did, and so be it. Some people can understand it, and some people aren't going to understand it, but that's just the way it is. It seemed like almost everybody was glad to see me back, and I was sure glad to see *them*.

J.R.: I personally did not want to do the *Confidential* TV piece we did when Steve walked out, but I had a job to do. The first thing I said when I sat down and we started rolling tape was to express to whoever was listening that I did not want to do this interview. That did not make the air. All in all, our staff at TV did an excellent job with the feature, and we had to cover it because it was a *huge* story that affected the fans and our company. I said what I felt and I meant every word I said. I did not see it coming and I hoped that someday the true story of "why" would come out. That was not a good day at the office. I wiped tears from my face on my drive home. Those were some personally challenging times I hope I don't have to experience ever again.

Eric Bischoff Comes Back into Stone Cold's Life

35

I'm trying REAL HARD not to
get violent right now.

—AUSTIN TO ERIC BISCHOFF ON *RAW*

For a long time there was heat between me and Bischoff because he had fired me back in 1995 when my arm got hurt in WCW. It wasn't just that he had fired me, which would have been bad enough because suddenly I didn't have a job or a lot of money coming in. But, on top of it, he fired me over the damn phone. That was the part that pissed me off the most.

I don't give a damn that he fired me. I understand being fired. But respect me enough to do it to my face.

So for the longest time I didn't see Eric Bischoff. He saw fit to run me down a couple of times on WCW television while WCW was pushing Goldberg, but that was his job. So finally he came to WWE and I was thinking, Oh, look, they brought ol' Eric in. Never say never in this business.

I wasn't thinking payback though. I had already left the company and walked away. Some months later, after I met with Vince, it turned out that WWE and Bischoff were going to be down in Bandera, Texas, shooting some video vignettes to tease my return. I wasn't in them, but they were about Eric looking for Stone Cold, as on TV he promised Vince he'd deliver me to *Raw* or lose his job. It's funny how we twist real life into our wrestling story lines, and rewrite history, but that's what makes them so much fun.

So I figured, Okay, I'll just go and see what's going on.

I got there and saw him, and I had no intention of blasting the guy or anything like that. I already knew what I was going to do. This wasn't going to be one of those situations where I acted like a fool. I wasn't mad at him anymore. It was water under the bridge.

So I saw him standing off to the side and I said, "Hey, man, can I talk to you for a minute?" I pulled him over where we could speak privately and I said, "Hey, Eric. I guess a lot of people think there's gonna be a lot of heat between you and me. You probably think so too. And for a long time, I was pretty mad at you for firing me the way you did.

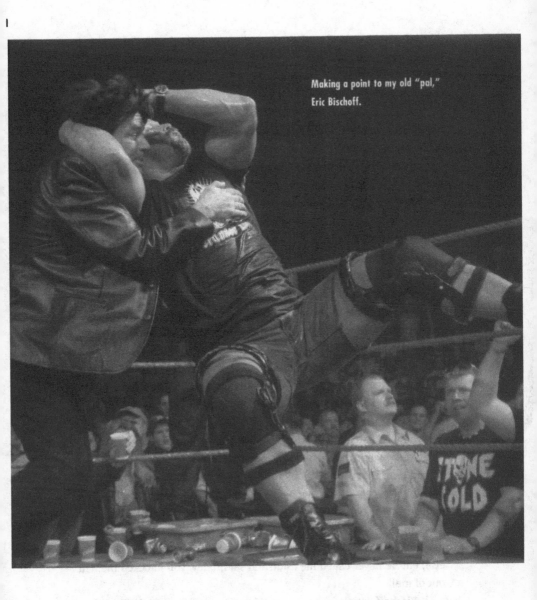

Making a point to my old "pal," Eric Bischoff.

"But that's a long time ago. I've been watching you since you came to WWE, and I think you're doing a great job. You know, what happened happened. That's in the past. As far as I'm concerned, if it's all right with you, let's wipe the slate clean and start from zero right here and put all

that other crap behind us. I got no animosity toward you, I'm not mad at you." And you could see a sea of relief wash over him.

Eric answered, "That would be great with me, Steve." And we shook hands.

We were headed toward the Pay-Per-View *No Way Out* on February 23, 2003, where we would finally work a match against each other. Eric called me a few times to talk about some ideas and stuff like that.

I said, "Has anyone said anything to you because of the old heat between you and me and that I might try to hurt you?"

And he said, "No, nobody's said anything."

I said, "I'm just telling you right now, Eric, I am stiff, and I haven't kicked or punched anybody in seven months. My timing might be off, but I'm not intentionally going to try to mess you up or hurt you."

He said, "Okay, it'll be fine. I'm sure it'll be okay."

Then we got to the match. As Eric had said, it worked out fine.

I know I caught him with a couple of really good stiff shots. Hey, it was my first time back and I needed it to look vicious and look good. But I certainly wasn't trying to take advantage of the guy. I know I gave him a couple of pretty good punches and a few stiff kicks, and he was pretty sore the next day, from what I understand. I'm sure some of the boys thought I had roughed Bischoff up on purpose. But that was not the case. I was rusty and I naturally work a little snug anyway.

But the hatchet was buried. I have a lot of respect for the guy for being tough enough to handle the beating. It all worked out and it was a good return for Stone Cold. I gave him a couple of Stunners and then pulled his arm up off the mat before the three-count, basically telling the audience I wanted to punish him some more. That was cool.

Still, Eric handled it very well. He never bitched one time about me landing spuds on him. He might have said something to someone else, but he never called me aside and said, "Hey, you knocked the hell out of me!"

Bischoff definitely wasn't one of my favorite people at WCW. When he first got there I liked the guy as an announcer, but when he got his power and the executive job and fired me, it all changed.

But, as it turned out, it was all for the best for me professionally and financially, and it made a good story line for us when he got to WWE. I now enjoy working with Eric as we have a lot of chemistry together.

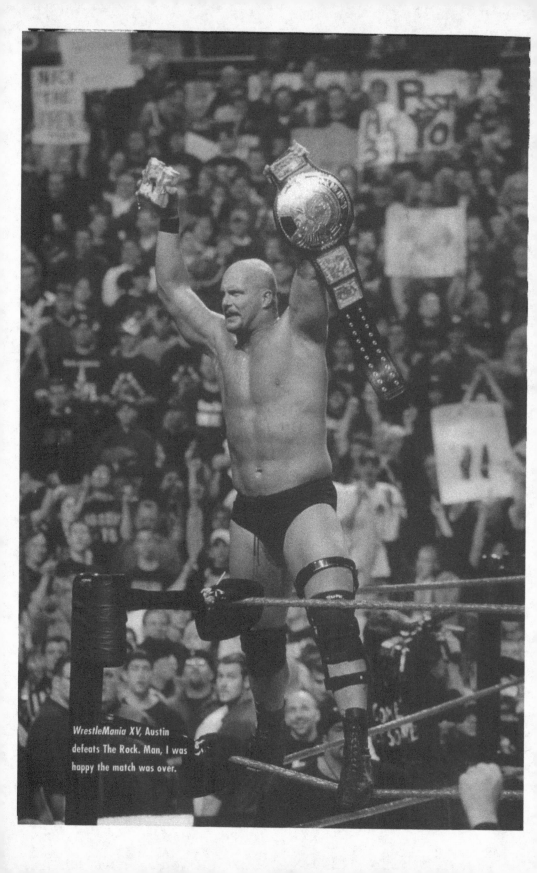

WrestleMania XV, Austin defeats The Rock. Man, I was happy the match was over.

The Fans
Welcome Back
Stone Cold **36**

Even before *No Way Out*, I had started doing paid personal appearances again. Those come from exposure on TV. When that dries up, it means nobody wants to see you.

That's not what happened in my case, thanks to the great fans out there, who I'll always appreciate and remember. When I came back to WWE and said I'd do a

program with Bischoff, leading to The Rock at *WrestleMania XIX*, the office allowed me to start doing some of those personal appearances without officially acknowledging that I was back with the company yet.

Even though I was gone for eight months, for Stone Cold's fans it was like I never left. Anywhere it was announced that Steve Austin would be appearing for autographs, it was a madhouse. I'm not bragging about that. It just makes me happy and extremely proud of the feelings my fans had for Stone Cold. They all wanted me to come back and kick someone's ass, and they didn't care who!

I was kind of lucky on that one. I loved doing these personal appearances and want to do more. I met literally thousands of fans all over the country and signed tons of autographs. I hugged babies. I posed for pictures. I was friendly and approachable—it was like I was these people's family. I loved being back with the fans and seeing so many turn out at malls, hockey games, baseball games, sports conventions, stuff like that. I want to thank my booking agent and good friend, Rich Minzer, for beating the bushes for me and getting me some great appearances. I needed to be with the fans. It was, and is, great therapy.

If someone throws rocks at you, someone else will stand up for you. My fans stood by me, thinking—whatever the reason—that I was going through some bad times and the company acted hastily in burying me on TV. They came out in droves to see me and tell me that they were so excited to hear I was back. I looked every single person in the eye and shook everyone's hand. As far as they were concerned, I got screwed somehow by Vince. Did I? No, as this could have been resolved in a much more sensible way.

But my fans are real loyal, and we're alike. We bond. I don't wear robes or suits. I drive a pickup truck. I wear jeans and boots or athletic shoes and a T-shirt, just like they do. They know I have the security and limos because I'm popular, but I'm just like them.

You'll find a large majority of my fans at Wal-Mart. It's my favorite store to shop at. If you've got a Wal-Mart in your town, that's everything you need, right there. You're more likely to see me shopping at a Wal-Mart than any other store. I'm very normal when it comes to shopping.

As a matter of fact, they just opened up a Super Wal-Mart ten miles from my house in San Antonio, and I can't wait to get a look at it!

Of course, not everybody was glad to shake my hand. A small percentage of the population thought that what I was doing was sacrilegious, that the "Austin 3:16" bit was wrong. Or they didn't like the way I flipped the bird. Or they didn't like my colorful language.

That's great, because I need those guys too. They make all the fans who really love me stand up for me even more. People are funny. If everyone likes you, that's not really a good thing, because they eventually get lukewarm on you. The crowd psychology is weird, at times.

March 30, 2003—
WrestleMania XIX
Sunday

t's *WrestleMania XIX* Sunday in Seattle.
I wake up after a fitful night's sleep to
learn that I've been medically cleared. I
can wrestle.

Originally they thought I had a pul-
monary embolism, a blood clot in my lungs. They did two
or three different tests and, thank goodness, everything

turned out to be okay. There was no heart problem whatsoever. It was one of those deals that just happened.

I check out of the hospital on Sunday at ten o'clock in the morning. Bob Clarke and Chris Brannan from WWE come to pick me up. They take me back to the hotel where I take a shower, shave, shampoo my hair (only kidding), listen to some CDs and made a few phone calls.

One of the people I call is Kevin Nash, because he heard what was going on and had left some messages, but I hadn't spoken to him. The hospital wasn't letting calls through. He's in his room, so I go upstairs and we talk about what happened. He offers me a ride to the building, but I tell him I've already told J.R. I would ride with him and Jerry Lawler to Safeco Field. Kevin says he'll just ride over with us, if it's okay. So we both go down and meet with J.R. and "the King," and we all ride over to the arena together.

In the limo, Jerry looks at me and says matter-of-factly, "You all right?"

I say, "Fine."

He doesn't know I've spent the night in the hospital. He's just asking me in general if I'm all right. The whole deal's been pretty confidential, pretty hushed up. Not too many people know what had happened. J.R., who has always looked out for the talent, hadn't even mentioned it to the King.

We get to the arena and I report to the agent for my match, which in this case is Pat Patterson. Pat always does The Rock's matches. Jack Lanza, my favorite WWE agent, always does my matches, but this time he's been asked to do someone else's. But I do ask him for some ideas and go over some things with him.

That afternoon, Rock and Pat and I go out and sit in the ring. It's kind of like a few years ago when Rock and I worked the main event at *WrestleMania X-Seven*, which set the all-time arena attendance record for the Houston Astrodome. For that match, Rock, Jack, Pat and I went out to a steak house in Houston. We had a private dining room all to ourselves, and we came up with the match. That match was a lot more complicated, with lots more twists and turns and false finishes than this

match is going to have. And we came up with that match over a steak and a couple of drinks.

So this time we're sitting in the ring in Seattle at Safeco Field. I know what the finish is going to be, but I'm brain-dead. I don't have a clue what else we're going to do in this match. With what had happened to me the day before, and my concerns for my health, I hadn't thought about what I could do or what we could do together. We talk different scenarios and I figure it out.

I say I'll get a couple of Stunners in on him and then he'll get me with three Rock Bottoms in a row. I'll barely get out of the first two somehow, but on the third one, I tell him, "You hang that elbow out there and hold it for six or eight seconds, so the people know that 'this is it' for Stone Cold Steve Austin. Then let it drop."

Whatever else we're going to do in the match, we come up with it in about thirty minutes. I want it to be a match that not only won't stink the joint out, but will be worthy of the spot it has at *WrestleMania XIX*. I'm worried about my health, but I'll be damned if I'm not going to wrestle Rock in a match that others like and I enjoy.

My leather vests are made for me by one of the WWE seamstresses, Terry Anderson. I have different ones, all of them with three different letters on them. Some of them say "DTA," for "Don't Trust Anybody." Others say "SOB" for "son of a bitch" or "BMF," for "bad mf—er." But the three letters always mean something. On the vest Terry's made for me for my last *WrestleMania* in Seattle, it says "OMR," for "One More Round." That's how I feel going into this match, that I'm going to do this "one more round," one more time.

More than likely, one *last* time.

But I'm not really sure I'm going to make it through the match. I'm a long way from the Sportatorium in Dallas. I haven't been in the ring in a real match for eight months. So to go out there and be in the main event, after being out of wrestling for eight whole months, I'm afraid I won't have my timing.

Then they crash the glass and hit my damn music. When my music goes on and 54,000 people light up like they're on fire, I tell myself I can

Teaching The Rock
a little respect.

do it one more time—one more round. I guess I'm a pretty stubborn SOB. My exes would agree, I'm sure.

When I walk in the ring, I know everything is going to be okay. I truly feel like I'm in a sacred place.

I go into the match adamant that Rock will go over, that he will win the match. I haven't discussed it with anybody, but I'm going to put The Rock over in the middle of the ring. If I couldn't do that, I wouldn't have entered the match.

That's a no-brainer. There's no other finish to this.

A lot of times when the office calls you to go over matches and lineups, the finish of the match is the last thing they talk about. This is one of those deals where the office don't have to talk about it with me. It's for me and Rock alone to talk about.

I know what's going to happen. I know what has to happen. And I want to do it because I've beaten The Rock a lot of times in big matches. It's the right thing to do, because this is business. It's the right time.

There's a story—a reason for the match. I've beaten Rock at two *WrestleManias*. Rock's going to go on the road next month and draw another Pay-Per-View against a different guy. He's gotta win.

Stone Cold Steve Austin might end up being the general manager of *Raw* or he might be selling T-shirts. Who knows what he's gonna do? So there's only one logical conclusion and that's to put The Rock over clean right in the middle of the ring. No cheating, no foot on the ropes, no pulling tights, no interference, whatever.

And that's what happens.

Two of the top guys in the business work their asses off in a sold-out arena. It's just a badass, see-saw, back-and-forth battle. People are going crazy.

In the end, Rock stands there for I don't know how many seconds with that elbow hanging over me. And when it falls, the fans *know* this is really "it" for Stone Cold.

After Rock pins me for the one-two-three, he leans over me real close and says, "I love you, man." I know he means it.

And I tell him I love him too, and he knows *I* mean it.

Then Rock says, "You'll never know how much this means to me.

WrestleMania XIX Seattle, my proud salute.

Thank you so very, very, very much. You don't know how much I appreciate this. I'll never forget it."

I'm glad to have been able to do it for him. The main thing, though, is that the fans seem to like it.

When I took a year off for that neck surgery, and then when I walked out for eight months . . . those were both career suicides. I'm fortunate to have worked hard enough to have a strong base of people who've stayed loyal to me. They've stuck with me, and I still wanted to find a way to entertain them.

After the match is over, I come up the ramp for the last time and I look at the fans. It's a sight I'll never forget. I give 'em the Double Birds and the crowd explodes. I get a huge cheer as if I had won the match, and that's wonderful to hear. And my music is playing as I'm leaving, which is cool.

Rock was the so-called heel in the match, or at least he was doing his best to get his fans to dislike him. But when we did that finish right in the middle, one-two-three, it set him up to do business down the road. The Rock beat Stone Cold at *WrestleMania XIX*. That's what the record book will always say.

It was never acknowledged on TV that this was my last match, but ol' J.R. knew. If you look at me on the tape coming up the ramp afterward, you can see it on my face. I was pretty emotional. Hell, I felt like crying. It was like someone had just taken a big weight off my back.

After the match was over, a lot of people said they liked it. But then, I lost it in grand fashion. The deal with me is that in my matches, you go from Point A to Point B. You can draw a straight line, and that's a match. Or you can go up and down and around and in curves and that's a match too. I just wanted to get through the match, from A to B, with a few turns in the road. We didn't do anything fancy. It was a basic formula and we told a simple story.

All of a sudden, all the pressures were gone, lifted off my shoulders. I had fulfilled my contract and my obligation to Vince McMahon and his family, had closure character-wise and didn't end up having to be stretchered out of the ring when the match was over.

But it was weird for me. I wished I could still wrestle a regular schedule. But I knew I couldn't, so I accepted that. I knew there were lots of people way worse off than I was. My time had passed, sure, but I was still one lucky South Texas redneck.

When the show was over, we had to wait for all the fans to clear out before we could return to the hotel. There were so many fans there, it took over an hour for us to go. But you don't mind waiting when the event was a sellout. So I took it easy after the show, I was in no hurry. I took a shower at the arena and put on an Ozzy Osbourne CD and then put on a Black Label CD and listened to a few songs.

I rode back to the hotel with J.R. I think it was appropriate that the last ride from *WrestleMania* for the wrestler known as the Texas Rattlesnake was with ol' J.R.

He asked me how I felt. He said I looked "relieved." I was. I'd been under the knife so many times with my knees, my neck and all this other stuff, it was great to know that I wouldn't have to go out there and perform at a substandard level.

I felt good that I had not only got through the match with The Rock without getting hurt, but had put on a pretty damned solid match. I had been off for eight months, but thank goodness my timing all just came back to me. I really liked what we did and was happy it was over, especially after so much apprehension about doing such a physical match at an event the caliber of *WrestleMania*.

We went back to the hotel and I went upstairs and showered again, changed my clothes and then went down to the company's big post-*WrestleMania* party. I kind of camped myself in one spot and talked to whoever came by.

It was fun. WWE really knows how to throw a party for all the hard-working people in the company who do such great work at *WrestleMania*.

Then I went up to my room. I put on some CDs and was just thinking, wondering what the next step was. What's gonna happen next?

I remember telling Vince more than five years ago that I only had three years left in the business as a wrestler—and despite that, I was still there in the main event at *WrestleMania*. But now it was over.

Was I sore the next day? Yes. Did I injure anything new or make anything worse? No. Is Stone Cold retired from active wrestling in the ring? Probably. You never say never in this crazy business, but I wouldn't bet on my wrestling again.

There had to be an ending. But this was closure. This was the finishing touch to Stone Cold's active wrestling career. It all made sense, story line-wise. My story now had an end as well as a beginning.

Nowadays, I miss going out and wrestling. And my fans miss it too, no doubt. The WWE fan base is extremely loyal, in general, but the Stone Cold fans are more intense and more loyal, than any of them, and I love them to death. So they might be disappointed that I can't go out there and raise hell, and drink and cuss, and challenge guys to wrestling matches.

I'm challenged now to be useful in another role. But I still want to entertain the fans who have stuck by me so long and through so much.

In my final match, I laid on my back and looked at the lights for three seconds and knew that my wrestling career was over. But what I did was right—for me, for WWE, for The Rock, for the wrestling business. It felt real good. I haven't always made the right decisions, but I nailed this one square on the head.

And that's how my in-ring wrestling career ended. But Stone Cold Steve Austin's story isn't over, believe me.

J.R: Knowing that this was most likely Steve's last match and that we weren't making a story line out of it or sharing the information with our fans was a challenging piece of business for me as a broadcaster. I did not even tell my broadcast partner, the King. I just wanted to get into the match, help the talent tell their story and add to the drama and emotion if I could. I tried to not think that this would probably be the last time I would ever call a Stone Cold match, but that really hit me after the third Rock Bottom by the "Great One" for the one-two-three. I had to keep The Rock "whole," as he was going on to headline another Pay-Per-View for the company the next month and at the time we did not know what role Steve would fill within WWE, if any. I did the best job I could selling The Rock in the postmatch,

because he is an awesome talent and he deserved it. Then after The Rock left the arena and Austin began to make his way out of Safeco Field, it was almost as if the 54,000 fans in attendance knew it was over. They didn't know officially, of course, but I think many of them felt some of the same feelings I was experiencing. For me, it was like calling the last at bat of my boyhood hero Mickey Mantle of the New York Yankees.

I was proud of both Steve and Rock that night for many reasons. They had a damn good match that I enjoyed very much and I think our fans did too. They came through in the face of great adversity, considering Stone Cold's health scare just hours before the event and his other serious health issues. But these two thoroughbreds got through it like the champions they are on a night I will never forget if I live to be a hundred.

Stone Cold's Bottom Line on the Wrestling Business

If I ran WWE in a perfect world, I'd take the business back ten or fifteen years. I'm not talking about eliminating the music or the pyrotechnics. I'm talking about the wrestling style, bell to bell. If we change that the way I'm suggesting, guys are going to sell the moves more.

That means slow down, take less chances and tell better stories. The way it was in the eighties, or when I was really hot in 1996, 1997 and 1998. *Raw* on Monday nights *was* raw. *Raw* is so damn slick right now, it ain't raw at all.

It used to be in WWE that three years out, they knew where everybody was going. They don't do that anymore. It's too bad. There was a big picture, a game plan. And you worked such a safer style then, because the guys were actually better workers. They didn't have to take as many crazy bumps, because they really sold the bumps that were available to them.

Then the high flyers came and everybody stopped selling the moves. The Road Warriors came and they stopped selling pretty much anything. It was good for them, but everybody spun off the good things that people did and turned them into everyday, regular stuff. Some people brought positives in, and other people made negatives out of it.

The first change I would make would be to have unscripted promos. I'd force guys to use their brains. Make it a spontaneous situation where guys are forced to use their hearts, their heads and their guts. When someone asks them a question, they wouldn't just be regurgitating some BS written on a piece of paper they had to memorize. I'd like to see WWE go back to being more of a wrestling company and less of a television company doing wrestling. And by no means is this a knock on the folks at WWE TV. My friend Kevin Dunn's crew is A-1.

And the promos—the talent would be given direction, "Make sure you cover these three points, and you've got two minutes allotted to your promo."

If the talent had a question, you'd give them direction on how to get from point number one to point number two. You'd give them the bridge. But what came out of their mouths would be their feelings, not what they committed to memory.

When it comes to cutting promos, I think we put a lot of guys in a position where they can't win. They're being asked to do something they weren't brought into the business to do. Their training is wrestling. We ask them to play a character, which requires acting skills. We don't have

any acting coaches or acting classes and these guys have no acting background. But we expect them to be actors.

Still, they could pull it off with some help. Hell, I can do it and I never took any acting classes. It's about having experience and having a gimmick that you can "become." Look at that damn Kurt Angle! He's a legitimate 1996 Olympic gold medal winner who never did anything but train, and he has terrific, natural acting skills.

It's better to let wrestlers be themselves. The cream will rise to the top. So I'd go back to the in-ring product. I'd slow down the process of putting guys in a main-event environment, if I had that luxury.

It would also be nice to have two separate locker rooms, one for heels and one for babyfaces, and have guys learn how to call matches again. Just like back in the old days when the referee came in the locker room and gave you the finish and gave the other guy the finish, and you went out in the ring and worked that style. To me, that's why there's no emotion in the matches anymore. They're so rehearsed and prefab, it looks like a performance.

You've made all your decisions before the match on the basis of the matches you've been in and also the stuff you've seen, so you're forming a decision without even listening to the crowd's response. You're not working them and you're not performing for them, and that makes a difference.

It's got to go back to being a work, the way it was when wrestling came out of the carnivals. Guys couldn't beat each other up all the time to make money, so they started "working" it. When you're working for a crowd, you listen to that crowd. And then, according to how the crowd reacts, you call a different sequence in the match.

"Hey, it's time to get some heat now. It's time for a little comeback. Time to cut the guy off. Time to go home." It's all based on how you're taking people on that ride. It might be a ten-minute ride, it might be a thirty-minute ride. But not all the decisions were made backstage. Guys have to think on their feet again and be able to call matches in the ring. That's one of the things I miss about the business these days.

I also think we have too many women wrestlers right now who

want to wrestle like the guys do and perform Lou Thesz presses, stuff like that. That's not sexy and it's not feminine. My ideal woman wrestler would work like Sherri Martel or Fabulous Moolah. They didn't wrestle like guys. They had their own style. That's my two cents on that.

I've talked about my frustration with the creative process. But I've spoken with several of the writers, and called a few of them aside, and we're all on the same page there. Yeah, I was critical of the writing. By the same token, people can be critical of me. I'm open to the criticism.

I also understand that most of our writers came from a different system than I came from. I came from the small circuits and the small territories—that's the way I learned the business. The writers are thrust into the system with a different perspective. They have to construct a show, and have to deal with the fact that we're so fast-forward these days, producing all the TV programs we produce.

But they've got to understand how the business works, and that the talent can't be turned into robots. They actually have to feel and learn and educate themselves. They have to be placed in different situations and get a chance to respond to them in order to turn into competent hands, whether they're heels or babyfaces.

So yeah, I run my mouth a lot, and I say what I feel, but I understand they have a job to do and they're working their asses off to do it. We're coming from different backgrounds, but I think everybody's on the same page now. We all have the same goal and that's for WWE to be successful.

The way I look at it, a wrestling gig is similar to a comedian's, going on the road and doing a one-night stand in a different town every night. If I'm a stand-up comic and I tell a joke, the one thing I'm going to do is pause before the second joke until the audience is done laughing at the first one. I want to get a laugh for each of my jokes. I'm not going to even think about telling the second joke until the laughter dies down.

If I tell enough jokes from my A material and the fans aren't buying it, then I gotta move to new material. Maybe they're not buying my generic humor, but they're buying my blue humor. And this audience tonight wants to hear F-bombs or locker-room humor. So I make an

audible call based on what I've heard and what I've observed. I change my routine.

It's like a concert. I went to see Fleetwood Mac one time and I didn't want to hear their new songs. I sat through them, I didn't hate them, but I really got into their classics. And I think they could tell the audience really got into their classics. But instead of giving them to us, it was like, "We're going to play these songs in this order, come hell or high water."

If you lay out a wrestling match like Fleetwood Mac did with their playlist of songs, saying, "We ain't changing this. The fans can sit on their ass, we don't care," you're cheating the fans.

That's what most people don't understand about wrestling. If you memorize your match in the back and you go out and do it verbatim, and the fans don't buy it, you've cheated them. You didn't listen to them, you didn't observe them, you didn't see what got them going and what didn't. One of the best things we can start doing on the road right now is give the talent the finish of the match and that's it. Bingo. Let them talk about it. And as they work their match, let them listen to the crowd and work with them.

I've also got a few pet peeves about the business. Imagine that. I don't like guys being late for work, but then again, I am a real time fanatic. I was always one of the first guys in the building my whole career.

I can't stand guys complaining all the time, bitching that they're not getting a break. Every now and then it's warranted, but more often than not it's a lack of work ethic or a lack of something else. Maybe a lack of talent. But they're going to bitch about it, even so. And sometimes all the backstabbing and the politics and the BS gets a little old.

Sometimes a guy hasn't been in the ring in a while, and the guy comes to the arena and he's not in good ring shape. I remember when I first came to WWE, I wasn't in ring shape and I was working with Savio Vega. Damn, I just ran out of gas. I was completely blown up.

There is no excuse to not be in condition in this business. There's no excuse for that at all. Of course, once you get on the road, all of the travel and the drinking and everything like that catches up to you. But as an excuse to be out of shape? No.

I mean, there are no prerequisites to get into pro wrestling. You don't have to have a college degree. You can be a car mechanic, you can be a football player, a schoolteacher, a Harvard graduate, whatever. You can be anything and get into this business, if you have talent. But once you get into the wrestling business, you'd better be in shape, and you'd better have your head on straight.

As I have said, my match against The Rock at *WrestleMania XIX* might have been my last. If I'm smart, I won't wrestle again.

Kurt Angle recently underwent a new type of surgery pioneered by a doctor in Pittsburgh. This doctor told Kurt he would be able to return to the ring in a few months, and sure enough, four months later he was wrestling again. So I went to talk to this doctor in June 2003, to see if he could do anything for me.

But unlike Dr. Youngblood in San Antonio, who had done my earlier surgery, as well as Chris Benoit's, Rhyno's, Edge's, Lita's, and Scotty 2 Hotty's, this doctor wanted to shave my discs. That didn't sound right to me, so I thanked the doctor and left, and decided to stay with the medical team I have.

I may be done with wrestling per se, but I like to create. Could I be involved in a booking meeting by conference call? Or could I work with whoever is head of merchandise? Could they send me ideas and ask me to critique them? Could I watch the shows and come up with ideas and gimmicks for all the merchandising possibilities? Yeah, I could like to do all that.

I'd like to be a consultant to Vince McMahon on a regular basis, despite the genius that he is, and tell him what I think about certain things they're doing. And I wouldn't be a yes-man. I think I know this business pretty well and will tell him straight out if something sucks.

I could talk to the guys as they come back from their matches and ask them about what they did, and help them to get it better next time. Or I could help with interview stuff. I could help people develop their characters, find out who they are and find a character they can grow with.

I told Vince on that XFL football deal, "Whew, man, why are you doing this?"

But you know, it wasn't my job to advise him about that. If it was, I'd have said, "Vince, damn it, focus on the product. Don't get involved with that other crap. Focus on wrestling."

It could be something like that. I don't know. It's hard to say. How do you help a genius out, except as a trusted advisor to him?

I would especially like to help build the career of whoever turns out to be the "next" Stone Cold Steve Austin. And if he's good enough, I hope he breaks every one of my records.

I don't think there's one guy on this roster who wouldn't want to have my level of success in the ring. If there is, we really ought to try to convince him to do something else for a living, because he's never going to make it. If you're not in WWE to become the champion and succeed, then you're in the wrong business.

And becoming champion isn't just a matter of carrying the hardware or making more money. It's the opportunity to assume a position of leadership. It's the chance to become responsible more than anyone else for putting an ass in the seats every eighteen inches. In old-school wrestling lingo, that means a full house is there to see *you*.

WWE is a billion-dollar corporation trusting you with the responsibility of representing that company. I don't think most guys realize just how much money you can make in that position. I never knew how much money *I* could make.

I always tell guys to listen to the audience and go with it. But there's so much posturing and gesturing in the ring, and guys looking over their shoulder at the crowd when it's not time to look at the crowd yet. And some guys shouldn't be looking at the crowd at *all* because they don't have the wrestling part down yet.

I understand that guys are trying to work a hundred miles an hour, but they're actually working too hard. They're working harder rather than working smarter. And nothing makes sense. They're trying to get noticed, but they're going about it the wrong way. They're trying to hustle, hustle, hustle, so they can draw some attention and be the "next guy."

I wonder how many guys actually practice their promos in the car, or at home, or in their head in the gym or on their way to the grocery

store? How many guys actually think about their character? I don't think enough guys are putting in time on their own to get better. That's all I used to think about. What was I going to say or do next? It's like playing chess. Plan several moves ahead and don't just wait on them. Also let Creative know your ideas, or they may get wasted.

Besides getting your character going and concentrating on wrestling, young wrestlers need to establish a relationship with Vince and J.R., and with Kevin Dunn and his Creative group. You become noticed much more at that level than you do in the ring. If I've got a billion-dollar company, I'm not going to trust some guy I don't know a damn thing about. I'm not going to say, "Hey, here's my billion-dollar company. I'm going to give you the responsibility of maintaining my reputation and my company's success, even though I don't know who or what you are."

I'd like to see the business enjoy another surge in popularity, but the only way that's going to happen is for some of these guys to do their homework. They need to *be* who and what they are and let WWE magnify that, put a rocket pack on the back of it and market the hell out of it.

Unfortunately, a lot of young talent are hanging back right now, while WWE needs those new number one, two and three guys to step forward and start taking over. It's there for them. On the other hand, the boys may lack the confidence to voice their opinions because the show is so writer heavy now.

That goes to what I was saying about guys doing their own promos—having the chance to use their hearts and their brains depending on the situation they're in. That's the way you get different personalities, not by one guy writing all the promos. If a wrestler is good and he's got natural talent and ability, he'll succeed and be a star. If he sucks, he'll fall to the side.

If you have one writer speaking for several talents, yeah, he meets with me in person and he knows that I'm from Texas and that I drink beer, and that The Rock is flamboyant, and that Triple H is going to talk about The Game or something like that. He's got an inkling of what to say, but he doesn't really know any of us.

You can read all the stuff I've spit out over the years. That was all

straight up out of my brain. If you had ten other guys, fifteen other guys, doing what I did and spitting their own stuff out of their brains, who knows how many guys you'd have knocking home runs out of the park?

I'd like to see the business get bigger, like it was a few years ago. The only way it's going to do that is if we have a whole lot of characters people care about—characters with lots of differences. It would also be nice to shave some of the size out there. Everybody's got big physiques now. Back in the old days, there were all sorts of body types.

And guys gotta sell. Not selling offensive moves kills the business. Hell, selling in the proper degree is a lost art. The boys who perfect it will take a huge jump forward to the Promised Land.

I remember talking to veteran wrestler Tojo Yamamoto in Dallas at the Sportatorium a long time ago. He said, "You have to know how to sell."

Then he told me to grab his ear. I grabbed his ear and he went crazy with pain and sank to the floor. I thought I had really hurt him.

Then he looked up at me and smiled. "You get it?" he said.

All I did was touch his earlobe and he made it look like I was tearing it off. A lightbulb went off in my head. I got it! I didn't hurt you, but boy, you made it look like I hurt you!

If a guy doesn't sell his punches, what does he have to do to hurt his opponent? Use a steel chair? So he hits his opponent with a steel chair. Okay. The main event comes and they use the steel chair—big deal, a steel chair was already used.

There's got to be a pecking order of moves established and used. All the bells and whistles and toys should be saved for the semi-main and main event. That's it, hands down. The first four matches or so ought to stay in the damn ring. That's their spot on the card, that's their role. Stay in the ring, put on a wrestling match and do the finish.

That's the way it ought to be. That's what our business ought to be doing now. At least that's how I see it, and I think I know what I'm talking about.

The other trap for young guys is they don't keep their heads straight. I've seen people come in here and have some success and go haywire. They haven't even scratched the surface of the success that I,

or a lot of other others, have had, but they go ego crazy. They've been on TV a couple of times, and all of a sudden they think they're the center of the universe.

The way my parents raised me, I take everything for what it is. I've been away from this business a few times, and each time it was like the world had been yanked out from under me. So I just try to keep a level head nowadays.

I can't stand to be with people who are overbearing and have a big head. Should they have an ego? Yeah, everyone's going to have an ego to a degree. But I don't get the big head. I know I'm just like everyone else. I've just been very fortunate.

Hell, anybody in that locker room today could be as successful or even *more* successful than I was. They just have to come up with the right idea, the right gimmick. I came up with a character that fits and works for me. I'm certainly not a rocket scientist. I got lucky.

But I made sure that all the right people knew what I was thinking.

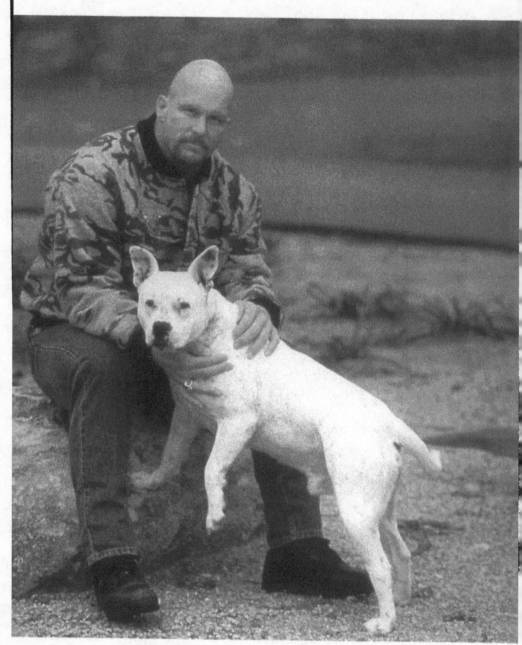

On my ranch with my pitbull, Sam.

Stone Cold on Traveling the Roads and Making the Right Decisions in Life

The wrestling business gets a bad rap by its critics, as they feel that our extensive travel schedule is an enemy. They say that travel is conducive to bad habits, that the bumps and bruises, and injuries, and soreness and dings to your body lead to a slew of pain medications.

To hear some people talk, the wrestling business is a self-fulfilling prophecy. It's going to breed drug abuse and broken marriages. All the time spent traveling up and down the roads takes away from your family, and you can't be the father you want to be because of your chosen profession. To me it's no different than being a major league baseball player, who's on the road for a hundred and sixty-two games. Basketball players, the same deal. Olympic athletes rarely have a home game. Actors go on location for months at a time. Rock bands go on world tours that last for months. I think sometimes our business takes a bad rap.

As far as I'm concerned, sports, entertainment and wrestling all fall under the same umbrella because you're out in front of a crowd. Whether it's a predetermined finish, a scripted play or a straight-out competitive performance, you're in front of a crowd. That crowd is there to see you perform and the crowd is being entertained. And to get in front of that crowd, you had to travel, then you had your downtime, then you had to go somewhere else to train, work out, practice or whatever.

Being up and down the roads, with the pain and the bumps and everything that comes with it, can be grueling. But that's true whether you're performing in a real-deal sport or wrestling. You're living out of a suitcase and you have a lot of time on your hands. You're psyched up and you're trying to come down from that crowd, so you have a couple of beers. You have a couple of drinks. Well, next night, you're going to do the same thing. And the night after that . . . and the night after that. You get the point.

In WCW, we were on the road up to twenty-seven days of the month. And I knew of guys who were on the road for a hundred-something days consecutively without going home. You're going to pick up some habits, not all of them good.

And not just because you're a wrestler. It's true also of football, baseball, hockey and any other professional sport. It's true of an actor on tour. It's true of rock 'n' roll bands. You come off the stage and you're amped up because of the adrenaline and everything else. You've got a lot of time on your hands and a lot of energy to get rid of.

If you live a regular life and you work nine to five, which is what a lot of people do and that's fine, you're really not exposed to all that

stuff. But some people still develop these issues just going nine to five. I think it's the same deal, but being on the road for too long and performing in front of a crowd tends to magnify the problem a hundred times.

I think it comes back to personal choices and how you were raised, and what your values are. I know I was raised like a million bucks and I've got the greatest parents in the world, but you know, I've done my share of stuff on the road—stuff that hasn't always been the best thing for my health. I've taken plenty of prescribed pain medications. I enjoyed having more than a few beers every night.

But that's not my parents' fault. That was my choice and I don't want anybody to feel sorry for me. Hell, if one day I develop a liver problem because of the drinking I've done, I'll look at myself in the mirror and say, "Well, you knew it was coming." It's not something I fear or something I think I have a problem with, but I'm also not an angel, not by any stretch.

You see some guys going out on their wives in the wrestling business. They've got their girlfriends in this town or that town. In the old days it was even worse than it is now. Let's say you ran Tulsa every Monday. You didn't live there, but you were there every Monday. You might see your girlfriend in Tulsa once a week.

The next night you'd go to Little Rock. And when you got to Little Rock, there was some other little gal who knew where you stayed—and you made sure she knew, or at least you didn't change where you stayed to get away from her. You stayed in the Holiday Inn near the airport every time you were in Little Rock. You could easily have stayed at the Howard Johnson's or the Sheraton or the Marriott, but the women all knew that you stay at the Holiday Inn.

But I think a lot of guys would have had the same philandering attitude if they had been working a nine-to-five job. I think it's just some people's nature to have a wandering eye. You see schoolteachers with wandering eyes, or lawyers or doctors or even presidents. I'm not sure, but I don't think the divorce rate in wrestling is higher than it is in a lot of other businesses. I think it goes back to your values and what your priorities are.

The same goes for drugs, whether you're talking about the pre-

scription kind or the illegal kind. There's the same chance for abuse as in any professional sport.

The talent takes hundreds of bumps a year, hell, maybe hundreds in a month. And yes, they go and work the next day and sometimes have a prescription for a pain medication from their doctor.

I've got no room to talk as I've taken my share of pain pills with all the surgeries I've had, but I get off them as soon as I can. I screwed myself up with those energy drinks you get at the gym that are loaded with Ephedra, which was why I had that heart attack scare. Who knows? I might have died if I didn't have people to call right there at the hotel.

I've seen the pattern that gets people in trouble. You've got an injury and you have to take a pain pill to control the pain so you can function. But instead of taking one pill every four hours as prescribed, you take two pills every two hours. You tell yourself that you're a tough wrestler. You're bigger and stronger, so you need more. Then you take two or even four pills instead of one. I don't think that kind of abuse is indigenous to wrestling as much as it's indigenous to many forms of entertainment and athletics.

But abuse of anything is bad. Just think, you've gotten this golden opportunity to be a professional wrestler for a big company. Don't blow it—and your life—by being stupid. Vince and J.R. are your "fathers" and you don't want to disappoint them by doing something dumb, and maybe ending up dead.

I've lost a lot of my friends in the past few years due to drugs' impact on their hearts. I hate to see people flush their careers down the toilet because they're screwing up with drugs, much less lose their lives at such a young age. And it's even worse when they leave families behind. As I said before, I will never stand by and watch someone screw himself up again. I just didn't think these people would actually *die*. They were so strong. But then I thought I was dying too.

That should tell you how unwise it is to mess with drugs, prescription or otherwise. Especially cocaine and some kind of crap called GHB. Too many of my friends have died that way.

Drink beer instead . . . in moderation, of course.

'Cause Stone Cold Said So, *Raw*, April 28, 2003

t is now Monday, April 28, 2003, almost a month after *WrestleMania XIX*, where I lost to The Rock.

I don't drink coffee anymore, and of course I've quit drinking those damn Ephedra-laced energy drinks. The only caffeine I drink now is in Coke or Pepsi. In the past month I've been seeing my doctor, getting things straightened out and work-

ing on what you're holding in your hands. I've also been in discussions with WWE on how to best use me, since I can't wrestle anymore.

It's time to get back on that ride, and they've got a seat saved for me.

WWE Raw is going to be broadcast tonight live from Boston on TNN. I've had a good workout and a good lunch. I'm ready.

In the *Raw* story line to this point, Eric Bischoff, the general manager of *Raw*, has been abusing his power. He fired me the day after *WrestleMania XIX* because of my health, saying I was a medical risk. The stuff Bischoff read on *Raw* about how bad my health was and why he was firing me were actual quotes from my most recent medical report. Up until then, it had been kayfabed, kind of a secret. All of a sudden it was being read on damned *Raw*.

Then J.R. "quit" the following Monday night while in a heated argument with Bischoff over how Eric treated Stone Cold. The third week after *WrestleMania*, Bischoff was back to his harassment, this time with Trish Stratus—a top WWE Diva who had been the WWE Ladies Champion more than once.

We're more than an hour and a half into the two-hour-and-five-minute broadcast when sleazy Bischoff is ready to take advantage of Trish, who's being held down by Jazz and Victoria. The camera switches to the back area, where a long, black stretch limo pulls in. Who the hell is it?

The car door opens and it's Linda McMahon, CEO of the company, stepping out. Bischoff sees all this on the big TitanTron screen they have in the arena, gets worried and demands that the referees help Trish.

While this is going on, Linda is walking to the ring. Linda gets there and announces to the crowd that Bischoff is being monitored by the WWE board of directors and tells Eric to get back to the ring. The crowd goes nuts with anticipation of what's going to happen and sings that "Nah-Nah, Good-bye" song.

Eric gets to the ring and kisses up to Linda, but she's too damn smart for him. Linda teases him, saying that there are members of the board who don't think he's fit for the job based on what he's done the past month. But then, she says, there was a compromise. *Raw* will have

a new general manager starting tomorrow morning, sharing authority and duties fifty-fifty with Eric. Eric begs, and the crowd buzzes about who it could be. Linda tells Eric that the new co-general manager is someone who'll be able to keep Bischoff in line.

Then you hear the sound of glass breaking and my music hits, and the Boston crowd goes totally wild. I walk down the ramp to the ring and cut a fun promo asking Eric to trust me in our new partnership. I give the audience all the pauses so they can say *"What?"* with me, and it's great.

I start out by saying, "How you doing Eric?"

He looks worried.

"What?" the crowd yells in unison.

Eric's face sinks, knowing what's coming. He won't be able to get a word in edgewise.

"You doing all right?"

"What?" the crowd yells.

"You feeling good?"

"What?" the crowd yells.

"Are you nervous?"

"What?" the crowd yells.

"Scared?"

"What?" the crowd yells.

"What's the deal?"

"What?" the crowd yells.

Eric starts to say something and I interrupt him, saying, "You don't have to say anything. I bet you think there's no way this can work."

"What?" the crowd yells.

"You're thinking there's no way we can be partners."

"What?" the crowd yells.

"Work together."

"What?" the crowd yells.

"As a unit."

"What?" the crowd yells.

"Put it there," and I stick my hand out to shake his hand.

He hesitates and says, "I don't know, Steve. This isn't a marriage made in heaven, you know what I mean?"

I respond with, "So right off the bat you're saying you don't trust me. I can read it all over your face. You don't trust me."

Bischoff is playing it down, so I holler to the audience, "If you think Eric Bischoff should trust Stone Cold Steve Austin, give me a 'Hell Yeah'!"

The audience roars, *"Hell Yeah!"*

Then I tell them I want to make sure I heard it right, so give it to me again. This time the *"Hell Yeah!"* is even louder. That was for emphasis. So much for Steve Austin not ever getting over in this business, right, Eric?

Then I go back to Bischoff and tell him, "So you're saying, by not shaking my hand, you don't trust me?"

He says, "You know, Steve, I want this to work. I really do . . ."

I come right back with, "Do you?"

"What?" the crowd yells.

"Promise?"

"What?" the crowd yells.

"Swear?"

"What?" the crowd yells.

"You mean it?"

"What?" the crowd yells.

"From the bottom of your heart?"

"What?" the crowd yells.

"You're telling the truth?"

"What?" the crowd yells.

So I stick my right hand out again and remind Eric that starting tomorrow we're going to be partners, fifty-fifty, and we're going to get along. I grab his hand and we shake. I then remind him that the key word is "tomorrow"—and to everyone's cheers, I kick him in the gut and put a Stunner on him.

And that's how the live show ends.

After we're off the air and it's just the audience in the building watching us, Bischoff is just getting up. I go to shake his hand and help him up, but he shakes me off. Finally he gets up and shakes my hand, and I Stun him three more times!

The crowd loves it, and that's what it's all about—giving the fans something extra and having fun with it. I can't wrestle, but I can sure hand out some managerial justice and a few Stunners here and there.

The following Monday night on WWE Raw, the first thing I do, as the new co-general manager, is to rehire J.R. as the *Raw* announcer. Screw Bischoff. Sorry, Coach.

As mentioned earlier, Bischoff fired me from WCW for real. He also contributed to the departures from WCW of Jim "J.R." Ross and this book's other coauthor, Dennis Brent. Now, in our WWE make-believe world, we can right the wrongs of the "real world."

I get home from *Raw* in Boston on Tuesday. I drop my stuff at home and go to the gym. While there, my probation officer calls me on my cell phone. I'm being released early from my probation for doing everything

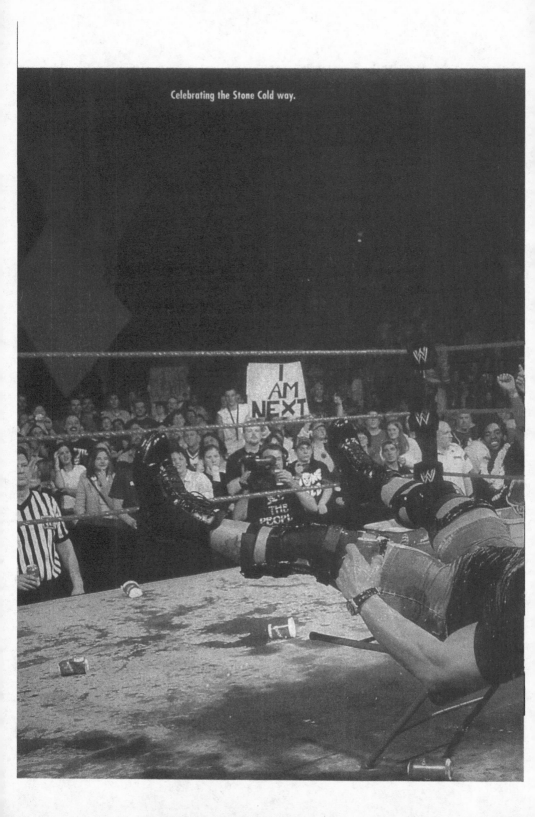

Celebrating the Stone Cold way.

the court asked me to do, and not messing up.

All of a sudden, my eyes light up. One of the terms of my probation was that I couldn't pop open a can of beer, so I'd been deprived of the trademark ending to my matches.

"Can you please repeat that?" I ask, absolutely jubilant.

My probation officer confirms it. I'm off the hook.

This is it! I am a free man and all that stuff is behind me now. My debt is paid. I felt like another tremendous weight has been lifted from my shoulders!

Stone Cold Steve Austin can now do the end of his act again! And I do it plenty the following Monday in Halifax.

I call up Vince and suggest to him that on next Monday's *Raw*, we have a real live kick-ass beer bash! I tell him that I just got off probation and if I'm not drinking about sixty beers in the ring next Monday, then there's something wrong. That's when they come up with these beer segments. One of

our Canadian sponsors, Molson beer, delivers forty cases of beer back-stage for our use—enough to make for a hell of a beer bash! *America's favorite beer drinker is back!*

When I was talking to Vince, I told him to keep a camera on me to get the shots because I was going to do all kinds of stupid stuff in the ring that night to celebrate. I told him that one of the things I was gonna do that night was that I was gonna swim in the beer.

He started laughing, and he said, "What?"

But that's what I do—and it works. Monday night comes, I come out and Bischoff and I have our little disagreements—but my rehire of J.R. stands. Then, later in the show, the beer bash begins. With all the celebrating and popping multiple beers for me and everyone else, there's so much damn beer spilled in the ring, plus we're all pouring cans out on the mat as we pop others open to share.

There's like a half an inch of beer there on the mat. At one point, I go down on my stomach and do arm strokes and paddle my feet like I'm the Olympic swimmer Mark Spitz or something.

So I'm out there on live TV, lying in the ring on my stomach, swimming in the beer—and the camera guy misses it! I don't know this until I get up and start doing something else, and I see the camera guy is waving to me and making swimming motions meaning "we need for you to do the 'swimming in the beer' deal again," because he missed it first time around. So I go and do it again.

The live crowd doesn't know what's going on, but they enjoy see-ing me flop down and do it some more. Next time, I tell myself, I should probably wear some flippers. Then I flip over on my back and do a "dead cockroach" impression, with my legs wiggling in the air as an inside rib to a friend of mine.

Stone Cold Steve Austin is always a "work in progress," and what's happening now is just another change on top of all the others. It's a different role since I'm not wrestling, but I've come to grips with that, and now I'm just going forward with the current story line. It's a lot of fun, and people seem to like it. I'm back on that ride and I'm real happy.

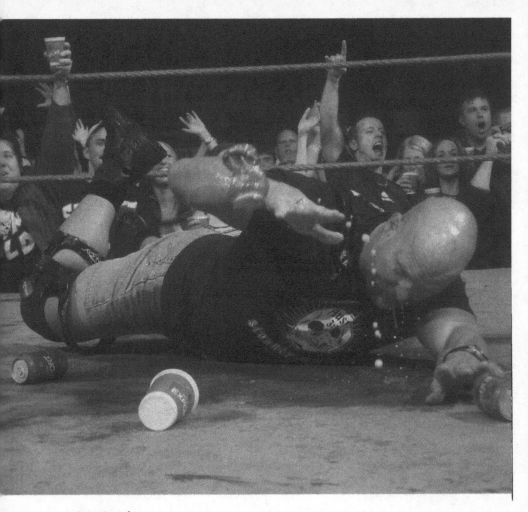

Swimming in beer.

At the end of the show I'm in the ring throwing down beers with Bill Goldberg, the big star from WCW who had finally come over to WWE, and that was a sight most people never thought they'd ever see—me included! Where do we go from here? We'll just see. It's been real interesting so far, and I'm having a blast.

My personal life has taken a turn for the better too. I've been fortunate enough to meet a wonderful girl named Tess that I really care about. Could she be number four—or will she be my next ex? Who knows at this point in my life?

Life has its challenges. I never read about anybody who amounted

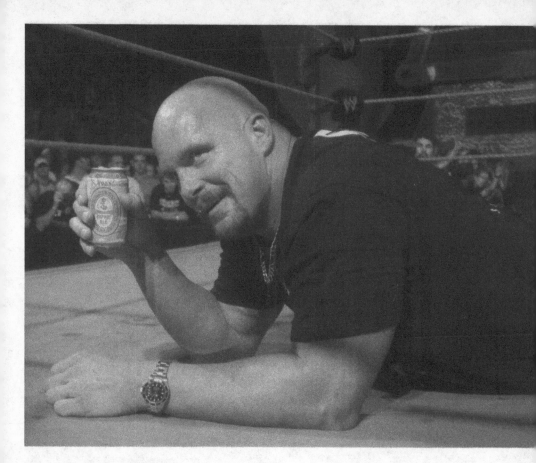

Another day at the office.

to anything who didn't undergo a journey that had its ups and downs, peaks and valleys. The key is how you respond to them. I've never walked away from my challenges or responsibilities.

Have I led an ideal life? No. Have I been a perfect husband? Hell no, far from it. But that's part of the journey we're on. Life ain't perfect and neither am I.

The way I see it, Stone Cold's ride is just beginning. *Oh, Hell Yeah!*